"Drawing from his profound personal experience of God, Klaus Issler brings Christian theology to real life via pursuit of deep friendship with God. Attentive readers will be powerfully challenged to enter into such dynamic friendship and its resulting community of God. This is theology that goes to the heart of a reader."
PAUL MOSER, *LOYOLA UNIVERSITY*

"For the cultures that are community- and relationship-oriented, as is the case in Africa, Dr. Klaus Issler's book will be an eye-opener on what really being a Christian is all about. It is my hope that any person seeking to have a more personal experience of God would read this book."
BENJAMIN M. MUSYOKA, *NAIROBI INTERNATIONAL SCHOOL OF THEOLOGY*

"*Wasting Time with God* is more than a solid piece of scholarship; it is a feast of personal, practical spirituality. . . . It is refreshing to see a book that addresses the head and the heart with such effectiveness."
J. P. MORELAND, *TALBOT SCHOOL OF THEOLOGY, BIOLA UNIVERSITY*

"The testimony of this book is that relationship, even friendship, with God is possible. More important, the stunning affirmation of the book is that the eternal God wants friendship with his people."
LINDA CANNELL, *TRINITY EVANGELICAL DIVINITY SCHOOL*

"*Wasting Time with God* is hardly a waste of time. It is a nuts and bolts discussion of how to grow in intimacy with God. It is clearly written and well grounded. This is a book well worth reading and wasting lots of time on. I highly recommend it."
DARRELL L. BOCK, *DALLAS THEOLOGICAL SEMINARY*

"In *Wasting Time with God*, Klaus Issler compellingly connects knowing and loving God with our ability as members of the body of Christ to know and love one another. Christian women in particular, who intuitively resonate with the community aspects of faith, will be enriched by the author's biblically sound insights into the correlation between rich relationships with one another and an increasingly intimate relationship with our God. This work of the heart is an honest quest to move beyond a primarily 'cerebral' faith to an increasingly intimate relational one with the divine—a quest made significant by its refreshing integration of intellectual excellence, sound theological scholarship and spiritual humility.

Issler has also created a welcome voice of balance on the person and work of the third person of the Trinity. For those who have tended to ignore the person and work of the Holy Spirit, *Wasting Time with God* is an articulate reminder that he is there to know and experience more fully."

BETH GRANT, *MISSIONARY/EDUCATOR TO SOUTHERN ASIA, ASSEMBLIES OF GOD*

"My greatest prayer for women is that they spend time with God. Life is so much better the deeper our friendship is with God. Klaus Issler explains to our hearts and minds who God is and how to deepen that friendship."

PAM FARREL, *CODIRECTOR OF MASTERFUL LIVING AND AUTHOR OF* WOMAN OF INFLUENCE

"So many Christians are consumed with the perceived busyness of their faith. They forget that their relationship with God is meant to be personal and intimate, characterized by a deep enjoyment of him. In his book *Wasting Time with God*, Klaus Issler reminds us of the simple joy and pleasure of being God's friend, and provides guidelines for communication and a closer, more intimate relationship."

BILL AND VONETTE BRIGHT, *CAMPUS CRUSADE FOR CHRIST*

WASTING TIME WITH GOD

A CHRISTIAN SPIRITUALITY
OF FRIENDSHIP WITH GOD

KLAUS ISSLER

InterVarsity Press
Downers Grove, Illinois

InterVarsity Press
P.O. Box 1400, Downers Grove, IL 60515-1426
World Wide Web: www.ivpress.com
E-mail: mail@ivpress.com

InterVarsity Press® is the book-publishing division of InterVarsity Christian Fellowship/USA®, a student movement active on campus at hundreds of universities, colleges and schools of nursing in the United States of America, and a member movement of the International Fellowship of Evangelical Students. For information about local and regional activities, write Public Relations Dept., InterVarsity Christian Fellowship/USA, 6400 Schroeder Rd., P.O. Box 7895, Madison, WI 53707-7895.

All Scripture quotations, unless otherwise indicated, are taken from the Holy Bible, New International Version®. NIV®. Copyright ©1973, 1978, 1984 by International Bible Society. Used by permission of Zondervan Publishing House. All rights reserved.

Cover photograph: © Darrell Gulin/CORBIS

ISBN 0-8308-2280-1

Printed in the United States of America ∞

Library of Congress Cataloging-in-Publication Data

Issler, Klaus Dieter, 1951-
     Wasting time with God: a Christian spirituality of friendship with God/Klaus Issler.
        p.   cm.
     Includes bibliographical references.
     ISBN 0-8308-2280-1 (pbk.: alk. paper)
     1. Spiritual life—Christianity.   I. Title.

   BV4501.2 I77 2001
   248.4 21; aa05-27—dc01

                                            2001024038

18	17	16	15	14	13	12	11	10	9	8	7	6	5
15	14	13	12	11	10	09	08	07	06	05			

With deep appreciation I dedicate this book to the following spiritual mentors who profoundly impacted my journey to know and love God.

In the early years,
To my parents,
William and Ruth Issler

In these latter years,
To Dallas Willard
and
To John G. Finch

For your faithful devotion to God

Foreword

There are books that look back, reminding us of a world that is past. There are others that are trendy, trying to keep up with the present. But there are books whose time has come, for they anticipate questions and issues that most readers are only just beginning to think about in hesitant ways. *Wasting Time with God* is one such timely, significant book.

Klaus Issler does not directly address the inquietude, even frustration, that many Christians feel about organized religion, church life and the whole gamut of institutionalized and professionalized expressions of faith. But "A Christian Spirituality of Friendship with God"—as the subtitle describes—is bound to stir up some inner disenchantment with whatever may be alienating our inner spirit as we gain deeper insights of God's ways with us in the intimacy of his love. As its title indicates, then, this book is gently subversive of those who are spiritually asleep in their contented, even though perhaps activistic, religious status quo.

To adopt Jesus' metaphor of new wine requiring new wineskins, this excellent book guides us suggestively, as if we are following our own heart's desire; yet it is prescribing "the Way of the Lord" in our cultural context. It is truthful and yet kindly, faithful to God's Word and yet flexible to various levels of personal intimacy with God himself. For as we become increasingly dissatisfied with impersonal structures, our quest for love—God's love—grows out of hunger for friendships that reflect such love. This process releases a spiritual dynamic that grows and matures while remaining structured and disciplined. Thus the reader is invited into an interactive reading experience that penetrates more challengingly than merely being informed. For that reason this is a dangerous book.

Wasting Time with God may catch you off balance and start you on a journey into a deeper walk with God than any you had imagined possible. For as we sometimes say of our search for something precious, "no stone was left unturned," it can be said likewise of this work. *Wasting Time with God* illustrates well a dictum of John Cardinal Newman: "Introduce God into your conscious life, and it admits a fact that transcends and excludes every other thought conceivable."

James M. Houston

Acknowledgments

In 1993, as a result of listening to tapes by Dallas Willard, and teaching the Homebuilders class on the subject of "Getting to Know God" (with the help of Thomas Morris's *Our Idea of God*, IVP, 1991), I found myself moving into a new season in my relationship with God. Begun in 1995, the book has paralleled my developing friendship with God; as I became a different person, so the book outline and contents became different, richer and deeper. And the following series of editors lent a good hand to get the book into your hands: Steve Webb and David Hazard were the first to believe in the project; Rodney Clapp shepherded it through the IVP acquisition process; and Andy Le Peau, a gracious and wise craftsman, carried the book to publication.

The following colleagues read the full manuscript (which appeared in different editions over the years), offering perceptive comments and criticisms: Linda Cannell, Scott Horrell, Bob Saucy and Bruce Ware. Although I did not always heed the advice, their probing helped make the book better. James Houston, a faithful guide in matters spiritual, was kind to lend his support by writing the foreword. Furthermore, over these past six years, a host of other people, friends, colleagues, students—too many to name individually but you know who you are—have had some influence on the present shape and texture of the book by discussing issues with me related to our relationship with God, by making suggestions and raising questions, by offering an encouraging word for the ministry of the material to your soul and by praying for me to persist in the project. Thank you.

Moreover, a book project requires a supportive environment conducive to research. Talbot School of Theology at Biola University is such a place (Dean Dennis Dirks and Dean of Faculty Mike Wilkins). The project was sustained by several university faculty research grants from Biola (Clyde Cook, president, Gary Miller, provost) and with multiyear grants from the Elizabeth Ann Bogert Memorial Fund for the Study and Practice of Christian Mysticism. Diligent research assistants Todd Vasquez, Jon Grenz and Darryl Keeney, along with Mrs. Jeane Jenkins, administrative assistant extraordinaire, with whom I have worked these many years in the Christian education Ph.D. program, all made the workload much lighter. Of course, I must mention the significant assistance of the three important women in my life: my mother, Ruth Issler, and my wife, Beth, who patiently read several versions of the book (Beth also reading multiple versions of every chapter), and my daughter Ruth, who sweated the details of the indices. Son Daniel offered a regular break from the work in our beloved pastime: playing table games of Acquire, Axis and Allies, Empire Builder and Settlers of Catan. And due to J. P. Moreland's inspiring encouragement from beginning to end, the book appears now instead of later.

But most of all, I thank God for being God—mysterious, majestic, personal.

1

THE QUEST

KNOWING GOD MORE DEEPLY

"Come near to God and he will come near to you."

JAMES 4:8

Given the opportunity—to live now or to live during the time when Jesus Christ walked this very earth—which would we choose? Some of us would jump at the offer to be with Jesus. To be comforted by his smile and reassured by his embrace. To see his miracles firsthand—the lame walking, the blind with sight. To chat with him as did Mary, Martha and Lazarus. Does your heart yearn for such intimacy and immediacy?

Yet why might Christians dream of seeing Jesus, touching him, hearing him? Is it because we detect some distance in our relationship with God? Do we want something more? Were first-century Christians better off because they actually saw Jesus and fellowshiped with him, while we have to limp along with our meager faith? In the final hours before his arrest, Jesus revealed to his disciples—and to all believers—the promise of a close and deepening relationship with God. "He who loves me will be loved by my Father, and I too will love him and *show myself to him*" (Jn 14:21, emphasis added). The Bible claims that a personal relationship with God is possible, yet a certain distance remains. Like Moses of old who asked to see God's glory (Ex 33:18), do we wish we could enjoy more of God's presence?

The Adventure of Knowing God

Although I am a seminary graduate who has served in full-time ministry for more than twenty years, I am mapping new terrain in my journey with God. My ideas about God have been stretched beyond comparison with former ways of thinking, and I feel much closer to God. A few years ago I sensed some turbulence in my soul, yet the practices I engaged in and the perspectives I had about knowing God were not helping me go deeper. Looking back I see how God brought people, books, ideas and events into my life to prod me forward into fascinating realms of new-to-me thoughts and experiences in knowing him. The year 1997 stands out in a special way. In January I was temporarily blinded in one eye for three weeks, and I learned to lean more on God. Seven months later I experienced a three-week spiritual retreat of solitude in which I sensed the presence of God as never before.

There is so much more God has in mind for us than I previously thought possible. I now live more in his grace and peace and love—a sense of duty motivates me less. I find myself in conversation with God more. As I rely more on God and pray more earnestly, I can discern specific answers to prayer. In a word, I feel more *connected* with God. Struggles and frustrations still dog my day, yet I sense less distance than before. With greater intensity, I appreciate how personal God is. I enjoy expending more effort to know God, the God who wants to know me.

This book is written to help believers respond to God's invitation to know him better and sense his presence more deeply. Furthermore, the majestic God of the universe will go to great lengths to enjoy a deep friendship with us. It is the greatest love story ever. "For God so loved the world that he gave his one and only Son, that whoever believes in him shall not perish but have eternal life" (Jn 3:16). "Now this is eternal life: that they may know you, the only true God, and Jesus Christ, whom you have sent" (Jn 17:3). In the future, God will bring to completion his long-term dream—*to live with us fully:* "The home of God is among mortals. He will dwell with them; . . . they will be his peoples, and *God himself will be with them"* (Rev 21:3 NRSV, emphasis added).

Our great God wishes to lavish on us his limitless love and to invite us into experiencing life to its fullest. The prophet Isaiah casts a vision of this wonder.

> On this mountain the LORD of hosts will make for all peoples
>   a feast of rich food, a feast of well-aged wines,
>   of rich food filled with marrow, of well-aged wines strained clear.
> And he will destroy on this mountain
>   the shroud that is cast over all peoples,
>   the sheet that is spread over all nations;
>   he will swallow up death forever.
> Then the Lord GOD will wipe away the tears from all faces,
>   and the disgrace of his people he will take away from all the earth,
>   for the LORD has spoken.
> It will be said on that day,
>   Lo, this is our God; we have waited for him, so that he might save us.
>   This is the LORD for whom we have waited;
>   let us be glad and rejoice in his salvation. (Is 25:6-9 NRSV)

Such joy awaits all believers, beloved of God, yet there is much to enjoy now as well.

What is it like to be friends with God? Bring to mind all of the good times you have had in the company of your friends—sipping coffee at an outdoor cafe, shopping till you drop at the mall, playing pickup basketball, sharing intimate secrets and on and on. Take all these moments, feelings and memories, wrap them up together, multiply them a thousand times, and then we might *begin* to get an idea of what friendship with God is like.[1] It is the best of the best, the cream of the crop. It is worth more than anything we could ever own or accomplish on our own.

The Beginning of Any Personal Relationship

The popular line in Christian circles—"God loves you; he can never love you any more than he does now"—conveys something right and something wrong. Of course, God's parental love for every believer is constant, but how well we know each other varies over time to the extent that God and believer each pursue an interactive relationship. For example, when a child is born into a family, a blood relation is established, but child and parent do not yet know each other. At the beginning, there is a built-in hiddenness. This is true with any new relationship, whether with parent and child or with a new neighbor, a new coworker on the first day at the job, or a new teacher and fellow students on the first day of class. A person's physical features are transparent, but the inner person is initially hidden. Time and common experiences together will provide the opportunity, but each party must decide whether or not it is worth the effort to bring down the barriers of self-hiddenness.

Some parents and children actually work at this opportunity and begin the process of friendship. Yet others are clueless about the need to be intentional and so settle for a shallow association of civility, missing out on the joys of genuine companionship. A growing relationship is based on continual and mutual self-revelation, and so it is with God. We can pursue a closer relationship with God, or we can settle for a superficial tie— and God's hiddenness remains. God gives us the freedom either way.

To change the metaphor, imagine a situation in which three consultants working for one client have all been invited for the first face-to-face lunch meeting with the client.[2] Consultant A corresponded with the client through letters and e-mail. Consultant B connected with the client many times by a cell phone. Consultant C used several videoconferences to contact the client. At the lunch meeting, how comfortable will each consultant be at the table with the client? Of course each consultant knows the client; yet there is a different quality of relational knowledge. Consultant A has only read the words of the client. Consultant B is familiar with the client's voice and tone. Consultant C was technologically present with the client and became accustomed to various nonverbal mannerisms. Likewise in our relationship with God, the relational quality will vary, depending on how each believer regularly chooses to connect with God.

Seeking God is not just a one-time affair; it must become a continuing lifestyle if believers want to deepen a friendship with him. Do we only associate the phrase *seeking God* with those who have not yet responded to God's gracious call to join his family? The need to seek God does not end when we are transferred into God's kingdom and family. Believers must continue to be seekers of God; it is our life purpose and brings to fulfillment our full potential for living.[3] The Bible teaches that a continuing relationship with God requires the participation of both parties: "Come near to God and he will come near to you" (Jas 4:8). Our love relationship with God can *always* grow deeper and deeper.

Furthermore, since God is mysterious, incomprehensible, transcendent, an infinite being of such independence and otherness, the Bible informs us that finite believers can never plumb all of the depths of who God is (e.g., Ps 145:3; Rom 11:33). As theologian Wayne Grudem explains, "For all of eternity we will be able to go on increasing in our knowledge of God and delighting more and more with him."[4] Believers can grow deeper in their relationship with God now and continue the process in eternity, yet never reach an end to knowing God.[5]

Growing in intimacy with God is possible. Redeemed humanity has been designed expressly by God—originally created in his image (Gen 1:26; Jas 3:9) and now being conformed to the image of his Son (Rom 8:29)—to be in continual communion with God (Jn 17:3). Furthermore, within the context of a deep and dependent relationship with God, the richness of life and all its potential is open to us. For example, the joy of friendship becomes enriched. Work flows more deeply from inner strength. Life and ministry in the body of Christ are uplifting. The One who created life knows best how to really live it. Without being consistently connected with God, we fall short of what we were designed to be.

Our Expectations of God

How well do we know God? What do we expect him to do? Our real conceptions of God are often revealed at those times when life turns upside down. For example, as Van walks down the hospital corridor toward his wife's room, he wrestles with the implications of her diagnosis. She may die in six months. They knew something was up—"Davy" became tired easily. In order to reduce the stress in her life, she quit her part-time job. They have always been deeply in love with each other. Only within the past two years had Davy and then Van come to a joyful knowledge of Jesus Christ as Savior. And these two, inseparable throughout fifteen years together, may be torn apart. As Van approaches her room, a depressing loneliness and fear claim his soul. God seems a million miles away.[6]

When jolted by the speed bumps of life, do we wonder why God does not clear the road? Do we expect God to be our celestial Superman, flying in at the right moment to save the day? How many no-shows does it take before we begin to doubt that God loves us or wonder whether he is really there at all? Forgiveness of sins and a future life in heaven without suffering are great gifts indeed, but we want a touch from eternity *now* as disappointment descends on our soul.

The quality of our life experience is linked to our view of God and what we expect God to do. For example, if God is viewed as an exacting, legalistic judge, he would keep track of every jot and tittle in our lives, including each lie, each angry moment, each lustful thought. Would not this "god" plague us with guilty reminders of our sins or punish us at each opportunity? Or maybe we conceive of God as a jovial grandfather type with a twinge of Alzheimer's disease and an elastic sense of grace. He would largely ignore whatever we do and excuse any wrong actions. Or maybe God always enjoys a good bargain: "Let's make a deal." If we do something good for him, then he will come through for us. But what happens when it appears that he does not hold up his end of the bargain? Turning Genesis 1:26 upside down, do we tend to create a god in our own image? A. W. Tozer (d. 1963) notes this peculiar penchant: "Always this God will conform to the image of the one who created it and will be base or pure, cruel or kind according to the moral state of the mind from which it emerges."[7]

Our ideas about God influence how we conduct our lives. Indeed, it may well be that the most important thing about us is what comes to mind when we hear the word *God,* as Tozer clarifies:

That our idea of God correspond as nearly as possible to the true being of God is of immense importance to us. Compared with our actual thoughts about Him, our [doctrinal] statements are of little consequence. Our real idea of God may lie buried under the rubbish of conventional religious notions and may require an intelligent and vigorous search before it is finally unearthed and exposed for what it is. Only after an ordeal of painful self-probing are we likely to discover what we actually believe about God. A right conception of God is basic not only to systematic theology but to practical Christian living as well. It is to worship what the foundation is to the temple; where it is inadequate or out of plumb the whole structure must sooner or later collapse. I believe there is scarcely an error in doctrine or a failure in applying Christian ethics that cannot be traced finally to imperfect and ignoble thoughts about God.[8]

Similarly, Dallas Willard warns that we position ourselves in a spiritual cul-de-sac if we neglect to correct and grow in our knowledge of God.

> Misunderstandings, mental confusions, and mistaken beliefs . . . about God . . . make a strong walk with him impossible, even if we've chosen, in effect, not to think about it. I have seen repeatedly confirmed, in often tragic cases, the dire consequences of refusing to give deep, thoughtful consideration to the ways in which God chooses to deal with us and of relying on whatever whimsical ideas and preconceptions about his ways happen to be flying around us. This is very dangerous to our health and well-being.[9]

False God-in-the-box ideas damage our spiritual life.

In December 1998, NASA launched a $125-million Mars Climate Orbiter to explore the planet of Mars. Yet after a journey of nine-plus months through outer space, the Orbiter disappeared September 23 upon entry into the Martian atmosphere. The embarrassed rocket scientists confessed to a profoundly simple mathematical error—failing to convert acceleration data from English units of force into metric units called newtons. "The bad numbers had been used ever since the launch in December, but the effect was so small that it went unnoticed. The difference added up over the months."[10] After traveling 416 million miles, the Orbiter arrived 56 miles too close to Mars and was destroyed. It was a minor error that resulted in devastating consequences. Might slightly off-course ideas about God yield analogous disaster for believers?

Confronting False Assumptions

Through his life example and teachings, Jesus consistently confronted wrong-headed notions about God and his plan. The Gospel writers highlight such encounters by recording how the crowds or the disciples were "amazed," "astonished" or "marveled" at his teaching (e.g., Mt 7:28; 12:23, 22:22, 33; Mk 6:2; 11:18; Lk 4:32; Jn 4:27). For example, note the disciples' reaction to Jesus' commentary after his encounter with the rich young ruler. " 'How hard it is for the rich to enter the kingdom of God!' The disciples were *amazed* at his words" (Mk 10:23-24, emphasis added). Normally within an Old Testament economy, material blessing was an indication of God's favor. Therefore, the rich were supposed to be automatically close to God due to their wealth. The disciples' reaction demonstrated how deeply ingrained this belief was. "But Jesus said again, 'Children, how hard it is to enter the kingdom of God! It is easier for a camel to go through the eye of a needle than for a rich man to enter the kingdom of God.' The disciples were even more *amazed*, and said to each other, 'Who then can be saved?'" (Mk 10:24-26, emphasis added). In other words, if this is true, can anyone be saved?[11] What deeply held false assumptions about God and his plan might Jesus expose today?

It is likely that this side of heaven all believers have some false conceptions about who God is. One reason for this problem is that we often retain our childhood view of God long after we become adults, as proposed by J. B. Phillips in his classic work *Your God Is Too Small*.

> The trouble with many people today is that they have not found a God big enough for modern needs. While their experience of life has grown in a score of directions, and their mental horizons have been expanded to the point of bewilderment by world events and by scientific discoveries, *their ideas of God have remained largely static.* It is obviously impossible for an adult to worship the [same] conception of God that [he had] . . . as a child of Sunday-school age, unless he is prepared to deny his own experience of life.[12]

The problem is complicated further in that, as Gordon Fee notes, "Most people, after all, prefer to reduce God to a size that their own minds can grasp, and thus control."[13] Do we tend to put God in a box, close it up and set the box in a safe place nearby?

Philosopher John Feinberg became angry at God when his wife was diagnosed with Huntington's disease—the premature deterioration of a portion of the brain. After working through the source of his anger at God, Feinberg confesses the relief of this realization: "I understood that much of my anger rested on a *misunderstanding of what God should be expected to do.*"[14] For author Philip Yancey it was a childhood view of God that needed to be debunked. "I grew up with the image of a mathematical God who weighed my good and bad deeds on a set of scales and always found me wanting. Somehow I missed the God of the Gospels, a God of mercy and generosity who keeps finding ways to shatter the relentless laws of ungrace."[15]

Reality consistently compels us to adjust perspectives and practices. Progress and change in the twenty-first century is so persistent that no one can remain unaffected amidst the continual fluidity of technological inventions and the uncertain business climate of fluctuating market share and mergers. What about our relationship with God? What has specifically changed about our view of God over the same time period? Although God's nature does not change, has our conception of God grown and become more mature as we have logged more time with God?

How could it be that any believer has plumbed the depths of the almighty God for all time? We could never wrap our hands or our minds around an infinite, majestic, all-powerful God. Knowing such an immense God is an ongoing project. God's unbounded nature requires that we continue to refine and reform our ideas about him. Otherwise our false God-in-the-box ideas will choke our spiritual life.

Of course God is our great King whom we lovingly obey and worship. "Now to the King eternal, immortal, invisible, the only God, be honor and glory for ever and ever. Amen" (1 Tim 1:17; cf. Ps 47; Ps 103). But perhaps we have only tapped a small portion of the possibilities for relating with God. In this book, we consider an additional prospect: *God also desires to be our friend, our companion, our confidant*: "The LORD . . . takes the upright into his confidence" (Prov 3:32). We worship the King, but can we also respond to God's personal invitation to draw near and become his friend (e.g., Jn 14:23; Jas 4:8), as did Abraham (Is 41:8; Jas 2:23) and Moses (Ex 33:11)? God's active participation in our lives can be as rich and rewarding as we want it to be, to the extent that we are willing to make room for all that God desires to be and to do in our lives. God is ready and available to visit us at our most intimate and vulnerable points, eager and willing to meet all of our needs.

The Affective Side of Christian Living

The "peace of God" is both a noted biblical construct as well as something we yearn to experience deeply. Scripture promises that it comes when we relinquish our anxieties in prayer to God: "And the peace of God, which transcends all understanding, will guard your hearts and minds in Christ Jesus" (Phil 4:7).[16] Healthy Christian living involves an

important experiential component, as noted by D. A. Carson in his assessment of contemporary trends in spirituality: "At the same time we should
be rightly suspicious of forms of theology that place all the emphasis on
coherent systems of thought that demand faith, allegiance and obedience
but do not engage the affections, let alone foster an active sense of the
presence of God."[17] And as J. I. Packer notes, "We must not lose sight of
the fact that knowing God is an emotional relationship, as well as an
intellectual and volitional one, and could not indeed be a deep relation
between persons were it not so."[18]

Emotions are a wonderful gift of God. Jesus himself experienced a
wide range of feelings (e.g., weeping, Lk 19:41; compassion, Mk 6:34;
righteous anger, Mk 3:5; frustration, Mt 17:17; and being troubled in
spirit, Mt 26:37), all without sin (Heb 4:15). Our emotions can often become windows to the current state of our soul (e.g., "Why are you down-
cast, O my soul? Why so disturbed within me? Put your hope in God," Ps
42:5, 11; 43:5). In addition, sometimes an experience offers evidence for
God's supernatural working, (e.g., Paul's obedience to his vision of Christ,
Acts 26:19; the acceptance of Gentiles as believers, Acts 10:47; 11:17;
15:8).

Furthermore, by undergoing certain experiences we come to appreciate truths at a deeper level. For example, for theologian Bob Saucy,
heaven is more vivid now since the untimely death of an adult child.
"Several years ago my wife Nancy and I lost our youngest daughter. I remember it vividly. With no indication of any health problems, she suddenly collapsed and died of heart failure when she was only 28 years old.
. . . It was like being hit with a .45 slug. . . . Heaven became more real to
me with a reality that I'm sorry to say was not there before. And that hope
has continued to shape my life ever since."[19]

The same could be said about our relationship with God. Nancy
Missler explains the difference between being aware of truths about communion with God and actually experiencing these truths at a deeper
level.

> A perfect analogy of this might be "the act of love" in a marriage. In a mar-
> riage, wives can make love, enjoy it and *even* bear children without ever
> having experienced the fullness, the intimacy and the ecstasy of complete
> union with their loved one. Positionally, yes, they are one with their hus-

bands, but experientially they don't have the slightest clue as to what it means to truly be "one."[20]

Our experiential communion with God is an important component of knowing God personally.

In this book I attempt to bring together a serious study of the doctrine of God with the pursuit of a vibrant and soul-satisfying relationship with God. Sound theology must inform our own conceptions of who God is, yet without experiencing such truths in daily life, the ultimate purpose of systematic theology is aborted.[21] Thus, although the general tone of writing will be more familiar and personal, I still intend to communicate substantive truths about God. Also, as a part of describing what a relationship with God looks like, at points along the way I share my own story, limited as it may be. If I can offer no experiential evidence for knowing God from my journey, why continue to read the book? For as Noel O'Donoghue notes, "A certain ponderous dullness and flatness of style is an infallible sign that a writer is not a true guide to the sacred places."[22]

Willingness and Readiness to Know God More

A student in my class once blurted out in frustration, "I want to know God more, but he doesn't seem to come any closer." I now understand that believers must become both willing and ready to make further progress in knowing God. Readiness involves undergoing a process of preparation to move to the next step. It will cost something to deepen our relationship with God, as Henry Blackaby and Claude King note in their book *Experiencing God:*

> Once you have come to believe God, you demonstrate your faith by what you *do*. Some action is required. . . . You cannot continue life as usual or stay where you are, and go with God at the same time. . . . To go from your ways, thoughts, and purposes to God's will always requires a major adjustment. God may require adjustments in your circumstances, relationships, thinking, commitments, actions, and beliefs. Once you have made the necessary adjustments you can follow God in obedience. Keep in mind—the God who calls you is also the One who will enable you to do His will.[23]

Furthermore, deeply held false notions can make us resistant to consider new truths. For instance, despite Jesus' many predictions of his upcoming death and resurrection (Mk 8:31; 9:9, 31; 10:33-34, 38-39, 45; 12:1-12; 14:3-9), this new idea never settled in the disciples' minds. When the women came back from the tomb to report to the disciples that Jesus had risen from the dead, they were greeted with skepticism. "But [the disciples] did not believe the women, because their words seemed to them like nonsense" (Lk 24:11). Peter was at least willing to explore the evidence at the empty tomb, but he went away, "wondering to himself what had happened" (Lk 24:12). But doubting Thomas remained adamant. Despite the eyewitness testimony of his comrades—"we have seen the Lord"—Thomas could make no sense of the claim that Jesus was alive again. " 'Unless I see the nail marks in his hands and put my finger where the nails were, and put my hand into his side, I will not believe it' " (Jn 20:25). When confronted by Jesus' appearance, Thomas was forced to reconsider his beliefs about life and death. Willingness to face false ideas about God is vital, but it may not always be easy.

Due to God's uniqueness, we must not only *want* to know God more, but we will also need to adjust our thinking and lifestyle to make room in our lives for God. For example, although there is still much more potential for growth, it has taken me over three years of concerted attention to matters described in this book to move to my present relationship with God. Desiring to know God is a commendable, necessary first step. But there is no instant spirituality; it is a journey of many steps.

Of course, any adjustments are worth the effort, as indicated in these comments from past students with whom I have shared materials from this book.

I became aware of another perspective to how much God loves me.

This course is great in learning more about the personal side of God and how you can work on improved closeness with Him.

This course is helpful because I began to think more deeply on my relationship with Christ. Questions were brought to mind that helped me evaluate my walk with God. Suggestions were shared which I plan to use to help me focus my writing in my daily journal (i.e., coincidences).

What Is Christian Spirituality?
In the title of this book, I retain usage of the word *spirituality,* despite

evidence in contemporary publications that it has been stretched to cover everything imaginable, even within Christian circles. D. A. Carson offers this caution: "'Spirituality' has become such an ill-defined, amorphous entity that it covers all kinds of phenomenon an earlier generation of Christians . . . would have dismissed as error, even as 'paganism' or 'heathenism.'"[24] The term is used within diverse religious and nonreligious associations: Jewish spirituality, Buddhist spirituality and even a New Age spirituality.[25] Among Christians, Catholics have used this term longer than Protestants. Bernard McGinn, John Meyendorff and Jean Leclercq note that "although . . . the words *spiritualis* and even *spiritualitas* were well known in Latin Christianity, 'spirituality' does not necessarily have a self-evident meaning for all Christians today."[26] The following working definition was developed by McGinn, Meyendorff and Leclercq for use by authors of chapters in the three-volume work on Christian spirituality:

> Christian spirituality is the lived experience of Christian belief in both its general and more specialized forms. . . . It is possible to distinguish spirituality from doctrine in that it concentrates not on faith itself, but on the reaction that faith arouses in religious consciousness and practice. It can likewise be distinguished from Christian ethics in that it treats not all human actions in their relation to God, but those acts in which the relation to God is immediate and explicit. [27]

This sketch suggests certain contrasts and boundaries I want to place around the term; it especially focuses on the believer's experiential relationship with God.

Christianity uniquely affirms a trinitarian God: Father, Son and Holy Spirit. Thus, any discussion regarding a distinctly Christian spirituality must help believers know and love each member of the one God who eternally exists as three distinct persons: "May the grace of the Lord Jesus Christ, and the love of God [the Father], and the fellowship of the Holy Spirit be with you all" (2 Cor 13:14).[28] Furthermore, any explanation of Christian spirituality grounded in the Scripture will include the Spirit.[29] Accordingly, the following working definition is proposed:

> Christian spirituality involves a deepening trust and friendship with God for those who are in Christ Jesus. More specifically, it is an ever growing, expe-

rientially dynamic relationship with our trinitarian God—Father, Son and Holy Spirit—through the agency of the indwelling Spirit of God.

Furthermore, believers need not be limited by their own relationship to deepen their knowledge of God. God is so grand and majestic, and each relationship is so person specific that there will be much to learn about God from the stories of other believers' experiences with God. The fullest knowledge of God attainable by human beings will only come about within a growing and God-knowing community of saints. Thus, to know God more fully cannot be accomplished without the larger community of believers.

Discerning the Truth of the Matter

Yet on what basis can we determine whether or not truth is evident in the advice of a friend, in a salesperson's claim or in publications such as this book? Biblically minded people generally adhere to a standard three-fold test of truth, of which the first test is foremost to the other two: (1) Biblical test: Is the claim in agreement with the data of Scripture (e.g., Acts 17:11)? (2) Intellectual test: Is the claim reasonable, logically consistent; does it make sense (e.g., Lk 24:11)?[30] (3) Experiential test: Is the claim realistic, fitting within our life experience as human beings created in God's image? Does it work in life?[31] Philosopher John Feinberg divides the category of experience into two questions: (a) "Does it square with the data of reality so that it is likely to be true, in a correspondence sense of 'true'?" (e.g., 1 Kings 10:6-7; Jn 20:24-25), and (b) "Can one practice such a view on a daily basis?"[32]

An event in Jesus' life—healing a blind and mute demon-possessed man—illustrates the use of these three tests of truth. None could deny their *experience* of witnessing this public event. "All the people were astonished" (Mt 12:22-23). Because of the healing, some in the crowd drew an inference from the Old Testament *Scripture.* "Could this be the Son of David?" (Mt 12:23). Although the Pharisees were opposed to Jesus, they could not deny their own experience of the miraculous healing. But they proposed another *logical* possibility, based on their Jewish theological tradition. They accused Jesus of being in league with the devil, "It is only by Beelzebub, the prince of demons, that this fellow drives out demons" (Mt 12:24). Jesus responded by demonstrating, in a number of ways, how il-

logical their claim was. For example, "Every kingdom divided against itself will be ruined, and every city or household divided against itself will
not stand. If Satan drives out Satan, he is divided against himself. How
then can his kingdom stand?" (Mt 12:25-26).[33]

The pursuit of truth requires the use of Scripture, reason and experience.
When presented with a new idea that is different from our core beliefs, we
can either dismiss the proposal outright or puzzle over the idea and consider whether there is any truth to it. For example, although acupuncture—
a technique using small pins placed in the skin to relieve pain—is a remedy
with a long history in Asia, our own Western medicine had never welcomed it. Scripture offers no comment on the subject. I tend to give more
credibility to our Western medical model, which asserts that procedures
should have empirical research substantiating them. Yet recently my father
received an acupuncture treatment for his shoulder and was surprised at
the positive effect it had for him. Now I am more open to considering further evidence regarding the pros and cons of this form of treatment.

In this book, there may be various new ideas to consider about God
that will need to be assessed in light of Scripture, reasoning and experience. To know God more, we need to search out all the evidence that can
be gleaned about our grand and majestic God.

A Compelling Vision of the Christian Life

What grand ideas grab our attention? Does our conception of the Christian life impact our daily experience? Although Richard Osmer of Prince-
ton Seminary addresses his comments primarily to mainline churches, his
diagnosis applies to all Christian churches.

> To a great extent, the many problems that are besetting the mainline
> churches today stem from the fact that churches do not seem to be able to
> offer their members a compelling vision of the Christian life. The Bible and
> theology seem remote from the realities of everyday life and do not function
> as sources of guidance in the pursuit of Christian vocation. . . . Their dimin-
> ishment [i.e., denominational loyalty and congregational commitment] has
> made it clear that denominations and congregations are increasingly depen-
> dent on their ability to project a vision that supports and transforms persons
> in their attempt to live to God in their own time and place.[34]

This book is my small contribution to address this problem.[35]

God loves us and yearns for a closer relationship with us. According to D. A. Carson, the love of God involves at least five differing expressions:[36] God's *intra-trinitarian* love, particularly between the Father and the Son (e.g., Jn 3:35; 14:31), God's *providential* love for all his creatures as Creator (e.g., Gen 1:31), God's *yearning* love to save the world through the cross of Jesus (e.g., Jn 3:16), God's *wooing* love to draw and secure the salvation of his people, and finally, God's *relational* love experienced with believers, subsequent to becoming a member of the family of God (e.g., Jude 21). The first kind of love is the basis and impetus for the other four loves—for God is love (1 Jn 4:8)—and sets an ideal pattern for all of our relationships (to be treated in the next chapter). Furthermore, believers are the immediate beneficiaries of God's kindness in all of the other four kinds of love.

Yet, the particular focus of this book is to explore Carson's final category of God's relational love further, for Christians who are already saved by God's grace. Scripture highlights the intimacy God desires with us.

> The LORD . . . takes the upright *into his confidence.* (Prov 3:32)

> If anyone loves me, he will obey my teaching. My Father will love him, and we will come to him and *make our home with him.* (Jn 14:23)

> Come near to God and *he will come near to you.* (Jas 4:8)

> Listen! I am standing at the door, knocking; if you hear my voice and open the door, *I will come in to you and eat with you,* and you with me. (Rev 3:20 NRSV)[37]

The majestic Creator of the universe desires our friendship. In fact, he is more interested in this endeavor than we are; he has been contemplating it and planning it for a long time. God is personal and has created us to enjoy deep friendship with him.

We have been specifically designed so that only an infinite God can truly meet all of our needs: emotional, relational, moral, intellectual. In the words of Scripture, "He [God] has also set eternity in [their] hearts" (Eccles 3:11). Augustine's pronouncement captures the sentiment well: "You have made us for yourself, and our heart is restless until it rests in you."[38] It is my prayer that your investment in working through this book will launch your pursuit of a deeper friendship with God as we explore some of the mystery of God's immanence, his desire to be near.

What Is up Ahead

How does a believer deepen his or her relationship with God? In this book I share the fruit of my quest to know God in order to stimulate fellow believers toward a more intimate level of friendship with God. I have puzzled over such matters as prayer, suffering, guidance and knowing a God who is three persons. Along the way I received much insight from the technical tomes of scholarship not readily available nor very readable for most Christians. Thus, in this book I draw on various sources of scholarship and try to make them accessible to the reader, especially for those desiring a biblically grounded, intellectually stimulating and experientially enriching relationship with God.

The book identifies certain essential components that must be considered and embraced by believers desiring to know God more.[39] The first part (chapters two through four) addresses the matter of intensifying a readiness for welcoming God into our daily experience. Since God is majestic and unique, there are certain foundational requirements to make room in our lives for God. These three chapters cover topics that actually are characteristic of any good relationship: preferential friendship love for the sake of the other (chapter two), humility (chapter three) and getting beyond outward (i.e., physical) appearances to connect with the inner person (chapter four). But these matters are also uniquely applicable in befriending God.

With readiness issues covered in part one, the matter of increasing our intimacy *and* conversation with God comes to the fore in the second half of the book. Chapter five proposes that believers must seek God with commitment, for God awaits our response to his initiatives. Sadly, our busyness and preoccupation prevent our movement forward. If we do not carry out our plans to "waste time with God," our relationship with God will languish. Furthermore, although seeking God is a daunting task, we are not left to our own resources, for God himself offers divine aid (2 Pet 1:3-4). God the Spirit, the third person of the Trinity who indwells each believer forever, guides and enables us to experience God's presence more fully (chapter six).

In the final two chapters, two practical arenas of life intersecting with God's plan are examined: suffering (chapter seven) and petitionary prayer (chapter eight)—matters related especially to the responsibility of God the

Father (e.g., Acts 1:7). In chapter seven we will consider several potential benefits accruing to believers who suffer. Although we still experience the grief that can be honestly shared with God, we may come to appreciate the "madness in God's method" in order more readily to welcome the good that can come to us through suffering. Finally, in chapter eight we consider the implications of Jesus' promise that prayer changes things (e.g., Jn 15:7).

I have alluded above to how references to God the Father and God the Spirit are included in the book. Furthermore, in each chapter I offer a relevant example from Jesus' life to highlight how he embodied the particular principle and practice under discussion.[40] Based on his earthly sojourn, Jesus became the Christians' sympathetic high priest (Heb 2:17-18; 4:15). Not only does Jesus show us God (Jn 1:18), but he also demonstrates for us what a dynamic relationship with God can be like. We can imitate him (1 Cor 11:1). If Jesus our Lord is also fully human, then he is the preeminent person to teach us about our subject. Consider that Jesus is the only person ever to live a fully human life and the only one ever to practice consistently what he preached. Truly we must "fix our eyes on Jesus," the pioneer of faith in God (Heb 12:2).

Throughout the book, sound theology directs the way to a deeper walk with God. The overall tenor of the book is not to bring guilt for what believers are not doing, but rather to offer liberating insights that can refresh and open up new ways to deepen a relationship with God.[41] Furthermore, to encourage an experiential response to the main ideas of the book, near the end of each chapter I include a pair of suggested practices—like a practical appendix—that may aid the reader in knowing God more.

Wasting Time with God

To deepen our relationship with God, we must become comfortable in new ways of connecting with God, in "wasting time" with God. Although wasting time is generally considered a Western sin, for the Christian, wasting time with God is always good and right. Furthermore, to follow Jesus, we must become like him. Yet, do we wish to emulate Jesus' *public* life of ministry without attending to his *private* life that provided the foundation for his public ministry? Luke 5:15-16 brings these aspects together: "Yet the news about [Jesus] spread all the more, so that crowds of people came to hear him and to be healed of their sicknesses. But Jesus often withdrew to lonely places and prayed." Jesus exemplifies the importance of attending to our private life.

The underlying belief of these "Wasting Time with God" sections is that we must make some lifestyle changes to know God more deeply. As Marjorie Thompson notes, "It would be nice if we could simply 'practice the presence of God' in all of life, without expending energy on particular exercises. But the capacity to remember and abide in God's presence comes only through steady training."[42] Furthermore, we must ask ourselves, is our life running on autopilot, controlled by our routines and habits of busyness and addictions? Or are we alert in the cockpit, being intentional about the direction of our life? Engaging in spiritual disciplines is one means to become aware of what is driving our life.

At various points in the New Testament an emphasis on training and discipline is affirmed (e.g., 1 Cor 9:24-27; 1 Tim 4:7-8; Heb 5:14). As Henri Nouwen notes, "Through a spiritual discipline we prevent the world from filling our lives to such an extent that there is no place left to listen. A spiritual discipline sets us free" [Rom 8:26].[43] For the most part, I draw on the classic spiritual disciplines that have served saints through-

Chapter	Topic	Spiritual Disciplines	
Chapter 1	Quest	Meditation	Asking Questions
Chapter 2	Friendship	Hospitality*	Spiritual Friendships*
Chapter 3	Humility	Confession*	Service*
Chapter 4	Faith	Watchfulness	Fasting
Chapter 5	Commitment	Personal Retreat	Journaling/Reflection
Chapter 6	Communication	Orienting Prayer	Working with a Spiritual Mentor*
Chapter 7	Apprenticeship	Lament	Advocacy*
Chapter 8	Partnership	Faith-Stretching Prayer	Practicing the Presence of God

* Usually involves some kind of interaction with others

Table 1.1. Overview of selected spiritual disciplines for each chapter

out church history (see table 1.1) and include two in each chapter.[44]

Wasting Time with God: Meditation

Among all the habits that foster a relationship with God, meditation on
the Word of God has been a premier spiritual discipline for both pastors
and laypersons. If we wish to learn more about God, the source of information to which we must look is the divinely inspired Scripture. Although
we can gain some important information from God's creation—general
revelation (cf. Rom 1:18-20)—the "authorized" source of information
about God and his plan is his written Word—special revelation.

> Happy are those [whose] / . . . delight is in the law of the LORD, / and on his
> law they meditate day and night. / They are like trees / planted by streams of
> water, / which yield their fruit in its season, / and their leaves do not wither./
> In all that they do, they prosper. (Ps 1:1-3 NRSV)

> Do not let this Book of the Law depart from your mouth; meditate on it day
> and night, so that you may be careful to do everything written in it. Then
> you will be prosperous and successful. (Josh 1:8)

Regularly repeating God's thoughts is a way to focus our attention on the
things of God. Meditation involves both internal and spoken "mutterings"
(Heb. *hagut,* "a muttering"). Note the parallelism in Psalm 19:14: "May the
words of my mouth and the meditation of my heart be pleasing in your sight."

Two key terms, *meaning* and *significance,* parallel the two parts of Bible
study, the more technical informational aspect and the more devotional
and meditative formational aspect. The meaning of the text refers to understanding the information the biblical and divine authors originally intended
to communicate to readers. The significance of the text involves applying
various implications of the passage to a particular situation of the contemporary reader.[45] As William Klein, Craig Blomberg and Robert Hubbard explain, "The meaning of any given passage of Scripture remains consistent
no matter who is reading the text, while its significance may vary from
reader to reader."[46] Without regularly engaging in meditation, the technical
aspect of Bible study becomes purely an academic exercise.

The art of meditation—discerning the significance of the Word for the
contemporary believer—is the art of formative reading. Peter Toon explains that it is an adaptation of "a modern form of Hebrew meditation. It

is to learn to read the sacred text slowly, prayerfully, and formatively—and preferably to read aloud."[47] Toon makes a distinction between *informative reading* and *formative reading*. The purpose of the first kind, whether one reads a letter, newspaper or book, is solely to gain information. On the other hand, "Formative reading is done in such a way as to allow the text to form us, to let God the Holy Spirit be in charge, and thus allow the Inspirer of Scripture to become for us its Illuminator so that its content (a little at a time) enters our souls."[48] Along these same lines, J. P. Moreland explains:

> In devotional reading one reads quietly, slowly, and with a sense of spiritual attentiveness and openness to God. The goal of devotional reading is not so much gathering new information or mastering content, though that may indeed happen. The goal is to deepen and nourish the soul by entering into the passage and allowing it to be assimilated into one's whole personality.[49]

In meditation we allow the Spirit to use his Word to penetrate our hearts. "For the word of God is living and active. Sharper than any double-edged sword, it penetrates even to dividing soul and spirit, joints and marrow; it judges the thoughts and attitudes of the heart" (Heb 4:12).[50] Consider reading a favorite passage (e.g., Ps 23) slowly with a receptive heart.

Wasting Time with God: Asking Questions

Since growing to know God is a continuing project, one way to maintain a lifelong learning perspective is to nurture the practice of questioning. Asking our own questions is what genuinely prompts our own learning. Do we forget how Jesus pursued his questions as a child of twelve? "After three days [Joseph and Mary] found him in the temple courts, sitting among the teachers, listening to them and asking them questions. Everyone who heard him was amazed at his understanding and his answers" (Lk 2:46-47). In his public ministry, Jesus prompted others to consider new ideas with his questions.[51]

> What do you think about the Christ? Whose son is he? . . . How is it then that David, speaking by the Spirit, calls him "Lord"? . . . If then David calls him "Lord," how can he be his son? (Mt 22:42-46)

> Which is lawful on the Sabbath: to do good or to do evil, to save life or to kill? (Mk 3:4; cf. Lk 14:3)

The disciples had their own questions for Jesus, prompted by the situation at hand:

Why do you speak to the people in parables? (Mt 13:10)

Why then do the teachers of the law say that Elijah must come first? (Mt 17:10)

Probably the best example of a group of people who manifested a spirit of teachability and a practice of questioning were the Bereans. During Paul's second missionary journey, after being jailed in Philippi and experiencing a near riot in Thessalonica, Paul and his companions came to the hospitable Bereans. "Now the Bereans were of more noble character than the Thessalonians, for they received the message with great eagerness and examined the Scriptures every day to see if what Paul said was true" (Acts 17:11).

Unfortunately, sometimes in school and in church we are discouraged from asking our own questions. Much of schooling involves memorizing answers in books that resulted from the questions asked by others—an important educational foundation. Yet one potential danger is that our natural, God-given curiosity about life—in prominent use as preschoolers (e.g., Ex 12:26; 13:14; Josh 4:6, 21)—may have been put aside as we got used to the habits of schooling. Perhaps a teacher awakened this learning desire, or some life crisis resparked this natural inclination. But the light for learning will be blown out unless we sustain it by developing an inquiring mind. By putting into words what puzzles or perplexes us, we are then in a position to seek answers.[52]

When in a teaching-learning situation, a good habit is to write down at least one question about something we would like to learn more about. Once a question gets a hold of us, we will become captivated to a life of learning and will engage in a process to demolish false God-in-the-box ideas.

In the next chapter, we explore what friendship looks like, whether with God or with anyone else, and how our human friendships can actually affect our relationship with God. Yet, a potential barrier confronts us: should Christians even have friends in light of Jesus' critique, "If you love those who love you, what reward will you get? Are not even the tax collectors doing that?" (Mt 5:46). In the next chapter we take up the subject of the nature of personal relationships.

PART 1

MAKING ROOM
FOR GOD

2

FRIENDSHIP

APPROACHING THE GOD WHO IS LOVE

"If anyone says, 'I love God,' yet hates his brother, he is a liar. For anyone who does not love his brother, whom he has seen, cannot love God, whom he has not seen. And he has given us this command: Whoever loves God must also love his brother."

1 JOHN 4:20-21

JESUS' EXAMPLE

"My command is this: Love each other as I have loved you. Greater love has no one than this, that he lay down his life for his friends."

JOHN 15:12-13

Where are you at about 7:00 a.m. Friday mornings? I am usually having a cup of coffee and an egg sandwich with my close friend Bill, who also happens to be my brother. For me, being in the company of such a good friend is not only a routine of life but also a treasured occasion, a time that seems to reach into eternity itself. When we are with a soul mate, we lose track of time. In other meetings we closely monitor the ticking of the clock, but not around our intimates. Here we metaphorically throw our watches away and feast on the fellowship. The older I get the more I treasure my close friends. Many things come and go in life, but our relationships with family and friends provide the core stuff of which life is made.

Yet, good friendships do not just happen; they are cultivated through thick and thin. I have enjoyed enhancing friendships with believers through working on projects together. For example, I have team taught classes with Bob, Pat, Gary and Kevin. Beth and I have served in ministry projects with Don and Lois, and Walt and Marty. Over an eight-year period, Ron and I worked on two book projects.

Furthermore, Beth and I have been recipients of the kindness of friends, such as Jack and Caroll, who loaned us their car to pull a trailer from Michigan to Kansas, and Alan and Bev, who always provide room and board on our way up and down the West Coast. Members of our church Bible fellowship group kindly provided meals or transportation when either Beth or I were having surgery or needed to get to the doctor's office. Our fireplace often reminds me of Gary, Sue and Amy's labor of love in removing paint from the bricks. Despite the pain of moving day, being with our Sunday evening friendship group made it special.

Until Bob and Collette moved away, we enjoyed their spontaneous visits, often with ice cream in hand: "Are the Issler's receiving guests this evening?" That momentous day I finally beat Keith at the game of Acquire is recorded for posterity in our picture album (grown men still play table games). And we go back a long way as friends with Brian and Anne, and J. P. and Hope.

We come into this world with nothing, and we leave with nothing, but our relationships can endure forever. Into eternity we take with us our relationship with God and our friendships with believers.[1] It is hard to put into words the feelings we experience when we are with good friends. I feel accepted. I feel comfortable; I can talk about anything without having to be politically or theologically correct. Friends listen with earnest eyes and ears, and comfort us with warm hearts. With friends we experience a foretaste of heaven: encouragement, sympathy, care, laughter, bonding, sensing someone's soul. Truly, "a friend loves at all times" (Prov 17:17).

Human nature, created in the image of God, has been so designed to make an intimate relationship with God possible. God invites us into a deeper kind of relationship with himself—a relationship of intimacy and love. "He who loves me will be loved by my Father, and I too will love him and show myself to him. . . . My Father will love him, and we will come to him and make our home with him" (Jn 14:21, 23). The stream of intimacy and close fellowship flows within these words of invitation to friendship with God.[2]

Yet if we wish to keep on moving toward a full-orbed friendship with God, we must grow in our relationships with others within the body of Christ in order to stretch our emotional and social capacities for befriending the God who is love. The main point of this chapter is that close friendships are essential for all believers, not only for the joy they give to us, not only for the contribution they bring to Christian community, but also for the help they provide in relating with God. If we do not increase our experiences of intimacy on the human plane,[3] we limit the kind of intimate relationship we can experience with God.

The Connection Between Loving God and Loving Others

Jesus indicated that loving both God and others is essential to living when he highlighted these two commandments in Scripture:

> "Love the LORD your God with all your heart and with all your soul and with all your mind [Deut 6:5]." This is the first and greatest commandment. And the second is like it: "Love your neighbor as yourself [Lev 19:18]." All the Law and the Prophets hang on these two commandments. (Mt 22:37-40)

These two commands may seem distinct and separate, but an important link actually connects the two. How we love God impacts how we love others. And how we love others impacts how we love God.

In Matthew 5:23-24, Jesus identifies such a reciprocal association in his teaching about strife among believers. "Therefore, if you are offering your gift at the altar and there remember that your brother has something against you, leave your gift there in front of the altar. First go and be reconciled to your brother, then come and offer your gift." Making things right with someone we have wronged is important enough to interrupt worshiping God. The apostle John makes this connection more explicit in the verse quoted at the beginning of this chapter. "If anyone says, 'I love God,' yet hates his brother, he is a liar" (1 Jn 4:20).[4] For believers, the level of intimacy we experience with God is largely affected by and limited to the depth of intimacy we experience in our human friendships.

Being aware of this essential link can motivate us to grow more loving relationships with believers in order to continue growing in our loving relationship with God. God experiences intimate and deep love within the Trinity—God already has a rich capacity for friendship. In comparison, we are the relational pygmies. Thus, the more our relational capacities are developed through human friendships, the greater will be our capacity to explore the rich potentialities within a deepening friendship with God. We first consider how God is love by examining this unique trinitarian friendship.

God Is One and Three

Although God is one divine being, God is not one person. God is an eternally existing fellowship or friendship of three persons. As J. I. Packer notes, "The one God ('he') is also, and equally, 'they,' and 'they' are always together and always cooperating."[5] Both Old and New Testaments indicate that God is a Trinity of persons (e.g., Is 48:16; 61:1; Mt 28:19; 2 Cor 13:14). Although the doctrine of the Trinity may be "one of the most important doctrines of the Christian faith"[6] it is also the most "incomprehensible" doctrine.[7] Immanuel Kant (d. 1804) ridiculed this teaching: "From the doctrine of the Trinity, taken literally, nothing whatsoever can be gained for practical purposes, even if one believed that one comprehended it—and less still if one is conscious that it surpasses all our concepts."[8]

Yet Scripture affirms three basic truths.[9] First, God is one (Deut 6:4; Jn 17:22). Millard Erickson notes, "The unity of God may be compared to the unity of husband and wife, but we must keep in mind that we are dealing with one God, not a joining of separate entities."[10] Second, the deity of each of the three persons is affirmed in Scripture (e.g., Jn 6:27; Heb 1:8; Acts 5:3-4, respectively). Third, as Erickson clarifies, "The threeness and oneness of God are not in the same respect."[11] Gordon Lewis and Bruce Demarest explain that "the Christian doctrine affirms oneness in respect to essence and threeness in respect to centers of consciousness capable of fellowship, communication, and intercession with one another."[12]

But this list of Bible facts does not exhaust the matter. For God is an eternally existing divine society of three persons[13]—Father, Son and Holy Spirit—who love each other maximally and who constitute the one Christian God. Furthermore, God invites his children to experience a close friendship relationship within the enduring divine friendship within the Trinity.[14]

The Bounty of the Love of God

Why did God create anything? For what purpose are we ultimately here? Some theologians, such as Jonathan Edwards (d. 1758), suggest that in all that God does, manifesting his glory is the prominent theme of Scripture: "to the praise of the glory of His grace" (Eph 1:6 NASB; cf. Is 42:8; 1 Cor 10:31). Others, such as John Wesley (d. 1791), highlight God's love as preeminent in God's plan: "God so loved the world that he gave his one and only Son" (Jn 3:16; cf. Acts 20:35). Roger Olson explains:

> Wesley placed God's love at the center of his preaching and teaching whereas Edwards made everything revolve around God's glory. . . . Wesley never denied or questioned God's majesty and greatness, but he tended to subordinate it to God's love. Edwards never denied or questioned God's love, but he tended to subordinate it to God's majesty and glory.[15]

One central theme may not capture all of God's purposes for creation. Olson suggests the inclusion of both majestic themes—God's glory and his love: "As the familiar children's prayer begins, 'God is *great* [his glory] and God is *good* [his love].' "[16] Certainly God's love—that God creates and acts out of the great wealth of his love—is given important emphasis in Scripture.

Yet God did not *need* to create anything in order to love, for his love is eternally manifested within the intra-trinitarian relations of the Godhead. C. S. Lewis (d. 1963) proposed using two terms—*need love* and *gift love*— to clarify the situation.[17] God's own need to give and receive love is fully satisfied through the eternal love of mutuality within the three persons of the Godhead. Our three-personed God—freely giving and receiving love among themselves—easily nullifies issues related to what philosophers have called the "lonely God problem." God has no needs outside of himself. As Wayne Grudem notes, "If there is no Trinity, then there were no interpersonal relationships within the being of God before creation, and, without personal relationships, it is difficult to see how God could be genuinely personal or be without the need for a creation to relate to."[18]

Yet out of the bounty of his own being, God's love to us is totally gift love. Daniel Fuller explains, "In other words, what motivates [God] is not the need for something he does not have or has incompletely but his delight in displaying what he already has. . . . It is the desire to take the blessing that one enjoys and extend it beyond oneself so that others will also benefit from it."[19] God's love is experienced by all in the warm sunshine and replenishing rain (Mt 5:45), and in the wonder of his rainbow, the sign of a divine promise (Gen 9:12-16).

The Mutual Love Between the Father and the Son

Furthermore, the love each person of the Godhead has for the other members of the Trinity is the benchmark for all loving relationships, giving believers a living model to which we can aspire and affirming the value of community and friendship among believers.[20] In his Gospel, John the apostle of love offers us glimpses of this dynamic loving relationship displayed between the Father and the Son (Jn 14—17).[21] Scripture highlights their oneness, their unity, their identification and their use of pronouns *us* and *we:*

> That all of them [the disciples] may be one, Father, just as you are in me and I am in you. May they also be in us so that the world may believe that you have sent me. I have given them the glory that you gave me, that they may be one as we are one: I in them and you in me. May they be brought to complete unity to let the world know that you sent me and have loved them even as you have loved me. (Jn 17:21-23)

We see a common possession, a true sharing of resources, within their love relationship.

> All that belongs to the Father is mine. . . . All I have is yours [the Father's], and all you have is mine. (Jn 16:15; 17:10)

Furthermore, an action toward or by one member of the Godhead is viewed as involving the other, indicating a strong sense of solidarity.

> If you really knew me, you would know my Father as well. . . . Anyone who has seen me has seen the Father. . . . If anyone loves me, he will obey my teaching. My Father will love him, and we will come to him and make our home with him. (Jn 14:7, 9, 23)

The Godhead is characterized by a robust interdependence through the mutual indwelling within the Trinity (*perichoresis* "as you are in me and I am in you," Jn 17:21). Is not the ultimate goal of any relationship, then, an emphasis on *we*, not *me*?[22] Since this form of community is exemplified in the longest lasting and most loving relationship that has ever existed, this love testifies to the healthiest and highest form of relating. Gerald Bray comments that "the doctrine of co-inherence [or mutual indwelling] is perhaps the most important single teaching of the Bible in an age which finds it hard to reconcile individual freedom and dignity with corporate commitment and responsibility."[23] And as D. A. Carson notes, "The relationship between the Father and the Son is the standard of all other love relationships. . . . There has always been an other-orientation to the love of God. All the manifestations of the love of God emerge out of this deeper, more fundamental reality: love is bound up in the very nature of God. God is love [1 Jn 4:8]."[24]

The lofty experience of love within the Trinity poses a challenge for us. For within any relationship between two persons involving differing levels of maturity, the lesser intimate and lesser mature person sets the boundary for how intimate the friendship can become, as illustrated in the relationship between a parent and a teenager. The more mature member is capable of greater intimacy, but the immature member cannot rise above his or her own present relational and emotional limitations.[25] Similarly, in a relationship with God, the believer—the limited member—is always the weaker party. Therefore, the more a believer develops mature relational and emotional competencies, the more he or she can enter into a richer love relationship with God.

School of Love and Friendship

To help us gain the relational and emotional skills we need for engaging in a closer relationship with him, God offers a school of love through experiences with our human friendships. Not only are human friendships a joy in and of themselves, they are also an essential means to deepen the most important relationship we can ever have, our friendship with God. Our intimate relationships with others—brothers and sisters, spouses, friends—are actually more essential to Christian living than we may have previously thought.

Yet contemporary examples of deeply intimate friendships are rare. Many of us are novices at intimacy, may I say, especially us men, for relationships are not highly valued in society today, as noted by physician Richard Swenson.

> A frightful consequence of the dramatic [technological] changes of the last few decades is how rapidly and thoroughly the relational life has come unglued. . . . Nearly all indices of the scripturally prescribed relational life have suffered major setbacks over the last three decades. Marriage—worse; parenting—worse; the extended family—worse; the sense of community—worse.[26]

Furthermore, although buzzwords like *community* and *love* abound in the church, deep relationships fair no better here.[27] Believers tend to gravitate toward ways of seeking God that are predominantly individualistic: personal Bible study, private prayer and times of solitude. Although helpful (and recommended in this book), these spiritual disciplines do not enrich the relational competencies we need to deepen our relationship with a God who experiences a deep fellowship within the Trinity.

Yet this God of love invites us into the divine fellowship to experience, in some measure, an everlasting love grounded in an already existing close friendship relationship. "Jesus replied, 'If anyone loves me, he will obey my teaching. My Father will love him, and *we will come to him and make our home with him*" (Jn 14:23, emphasis added). The key point of this chapter is that we must develop closer friendships with other believers in order to make room in our lives for God. Greater intimacy experienced with others increases our capacity to become more intimate with God.

What is needed, then, is a healthy, biblically based view of friendships. In the following pages I propose a way of understanding friendships to accentuate the rich potential of good that comes with deep friendships. Since the word *friend* is used for a multitude of associations with others, whether they are intimate or not, we need to mark out appropriate distinctions for the kinds of personal relationships we experience, among which "deep friendship" will surface as one particular category. Then we will consider what Scripture teaches about the characteristics of friendship and return to the theme of how friendships are essential to Christian community and knowing God more intimately.

Talking about friendship in a book can never do justice to its dynamic wonder. In working through this chapter, the reader may wish to personalize the topic by keeping in mind the names and faces of valued relationships: parents, brothers, sisters, spouse, children, close relatives, close friends, colleagues at work, small group members, church members, club members, neighbors—persons who are special and with whom one spends a lot of time. Or it may be worthwhile to focus primarily on the close companions of one's life. For example, which persons would be invited to

☐ attend a special birthday celebration?

☐ serve together on a short-term overseas missions project?

☐ spend a day at Disneyland, or go shopping, or enjoy an evening of dinner and conversation?

☐ pray for a confidential prayer request?

My fortieth birthday party is a continuing special memory for me because I was in the company of some exceptional friends. To make this singular event a reality, our family spent Easter break at my folks' place—a good two-day drive from our house in another state. But for me, it was worth the effort. Here I sat around the table—overloaded with pizza, my favorite meal—with some buddies with whom I have been through thick and thin: J. P., Bill, Keith, Scott and Walt. A number of years had passed since we had worked at the same place, but now we were together again—greeting each other with a warm embrace, reliving shared moments, laughing and ribbing each other, and sharing openly and honestly about deep matters. Memories flooded my soul of the good times and of the difficult times. I am glad these men continue to love God. But just as important to me, these men love me.

Taking out the scrapbook of our memories and reliving special moments with these significant others can bring a personal touch to the reading as we consider a biblical perspective on friendship.

Distinctions Among Relationships

But first we must clarify the range and diversity among human relationships.[28] Scripture presents one scheme by way of three terms: *friend, brother* (or family) and *neighbor:* "Do not forsake your friend and the friend of your father, and do not go to your brother's house when disaster strikes you—better a neighbor nearby than a brother far away" (Prov 27:10; cf. Ex 32:27; Jer 6:21; Lk 14:12). Based on distinctions stemming from differing sets of obligations or expectations within a given relationship, three broad types of relationships are proposed: (1) close friendship love, (2) family kinship love, and (3) neighbor love.[29] To provide a tighter boundary around the first category, *close friendship* will refer to those with whom we tend to socialize often. Then the third category will include all other relationships we have beyond family. Each of these three spheres demands different claims on our loyalties.[30]

1. *Close friendship love* is a love mutually engaged in and voluntarily chosen, usually among those we tend to socialize with freely and frequently.

2. *Family kinship love* is a love springing from the given ties of family and kinship relations (blood and marriage). Kinship ties bear an implied covenantal relation of reciprocity in which, during times of crisis, the family pulls together.

3. *Neighbor love* is a love of hospitality to others and is a broad, catch-all category of love, which includes (a) those for whom there may be a limited expectation of return of favors, but much less than with close friends or family, and (b) those with whom we have frequent contact for various reasons (e.g., work, church and neighborhood). Additionally, it consists of (c) all one-way love relationships with those we do not know well, strangers for whom we expect no return. Finally, (d) enemies would also come under this rubric.

The categories of close friend and family are easily discerned in Scripture. For example, "There is a friend who sticks closer than a brother" (Prov 18:24). Shared elements within these categories permit Scripture to group them together in parallelism on occasion. "A friend loves at all times, and a brother is born for adversity" (Prov 17:17). "A poor man is shunned by all his relatives—how much more do his friends avoid him!" (Prov 19:7). In the Old Testament, sometimes *friend* and *neighbor* overlap in meaning, but context does identify when a close friend is in view, as Derek Kidner explains: "The common word for 'friend' (Heb. *rea'*) means, equally, 'neighbor': it has very much the range of meaning of our word 'fellow' [British]. At the far extreme, it signifies merely *the other fellow*; at its nearest it stands for a person with whom one has close friendship."[31] Each kind of love is more complex, adding more commitment and intentionality, as represented in the three sets of concentric circles in figure 2.1.

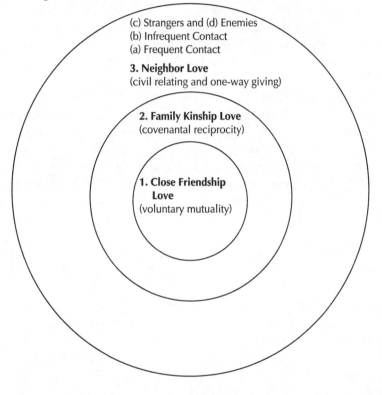

(c) Strangers and (d) Enemies
(b) Infrequent Contact
(a) Frequent Contact

3. Neighbor Love
(civil relating and one-way giving)

2. Family Kinship Love
(covenantal reciprocity)

1. Close Friendship Love
(voluntary mutuality)

Figure 2.1. Circles of love: Friends, family, neighbor

Most do not need a divine command to love friends or to love immediate family members, not even ourselves for that matter. But we do need a command to love those outside these circles—to love our neighbor as ourselves. This command is first recorded in Leviticus 19:18 and repeated in the New Testament on several occasions (Mt 5:43; 19:19; 22:39 [parallel, Mk 12:31]; Lk 10:27; Rom 13:8-10; Gal 5:14; Jas 2:8; cf. 1 Cor 10:24; Gal

6:10). The command prompts us to increase our circle of comfort and extend hospitality to those who do not normally return our favors.

We come into this world as helpless children, totally dependent on parents and the care of others. From the outset, love is offered without our loving in return. (I can appreciate this point more now as a parent having my own children.) But along the way we take small steps in learning to love others. Describing the process sounds simple: we learn how to love as we have been loved (cf. Jn 13:34). But becoming a master at loving others takes a lifetime, perhaps an eternity.

The Predicament of Loving
The practical challenge is how to continue obeying the command to practice universal Christian love to all while at the same time allowing for distinctions in our various spheres of relationships (e.g., friends, family, neighbors) for whom the Bible also obligates us to love. The dilemma comes to light in Jesus' words, which seem to downplay the importance of friendships. "If you love those who love you, what reward will you get? Are not even the tax collectors doing that? And if you greet only your brothers, what are you doing more than others? Do not even pagans do that?" (Mt 5:46). A tension, then, arises between a universal, unconditional form of love, "Christian" love (popularly associated with the Greek term *agape*),[32] and a friendship-oriented, mutually returned, more exclusive form of love that Jesus seems to be critiquing in Matthew 5.

Consider the following contrasts between these two types of love:
□ Universal Christian love must be given to anyone, even to our enemies; exclusive friendship love is usually restricted to a few select friends.
□ Universal Christian love is love given without any thought of receiving love back; exclusive friendship love is a mutual love—it expects that love will be returned.
□ Universal Christian love is steadfast and faithful—it can never end; exclusive friendship love changes with time—and sometimes may end.
A legitimate tension stares us in the face.

At one level of comparison, a universal type of love tends to be a form of impersonal love, or rather a nonperson-specific type of love. That is, universal love is offered regardless of who the particular recipient is. It is a faithful, enduring form of love that keeps on giving like the Energizer battery-operated bunny, no matter if any love is returned. As helpful and necessary as that kind of love is, we desire much more as we grow in our capacity for deep love. We wish to be loved *because* of who we are, not in spite of it. At the human level, that requires a version of friendship love. In his *Spiritual Friendship*, a profound medieval treatise on friendship, Aelred of Rievaulx (d. 1167) draws a distinction between these two kinds of love, friendship and charity (universal Christian love). "In the perfection of charity we love very many . . . but yet we do not admit [all of] these to the intimacy of our friendship."[33] At our deepest level of being, we yearn for a mutual and intimate kind of companionship that deep friendships can offer.

Matthew 5 does not prohibit friendship love altogether, it only condemns an exclusive focus on friendship love as the totality of one's sphere of relationships. Expanding our range of love is the point.

Actually, friendship is a school through which we learn how to offer love of a genuinely Christian and universal kind to all. Theologian Gilbert Meilander explains:

> Attachment to friends is a school in which we are trained for that greater [heavenly] community. Steadfast faithfulness in [universal] love is necessary even when friendship ceases. But faithful friendship is the goal—a goal which can be realized only when a friend is loved in God. . . . Life is a journey, a pilgrimage toward that community in which friends love one another in God and time no longer inflicts its wounds on friendship. Along the way, friendship is a school, training us in the meaning and enactment of love. Friendship is also a foretaste of the internal reciprocities of love which have yet to be fully realized.[34]

Thus, friendship is a great reward in its own right, an end in itself, yet it also serves as the crucial means to expand our loving—to reach beyond our circle of comfort.

Furthermore, an exclusive love is the only appropriate kind of love to offer God, and—for those who are married—only an exclusive love will satisfy our spouses. For these particular instances, a universal, open-armed love for all will not suffice. Actually, marriage offers a helpful case for analysis of relationships since marriage is only for this life (Mt 22:30). Aside from the aspects unique to this life (e.g., procreation and parenting), marriage affords a contained context for two people of vastly different backgrounds—a crosscultural relationship of gender[35]—to work over a lifetime at becoming deep friends. With a commitment to an exclusive marriage covenant, each spouse can and must explore how to become genuine companions, how to grow into a loving unity and mutual indwelling of each other that mirrors the Trinity. Of course, this deep friendship aspect is not unique to marriage; it can be experienced by any two persons willing to commit themselves to work at becoming close friends (e.g., 1 Sam 18:1-4). In the scheme of things, God has instituted the marital context to bring two diverse people together to work at becoming one. Similarly in the church, Christian unity is the result of believers of differing backgrounds who work at loving each other, sustained by God's grace.

Thus, we must continue maturing in love by extending it to those beyond our circle of friendship and family—to neighbors, to strangers and to enemies, as suggested in figure 2.1. Our growth in universal love, an unconditional kind of love, also actually helps sustain these differing love relationships. Furthermore, both kinds of love are necessary in a deep relationship, an exclusive love as well as a universal and enduring love for all, for there are times of crisis when a friend cannot give love but needs to receive it.

Before suggesting a more comprehensive way of understanding friendships, we look at our topic from two additional angles.

Aristotle on Friendship

Today the word *friend* covers a multitude of relationships with varying degrees of loyalty. To provide some boundaries within this expansive terrain, we consider one classical threefold typology from Aristotle (d. 322 B.C.) that focuses on what about the other attracts us. The first classification of friendship is based on the enjoyment of common interests or pleasures, such as golf partners, members of a quilting club or the group that gets together Saturday evening for cards. Most of our Christian friends or church members might be included here since the association is based on a common interest in loving and serving God.

A second group involves relationships based primarily on benefits or advantages that may accrue to us because of the friendship—a friendship of usefulness. The benefit may result from skills the person has, for example, a business partner, a teammate in a soccer club or colleagues in a ministry team at church. Or we may barter benefits with our own resources: trading days off, lending a pickup truck or gardening tools. These two categories of relationships—both probably relating to the biblical term *neighbor*—are common in life. Close friendships typically develop from either friendships of common interests or friendships of mutual benefit.

In Aristotle's final category, people seek the friendship for its own sake, a friendship of character, for the sake of the friend himself or herself—not solely for common interests or benefits to be received. The initial relationship, taking seed elsewhere, blossoms into a full-flowered friendship of character in which close friends seek the good together. Within this kind of relationship a deep and mutual love can grow. Genuine deep friendship is characteristic of this third category.

Friendships, then, will range among all three Aristotelian classifications. Or, for our purpose, they can be viewed as ranging within two categories: (1) closer friendships (of mutual advantage or interest) and (2) deep or spiritual friendships of character.

Relationships of Status
Another useful ingredient for the recipe involves classifying relationships according to aspects of status. For example, in most cultures one's age is a significant factor for making distinctions, partitioning people into those who are older, those within the same age span and those who are younger. This issue figures prominently in our own country, especially during the years of junior high and senior high school. Within Asian cultures, it is a sensitive issue across the age spectrum. Of course, people are also grouped other ways, for example, according to competencies (e.g., gradations in educational degrees or vocation certifications), position or role (e.g., CEO and employee, pastor and church member, Bible study leader and group members), and socioeconomic status or social class in society (e.g., according to annual salary, to longevity within a community or, in India, to one's caste).

Consider the arena of mentoring as a way of capturing a status-based assessment of relationships, without creating a permanent stereotype often attached to particular roles mentioned above. The mentor usually offers sage advice based on a little more expertise and experience, while the related role of protégé or mentoree belongs to the apprentice who defers to the wisdom of the greater. Healthy flexibility in mentoring roles is evident in the relationship between Barnabas and Paul (also known as Saul). Barnabas (Acts 4:36-37), a respected church leader, was the first to welcome the new convert Saul into Christian fellowship (Acts 9:26-27). After Barnabas was commissioned by the Jerusalem church to head up the new church in Antioch, he invited Saul to join him in the teaching ministry (Acts 11:19-26). While ministering together in Antioch, the Holy Spirit commissioned Barnabas and Saul to begin a missionary journey to the Gentiles (Acts 13:1-3). Apparently while on that first journey, Saul (now named Paul, Acts 13:9) became the chief speaker (Acts 14:12) and the leader of the missionary team ("Paul and his companions," Acts 13:13).[36] Eventually two missionary teams were commissioned, one headed by Paul and the other by Barnabas (Acts 15:39-40). On one occasion, Paul mentored Barnabas when he and Peter erred in a matter (Gal 2:11-14). In sensitivity to cultural mores, Scripture also encourages mentoring relationships along lines of age: between older women and younger women (Tit 2:4), and younger men and their elders (1 Pet 5:5).[37]

Along with the mentor-mentoree relation is the peer-peer relationship, in which status basically plays no part. It is within this particular type of relationship that deep friendship emerges, for equality is an essential feature. As Jerome (d. 420; translator of the Latin Bible) explains, "Friendship either finds equals or makes them. Where there is inequality, one takes pre-eminence, and the other bears subjection."[38] Or as Aelred of Rievaulx informs us, "It is also a law of friendship that a superior must be on a plane of equality with the inferior. . . . Therefore in friendship . . . let the lofty descend, the lowly ascend; the rich be in want, the poor become rich; and thus let each communicate his condition to the other, so that equality may be the result."[39]

The friendship of Jonathan and David illustrates this movement from a status distinction to one of equality as friendship deepens (1 Sam 18—20). We witness the kindness of Jonathan, heir to the throne, taking into his bosom a companion of lowly estate—a shepherd boy (also serving as court musician for the king). They establish a covenant with each other (1 Sam 18:3) that spanned a generation and eventually benefited Jonathan's son after Jonathan was killed in battle (2 Sam 9:1-7). Due to his deep friendship with David ("[Jonathan] loved him as himself," 1 Sam 18:1), Jonathan risked the wrath of his own father, King Saul—a bond of kinship—to protect his friend from harm's way. Despite his position as the natural heir to the throne, Jonathan submitted himself to God's sovereign plan for Israel and recognized David as God's anointed and future king (1 Sam 20:13, 15)—a demonstration of genuine friendship, bearing no conflict of interest. Sadly, over this very issue King Saul forced David to flee for his life, separating these best of friends.

Proposing a way to reflect on various kinds of relationships is no easy task. As a starting point, let me suggest a three-by-three relationship matrix in which the different categories previously described are combined as a means of assessing our relationships (see figure 2.2). This side of heaven we probably cannot maintain more than a handful of deep, spirit-

Status Attraction	A **Mentor** to Me	**Peer-Peer** Relationships *"Closer Friends"*	Someone I Tend to **Mentor**
Family/Kinship	Parents, grandparents	Brothers, sisters cousins	Children, nieces, nephews
Neighbor/Friends — Common Interest or Pleasure	Pastor, church leaders, teachers	Fellow church members, home Bible study group members, gardening group, golfing buddies	Team you coach, class you teach
Neighbor/Friends — Mutual Benefit or Advantage	Employer, board of directors, sports coach	Fellow ministry team members, fellow employees, team members in sports, business partner	Employees you supervise, those you lead
Spiritual Friends		Friends of character*	

*Genuine spiritual friendships of character will usually be a few among those within the peer-peer relationship column, due to the essential feature of status equality. Of course, those in columns on either side could become "closer friends" (as indicated by the dotted lines), but it will involve a status change toward equality.

Figure 2.2. Relationship matrix

ual friendships of character. As Thomas Aquinas (d. 1274) noted, "Perfect friendship cannot be extended to a great many persons."[40] All forms of associations will help us develop our relational skills, but it is our spiritual friendships that will mark us more deeply.

Not long ago I was reminded of how important deep, spiritual friendships are by the following e-mail from Alan. He almost left this earth early through a heart attack. But God graciously gave an early warning, and my friend was ushered immediately into the operating room to undergo bypass surgery. We kept in contact during this trying time, and one day I was overwhelmed by this e-mail:

> Time has elapsed, but your true friendship and love has not gone unnoticed. I want to take this moment to express my deepest thanks for your sacrificial love and thoughtfulness in probably one of my closest moments of life. Thank you for living up to the ideal of what true friendship and fellowship is about. I am glad we experienced some of the most joyous moments together (at graduation, at your wedding, even the celebrations of many events at life). Thanks for checking up on me, and sharing a few of those closer moments of life on this side of eternity. I can't ask for a finer brother who in his own way shows his loyalty and commitment. Truly I say thank you![41]

Although my dear friend speaks with hyperbole, these words testify to the results of years of working at being friends. Good friendships are cultivated through shared experiences over time, and so it is with our relationship with God.

Now we turn to examine more specifically what Scripture teaches about friendship and then consider how friendship plays a role in building Christian community.

Friendship in Scripture

Surprisingly, the common Greek terms for "friend" (*philos*) or "friendship" (*philia*) rarely appear in the New Testament.[42] Instead the Bible addresses the important issue of friendship *thematically*. Teaching on friendship must be culled from a variety of sources: examples of friendships (e.g., Jonathan and David, as noted above), sparse explicit biblical references to friendship, mostly in the wisdom literature of the Old Testament (e.g., "A friend loves at all times," Prov 17:17), the underlying texture and tone of certain biblical writings (e.g., the book of Philippians, to be developed in the next section), contributing features of a healthy Christian community (e.g., New Testament "one another" verses) and the intratrinitarian love of the Father and the Son (as was treated earlier). In the following section, we explore some of these sources.

Paul and Friendship

A rich treasure of common friendship language from the ancient world is evident in the apostle Paul's letter to the Philippians (1:27—2:2).[43] By selecting the common terms of their day associated with deep friendships, Paul urges these folk to continue growing in their friendship with each other as a body of believers. Consider these parallels with the ancient world. In his discussion of friendship, Aristotle used the phrase "two friends, one soul."[44] Paul used "one soul" *(mia psyche)*[45] in his encouragement to stand "firm in one spirit, with one mind striving together for the faith of the gospel" (1:27 NASB). Variations of this term occur in 1:27, "one spirit" *(en eni pneumati); in 2:2, "being one in spirit" (sumpsyche, "fellow soul"); and in 2:20, "kindred spirit" (NASB; isopsyche, "equal soul").

"Agreement or union in thought" was another common expression of friendship used by Cicero (d. 43 B.C.) in his classic treatise *On Friendship.*[46] Twice Paul employed this same phrase *(to auto phronein),* first in 2:2, "being like-minded," and then in 4:2, "to agree with each other," specific words offered for the two women experiencing relational difficulties. "Having things in common" *(koina ta philon)*[47] was also a broadly employed criterion of friendship. Phraseology using a similar *koine* ("common") motif appears in 1:5, "your partnership" *(koinonia); in 2:1, "fellowship of the Spirit"; and in 1:7, "all of you share" (sygkoinonous; see also 3:10 and 4:14-15). In addition, a key criterion of "frankness of speech" *(parrēsia,* "boldness") appears in 1:20 ("courage"), and is illustrated in the public rebuke of Euodia and Syntyche, with whom Paul must have had a close relationship for them to bear such public shame. Although Paul avoids using the common word for *friend* in his letters, the particular terms he employs in this letter suggest his own close relationship with these believers, as well as his exhortation to the body of believers to continue becoming closer friends.

Love One Another

Another source of biblical information useful for guiding friendships includes the various "one another" verses scattered throughout the New Testament (see table 2.1). Such a checklist indicates the breadth and depth of growing relationships. Some of these exhortations can be experienced at almost any level of relationship, such as "Encourage one another" or "Offer hospitality to one another." But some require a greater depth of trust and intimacy to engage freely in more personal aspects of loving: "Admonish one another" or "Confess your sins to each other."[48] Within our varied relationships, are we able to practice each command

Love One Another (Jn 13:34; Rom 13:8; 1 Thess 3:12; 1 Pet 4:8; 1 Jn 4:11)

Accept one another. (Rom 15:7)
Admonish one another. (Rom 15:14 NASB; Col 3:16)
Pursue the things which make for peace and the **building up** of one another. (Rom 14:19 NASB)
Carry each other's **burdens**. (Gal 6:2)
Have equal **concern** for each other. (1 Cor 12:25)
Confess your sins to each other. (Jas 5:16)
Be **devoted** to one another. (Rom 12:10)
Encourage each other. (1 Thess 4:18; Heb 3:13; 10:25)
Forgive one another. (Eph 4:32; Col 3:13)
Greet one another. (Rom 16:16; 2 Cor 13:12)
Don't **grumble** against each other. (Jas 5:9)
Live in **harmony** with one another. (Rom 12:16)
Honor one another. (Rom 12:10)
Offer **hospitality** to one another. (1 Pet 4:9)
Clothe yourselves with **humility** toward one another. (1 Pet 5:5)
Be **kind** and **compassionate** to one another. (Eph 4:32; 1 Thess 5:15)
Do not **lie** to each other. (Col 3:9)
Stop **passing judgment** on one another. (Rom 14:13)
Be **patient, bearing with** one another. (Eph 4:2; Col 3:12-13)
Live in **peace** with each other. (1 Thess 5:13)
Pray for each other. (Jas 5:16)
Regard one another as more important than yourselves. (Phil 2:3 NASB)
Serve one another in love. (Gal 5:13)
Do not **slander** one another. (Jas 4:11)
Speak to one another with psalms, hymns and spiritual songs. (Eph 5:19; Col 3:17)
Spur one another on toward love and good deeds. (Heb 10:24)
Submit to one another. (Eph 5:21)
Teach . . . one another. (Col 3:16)

Table 2.1. New Testament "one another" passages

somewhere? In this regard, marriage may offer the best opportunity to experience and practice all three categories of love within one relationship—the very particular love of deep intimate friendship, the familial covenant love that binds for life ("till death do us part") and also a version of hospitality—offering love with no strings attached. The "one another" list may prove useful as a diagnostic tool as well, identifying areas of lack or limits in our present relationships.[49]

Jesus Builds Community with Friendships
Jesus himself shows the way in befriending and loving others. His example lends support for an emphasis on two distinct relational themes: community and friendship. Unfortunately, the command "to make disciples" (Mt 28:19-20) is often narrowly misconstrued today, so that discipleship is viewed as primarily involving a one-on-one mentoring relationship. Although such mentoring is one important component of the process (e.g., Jesus' face-to-face encounter in the restoration of Peter, Jn 21:15-19), it misses Jesus' major thrust. For Jesus, discipleship or disciple making primarily takes place within the context of community. During his earthly ministry, Jesus appointed twelve individuals from among his various followers, "designating them apostles—that they might be with him and that he might send them out to preach" (Mk 3:14). Michael Wilkins notes:

> Jesus called individuals to discipleship, yet responding to that call brought disciples into a community of faith. . . . As Luke continues his story from the Gospel to the book of Acts, he allows us to see the crucial necessity of the community for discipleship. . . . Through the Spirit, the community would now provide the fellowship, encouragement, edification, and mutuality necessary for following the Master in the new era.[50]

In Christ and through the Spirit all believers are joined to this new community. Jesus institutes a new or surrogate kinship community in which those who do "the will of my Father in heaven [are] my brother and sister and mother" (Mt 12:50). Such a community is the larger context in which discipleship takes place.

Yet another trend is noted in Jesus' example. The Gospels record that within the Twelve, Jesus had an inner circle of deep friends: Peter, James and John. On three occasions Jesus specifically invited these three to join him (Mk 5:37; 9:2; 14:33). Among these three, John became the closest friend of Jesus (known as "the disciple whom Jesus loved," Jn 13:23; 19:26; 20:2; 21:7, 20, who emphasized the concept that "God is love," 1 Jn 4:8). One critical occasion with these close friends took place in the Garden of Gethsemane. Jesus confessed, "My soul is overwhelmed with sorrow to the point of death. Stay here and keep watch with me" (Mt 26:38). As Robert Stein notes, "At Gethsemane we see, perhaps for the first time, an occasion when Jesus needed his disciples. . . . But they failed him, for 'he came and found them sleeping' (Mk 14:37, 40; compare 13:36)."[51]

Near the end of his ministry, Jesus proposed to the twelve disciples a "new" command to "love one another" (Jn 13:34). The new element or standard within the command came from Jesus' own example—"as I have loved you" (Jn 13:34; 15:12; see also Jn 13:1; 15:9). During the Upper Room Discourse, just prior to his death, Jesus introduced the term *friendship* to his disciples.

> My command is this: Love each other as I have loved you. Greater love has no one than this, that he lay down his life for his *friends*. You are my *friends* if you do what I command. I no longer call you servants, because a servant does not know his master's business. Instead, I have called you *friends*, for everything that I learned from my Father I have made known to you. (Jn 15:12-15, emphasis added)

Outside of the circle of the Twelve, Jesus had other friends, including women who offered financial support (Lk 8:1-3). The Gospel of John notes especially Jesus' friendship with Mary, Martha and Lazarus (Jn 11:5). It may be that Lazarus was chosen by God the Father to die and rise from the dead due to Jesus' special love for him (Jn 11:3, 36). Among some of his followers and disciples, Jesus developed closer friendships, thus demonstrating the need for deep friendships within the larger body of Christ.

Linking Community and Friendship
What is the relationship, then, between friendship and community? It seems that a symbiotic connection exists between the two in that each provides something the other requires. Any committed intimate friendship requires a larger community for the friendship to grow and flourish.[52]

Conversely, community requires various sets of deep friendships and familial bonds scattered among its membership. These relational ties provide the human glue that sustains the community both relationally and experientially, for "a friend loves at all times" (Prov 17:17) and can help leaven the whole lump toward deeper community. The concept of a Christian community of love is a deeply relational one; it is more than a bunch of individuals who happen to occupy a similar geographical space and who act civilly toward one another for a time. A Christian community needs long-term, genuine love, a love that matures through intentionality and shared experiences over time.

Thus, New Testament community is an emergent interdependency of people in Christ who are in the process of loving each other genuinely, a process of becoming one. Just as with any earthly family, where relational love is never automatic but must be cultivated by all parties, so in the family of God, *relationships must be cultivated.* Theologically speaking, believers are already one in the Spirit (Eph 4:3), a unity based on our position as members of God's family. Yet experientially we must become one by growing in our love and friendship for each other. It is similar to our status of being saints or holy ones by virtue of Christ's imputed righteousness. Although called saints, we still must become sanctified in practice. Likewise, we are one in theory, but not yet fully in practice. Our communal love must grow through the working of each part (Eph 4:16). Thus, various sets of friendships must be evident and interspersed throughout the members of the community for the community to be growing up in love—it can be no other way when people are involved.

Moreover, Scripture affirms three relational entities or clusters (e.g., Eccles 4:9-12) that need to be factored into the mix, each receiving some prominence in Scripture:

☐ individuals (e.g., "each one may receive what is due," 2 Cor 5:10, and "as each part does its work," Eph 4:16)

☐ dyads, relationships between two persons (e.g., marriage, friendships)

☐ groups (three or more persons, e.g., Trinity, family, church leaders, local church body)

Regarding the entities of dyads and groups, figure 2.3 depicts a formula as one way of portraying the relationship between friendship and community.

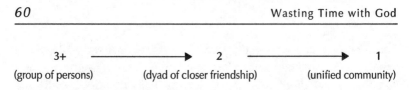

Figure 2.3. The essential linkage of friendship within community

The point is that for a group of people to become truly one, to grow genuinely into a unity of mutual indwelling, they must first develop closer friendships with many and deep friendships among a few. This middle step *cannot* be skipped. Thus, if various sets of closer and deep friendships are not being developed throughout the membership of a local church, then little genuine community can exist; instead, there is only an aggregate of individual believers. Perhaps because of this factor Jesus selected two sets of brothers (Peter and Andrew, Mt 4:18; and James and John, Mt 4:21)—involving already existing close relationships—to be included in the twelve disciples in order to jump-start his community. Furthermore, it is interesting to note that it was within this already intimate circle of brothers and business partners[53] that Jesus developed deep friendships. Community, at the human level, is developed through various sets of close friendships, as Simon Chan explains:

> Exclusive friendships in the Christian community can be inclusive if the community is conceived as a series of concentric circles or small interlocking circles of friends. Each Christian has circles of friends of varying degrees of intensity. At some point these circles intersect one another, linked together by common friends. Thus everyone has some exclusive friends.[54]

Furthermore, healthy family units within the local church are also essential for a healthy church body.[55] Within the family unit itself, made up of parents and children, the interconnection of friendship and community is evident on a smaller scale. Home is where children can learn about hospitality, friendship and community by experience. The marriage can supply the friendship as the foundational center of this larger family community. A great potential for fullness as a deep friendship, at the human level, is in marriage, for the two "will become one flesh" (Gen 2:24). Michael Wilkins, a former drill sergeant and now seminary professor, shares how God used the love of his wife, Lynne, to help him grow as a new Christian.

During that first year of marriage, I would get so frustrated and angry that I'd look for the first thing available to take my rage on. . . . But it was then that I began to understand God's love for the first time. Lynne had God's heart, a heart that never stopped loving. . . . God's love continued to pour into her heart, which she then was able to pour out to me, in patience, kindness, soft answers, and spiritual guidance. . . . Her love was the example I needed of how love worked. . . . For twenty years, the fruit of her yieldedness to God has been a husband whose heart and life have been transformed by love.[56]

The Goodness of Friendship

Without growing deeper in close friendships, believers will never be able to enter into abundant Christian living that Jesus promised, for friendships operate as our school to train us in love. Good friendships are not only a joy in and of themselves, but they yield three important benefits for Christian living, two of which were treated in this chapter. First, good Christian friendships help us develop a greater capacity for intimacy with God. The more we deepen our friendships and thus grow in our relational competencies, the more we can enter into the joy of a relationship with God.

Second, deep friendships are essential to the development of a rich quality of community within the body of Christ. As noted in Philippians 2, Paul urges the church toward becoming a more loving community by embodying the essential characteristics of genuine friendship. "Then make my joy complete by being like-minded, having the same love, being one in spirit and purpose" (Phil 2:2). Pockets of close friends throughout the church membership provide the nurturing context for community to be enriched.

Finally, deep friendships help us grow in our own maturity, for such soul mates become another self to reflect back to us the depths of our own journey in character formation. Paul Wadell develops this idea in his book *Friendship and the Moral Life*. "The moral life is the seeking of and growing in the good in the company of friends who also want to be good. Friendship is the crucible of the moral life, the relationship in which we come to embody the good by sharing it with friends who also delight in the good."[57] As Scripture teaches us, "Better is open rebuke / than hidden love. Wounds from a friend can be trusted" (Prov 27:5-6). "Pursue righteousness, faith, love and peace, along with those who call on the Lord out of a pure heart" (2 Tim 2:22).

The move to another state prompted Pastor Jack Deere to reflect on the key values of life.

> The two greatest sources of joy in life are God and friends. When I look over my life, the times I've been happiest were the times I was closest to God and had close friends I loved very much. Every time I've tried to find a greater happiness in something else—a career, a possession, a hobby—I've been disappointed. God made my heart that way, and he made your heart that way too. Real joy only comes through an intimate love relationship with God and friends.[58]

Good friendships are important not only for this life but for the next life too.

Wasting Time with God: Hospitality

Hospitality is creating a context in which other Christians are welcome and can nurture the beginning and growth of closer friendships. The New Testament Greek term for *hospitality* literally means "love of strangers" *(philoxenia)*. It is helping people who do not know each other to form bridges upon which further relationships can take place. As Henri Nouwen notes, "The church is perhaps one of the few places left where we can meet people who are different than we are but with whom we can form a larger family."[59] Although we may only handle a handful of deep intimate friends, such dyads offer the relational support for reaching out to others. We have the capacity for many relationships, and God urges us to continue to enlarge our comfort zone of friends and neighbors. "If you love those who love you, what reward will you get? Are not even the tax collectors doing that?" (Mt 5:46). Such a ministry of bringing Christians together may involve a wide variety of avenues, such as social events (watching a movie or sports events on TV together, going out for coffee, playing a game at home), hobbies (gardening, fishing) and projects (making a quilt, fixing a plumbing leak, yard work).

Church leaders need to make room for a variety of open groups for which believers can join at any time to meet others and initiate particular friendships. In this regard, two factors must be noted. First, it is possible to improve one's relational skills. According to Steve Duck, a major researcher of friendships, "Because it is a skill, relationshipping . . . is something that can be improved, refined, polished (even coached and practiced) like any other skill, trained like any other, and made more fluent."[60] Based on his research, he identifies various components and offers detailed information for the three general phases outlined: attraction, developmental period, and deepening and intensifying relationships. Second, developing friendships takes effort and time. Because developing friendships seemed so easy during our growing-up years, we now assume that good relationships just happen, that we have no actual part in their development or demise. In his summary of a twenty-five-year research of optimum human functioning, University of Chicago Professor Mihalyi Csikszentmihalyi destroys this myth:

> People believe that friendships happen naturally, and if they fail, there is nothing to be done about it but feel sorry for oneself. In adolescence, when so many interests are shared with others and one has great stretches of free time to invest in a relationship, making friends might seem like a spontaneous process. But later in life friendships rarely happen by chance: one must cultivate them as assiduously as one must cultivate a job or a family.[61]

If it takes planning and work to become proficient as a musician, or basketball player, or plumber, or office manager, why not for building good friendship?

How regular are we as members of a Christian fellowship? Have we identified with a local church? Within that local church, do we regularly fellowship with a smaller set of believers to become known and to come to know others in regular face-to-face encounters? The church is a family, and growing in love requires ongoing conversation and caring among its members. Just attending the main weekly worship service will not permit love to grow; it requires regular participation in the lives of believers (Eph 4:16). Getting connected to a smaller group of believers is imperative if we wish to obey Christ's command to love one another and to love God. From within such groups, those with whom we can move toward deep friendships may be discovered and those relationships developed. Furthermore, repairing relationships with other believers is imperative when possible (e.g., Rom 12:18). James Houston warns us, "Our relationship with God can never be right when our relationship with other people is wrong."[62]

Wasting Time with God: Spiritual Friendships

In addition, if we wish to deepen our friendship with God, we will also need to intensify our special companions to move to even deeper levels of openness and intimacy. Such friendships offer the potential for experiencing the kind of mutual indwelling characteristic of the Trinity ("that they may be one as we are one," Jn 17:22). For example, at one point I was satisfied with my marriage to Beth, going on twenty-five years now. When the truths of this chapter pierced my heart, I realized I could not leave our marriage relationship as it was. Since I yearn to know God more, I had greater motivation to initiate more conversations, though I tend to be the less talkative one, to work through conflicts and honestly admit my stubbornness and desire to be right, and to give more thought about how to do my part in developing a more intimate relationship with Beth.

Since frankness of speech is one essential criterion of a close friendship, we may wish to monitor our talk with friends. Does the conversation stay at surface levels, or do we at times penetrate to confidential matters of our soul? Intimacy among friends involves honest and loving self-disclosure.[63] God set the pace for our friendship with him by revealing himself to us. Furthermore, Jesus offers to share more of himself with us, if we wish: "Whoever has my commands and obeys them, he is the one who loves me. He who loves me will be loved by my Father, and I too will love him and show myself to him" (Jn 14:21). Our natural tendency is to hide our mistakes, our foibles, our sins. But that prevents us from developing deeper integrity, which is characterized by "truth in the inner parts" (Ps 51:6). "Therefore confess your sins to each other and pray for each other so that you may be healed" (Jas 5:16). In the company of a good friend, we are accepted as we are. We can explore our sins and gain caring counsel to move on.

For example, one of my spiritual friends has been in my face and by my side. He was kind to invade the privacy of my finances, to ask penetrating questions and work with me to suggest strategies to get on a more sound financial basis. Also, without my asking he kindly attended a conference session where I presented a paper launching into new arenas of research for me. He was there to bail me out in case I faltered during the question time. In the company of deep friends, we can flourish.

If we wish to nurture spiritual friendships in our church settings, besides sponsoring open groups various closed groups will need to be fostered among the body in which group memberships will remain unchanged for longer periods of time. Consider the Club as one example of a closed group. For over the past forty years, the same fourteen women have met once a month.[64] These former schoolmates from a local high school in southern California made a commitment to stay connected. In earlier times, while the vitality of youth pervaded, they gathered for long evenings. Now mostly in their 60s, they plan afternoon engagements. Lucille Basye, whose priorities are God, family, Club, shares, "Our marriages aren't perfect and neither are our kids, and we love each other more than we did then." They value the peace and comfort they derive from these long lasting and dear relationships. Stella Carucci philosophizes, "This group keeps us young. It is the relationship that helps us deal with all the others . . . even the one with ourselves." Anything valuable requires our best effort. Friendship is worthy of this kind of investment. What advice do they offer for budding friendships? "Forget one-upmanship. Never judge. Think nothing of different income and education level. Be brutally honest. Give, give, give when others hit hard times. Learn to razz and be razzed. Check your ego at the door." Their pearls of wisdom resonate with many of the points developed in this chapter.

We may use the relationships matrix in figure 2.2 (p. 53) as a diagnostic tool to identify which friendships may need to receive more attention. Who are our identifiable mentors? Do we happen to be a mentor for someone? In which contexts with believers are we growing closer friendships? Furthermore, do we have any spiritual friendships, soul mates, who fit Paul's injunction in 2 Timothy 2:2: "Pursue righteousness, faith, love and peace, along with those who call on the Lord out of a pure heart"?

Conclusion

If our friendship with God can only rise to the level of the most intimate relationship we have on this earth, then we must intensify our friendships. Believers need to develop closer friendships with many and deep or spiritual friendships with a few. Such deep friendships of the few provide a rich context for maturing trust and intimacy. In addition, believers must also reach beyond this circle and grow closer in relationships with other believers.

To facilitate these two emphases within a local body of believers, church leaders will need to nurture a context of relational growth. This will require opportunities for both kinds of loving groups: (a) open groups for hospitality, for which an invitation for others to join is always extended, and (b) closed groups in which covenant friendships can be nurtured by retaining the same members over an extended period of time for the development of deeper trust and love. Without room for such closed groups within the local body, mature love cannot flourish. As Houston explains:

> There is a close connection between our need for richer human relationships and our need for intimacy with God. Each dimension (our relationship with people and with God) reinforces the other. . . . Each dimension deeply affects the other. If we find it hard to form lasting relationships with those we see around us, then we will find it very hard to relate in any depth to the God we cannot see.[65]

By improving and deepening our human relationships, we make more room for friendship with God.

Growing in our friendship with God also requires us to look inward, into the recesses of our heart. If we are honest, we can acknowledge that our hearts are crowded with our own self-importance, leaving little room for God. The psalmist claims, "In his pride the wicked does not seek him; / in all his thoughts there is no room for God" (Ps 10:4). The haughty sin of pride does not only afflict the wicked; it continues to plague the believer. It is a type of spiritual cancer that gradually damages our relationship with God. It must be removed if we wish a deeper friendship. And God offers his help. "God opposes the proud / but gives grace to the humble" (1 Pet 5:5). The prescription for health is to humble ourselves—an important life skill not normally taught in our culture. Growing in humility before God is the subject of the next chapter.

3

HUMILITY

HONORING THE GOD WHO IS HOLY

*"God opposes the proud
    but gives grace to the humble. . . .*

Humble yourselves before the Lord, and he will lift you up."

JAMES 4:6, 10

JESUS' EXAMPLE

*"And being found in appearance as a man,
    [Jesus] humbled himself
    and became obedient to death—even death on a cross!"*

PHILIPPIANS 2:8

Although I have served God as a pastor, and now a seminary professor, I was not exempt from the vile sin of pride. I was clueless about the deep layer of self-righteousness that permeated my soul, deluded in thinking I had something to offer to God. At age eleven I came to a saving knowledge of Jesus Christ, having grown up in a good Christian home. There was no extended time of rebellion during my teenage years when I was involved in our church youth group and also served as a Sunday school teacher for ninth graders. During college I served as a student volunteer with a college ministry. Following four years of seminary, I served first as a pastoral staff member and now for many years as a seminary professor. Yet under the surface a subtle pride limited God's work in me and through me, a layer of pride I could not sense though others could.

Then a couple of years ago I had the opportunity to take a three-week retreat of solitude in a remote cabin. Here, while I was earnestly seeking God, he performed open-heart surgery and laid bare my soul, exposing these dark broodings of pride. Within this unique and painful encounter, God visited me in a special way. Being prompted to read Romans 1—2, I knelt at my bed and began reading. Suddenly words of the text came alive and pierced my heart: "boastful," "unmerciful," "unloving." For two hours, I wept in God's presence like never before. The Lord made me aware, at a deep experiential level, of my own pride and sinfulness and my desperate need for his mercy and continuing work in my life as a believer. Some have blocked arteries; I had clogged spiritual veins. The cholesterol of self-righteousness minimized (and still minimizes) the work God could do through me.

Too Comfortable?

Believers are forever saved from the penalty of sin, but are we too comfortable in our transgressions? After working in a barn for a while, the stench of manure is no longer noticeable, but the manure is there nonetheless. Have our noses become so accustomed to the putrid odors and smells of pride? Perhaps Pastor Jim Cymbala's experience may help us sense what God's nose smells—that a holy God is willing to associate with us despite the stench of our pride and sin.

On Easter Sunday evening, 1992, at Brooklyn Tabernacle in New York, Roberta Langley, a red-haired, long-time drug abuser shared her dramatic testimony.[1] At the back stood a homeless man listening intently to her. Sometime after the service, as people were still milling around, Pastor Cymbala finally sat down on the platform to rest his weary body. It had been a long day of ministry. About four rows back stood a homeless man, disheveled, hair awry, waiting to approach the pastor. The church often provided money and help for the homeless, but the pastor was a little disappointed that such a great Easter day would end with this handout. He waved the man forward and reached for his wallet. But the approaching smell was unbearable. Cymbala notes, "The mixture of alcohol, sweat, urine and garbage took my breath away. I have been around many street people, but this was the strongest stench I have ever encountered. I instinctively had to turn my head sideways to inhale, then look back in his direction while breathing out."

It turned out that David, the homeless man, did not want any money, "I want the Jesus that red-haired girl talked about." Pastor Jim was just trying to get rid of David with a handout; now Jim's heart melted in compassion for him.

> David sensed the change in me. He moved toward me and fell on my chest, burying his grimy head against my white shirt and tie. Holding him close, I talked to him about Jesus' love. These weren't words; I felt them. I felt love for this pitiful young man. And that smell . . . I don't know how to explain it. It had almost made me sick, but now it became the most beautiful fragrance to me. I reveled in what had been repulsive just a moment ago. The Lord seemed to say to me in that instant, *Jim, if you and your wife have any value to me, if you have any purpose in my work—it has to do with this odor: This is the smell of the world I died for.*[2]

Our gracious God has drawn us to himself, putrid aura and all. Although God graciously puts up with our sinful ways for a season, it still stinks to high heaven.

How oblivious are we to the sin that still lurks in our souls? In a recently published empirical research study conducted at Cornell University, two psychology professors concluded that we tend to be ignorant of our own incompetence. The study explored "why people tend to hold overly optimistic and miscalibrated views about themselves."[3] The professors concluded that "those with limited knowledge in a domain suffer a dual burden: Not only do they reach mistaken conclusions and make regrettable errors, but their incompetence robs them of the ability to realize it."[4]

Jesus made a similar point in relation to our uncanny ability to find fault so easily in others, yet remain clueless about our own ineptitude and sinful ways. "Why do you look at the speck of sawdust in your brother's eye and pay no attention to the plank in your own eye?" (Mt 7:3). We tend to smell sin effortlessly in others, but not so easily in ourselves.

Two Layers of Sin
The Old Testament made distinctions between two categories of sins. For

unintentional sins—sins of ignorance—there were sacrifices that could be offered to cover the guilt (Lev 4—5; Num 15). Yet for sins of arrogance, no sacrifice was ever specified. Death was the usual penalty. Old Testament professor Ron Allen explains, "The Hebrew idiom is 'sins with a high hand,' a posture of arrogance, blasphemy, and revolt. Unlike the unintentional sins, for which there are provisions of God's mercy, one who sets his hand defiantly to despise the word of God and to blaspheme his name must be punished. The punishment is one of death, not just banishment or exile."[5]

Scripture records one occasion when God graciously pardoned someone worthy of death: David, the king and leader of Israel. When confronted by the prophet Nathan of his adulterous sin with Bathsheba and his cover-up murder of her husband Uriah, David humbled himself, " 'I have sinned against the LORD.' Nathan replied, 'The LORD has taken away your sin. You are not going to die' " (2 Sam 12:13).

Likewise, God has been offering us that same magnanimous pardon. When arrogance arises in our heart as believers before God—whether we are aware or unaware—we deserve death. For at the root of pride is the exaltation of the self above all else, above what is right in the presence of God. At the core of this spiritual cancer is the ambition "I am God," epitomized in phrases like "I'm more important than others," "I deserve better treatment," "Me first." Of the various sins we engage in, pride is the worst smell of all in God's nostrils.

The chief of sins is pride, a key characteristic of Satan himself (1 Tim 3:6). Of course, a different sort of pride is good and common to life. It may include satisfaction over an accomplishment well done, as evidenced in that "pride of ownership" phrase realtors employ, or the kind related to one's patriotic solidarity of national pride. But the bad pride now under examination is evil, arrogant, self-exalting, self-righteous. No good exists here, only delusion and self-destruction.

Divine Opposition to Pride

This chapter points out that pockets of sinful pride continue to hold believers hostage from experiencing God more fully. For "God opposes the proud" (Jas 4:6; 1 Pet 5:5), whether it be a proud believer or nonbeliever, since pride leaves no room for God (Ps 10:4; Hos 13:6). Furthermore, for believers, our pride sadly hinders full enjoyment of God's blessing and fellowship. Yet God does not expect us to deal with this crucial project without divine assistance. God "gives grace to the humble" (Jas 4:6; 1 Pet 5:5) to enable us to come near to him.

Pride and humility are mutually exclusive qualities. Humility can never grow and flourish where self-exalting pride dominates and destroys the good in its path. Especially those of us in Christian leadership must recognize that pride continues to rule how we think, how we feel and how we live. Humility is one Christian virtue not highly prized outside of Christendom nor highly practiced within Christendom. Facing our pride requires a kind of personal openness before God not usual in contemporary society, to agree with God about our sin, the basic meaning behind confession (1 Jn 1:9). James scolded his hearers:

> But if you have bitter envy and selfish ambition in your hearts, do not be boastful and false to the truth. Such wisdom does not come down from above, but is earthly, unspiritual, devilish. For where there is envy and selfish ambition, there will also be disorder and wickedness of every kind. But the wisdom from above is first pure, then peaceable, gentle, willing to yield, full of mercy and good fruits, without a trace of partiality or hypocrisy. (Jas 3:14-17 NRSV)

Following David's sin and subsequent repentance, this king of Israel penned a psalm of remorse and contrition before God. In the midst of baring his soul, David insightfully highlights the key issue: "Surely you desire truth in the inner parts; you teach me wisdom in the inmost place" (Ps 51:6). And later, "The sacrifices of God are a broken spirit; a broken and contrite heart, O God, you will not despise" (Ps 51:17). The task, then, is to sustain a transparent and tender heart before God.

The Parable of the Prodigal Son

Two of Jesus' parables recorded in Luke expose the hidden darkness of pride and arrogance, embodied in the religious leaders known as the Pharisees. Although today that group may evoke feelings of disgust for their petty selfishness and opposition to Jesus, in that day Pharisees were highly esteemed by Jews as righteous and God fearing.

Jesus presents the parable of the prodigal son primarily for the benefit of the Pharisees, who grumbled that Jesus associated with sinners (Lk

15:1-2). A picture displayed in our den at home often reminds me of this important parable. Awhile back, my friend Bill Roth returned from a trip to Eastern Europe. As a memento of this trip, Bill gave me a framed eight-by twelve-inch picture he had taken of Rembrandt's (d. 1669) famous painting *The Return of the Prodigal Son,* displayed at the Hermitage in St. Petersburg. This picture now symbolizes the richness and greatness of God's love for me. It was Henri Nouwen's book by the same name that introduced me to the wonder and meaning of this painting and the deeper significance of Jesus' parable.

Most remember the first part of the story describing the exploits of the younger son who, after requesting his portion of the inheritance, squanders his wealth in a foreign land. When he came to his senses, he realized his father's servants were better off than he. Returning home, his father welcomes him and restores him as his son. But Jesus' main point is directed at the elder son, the one who embodied the arrogant and unforgiving heart of the Pharisees.

Kenneth Bailey[6] elaborates from cultural custom how the elder son is just as rebellious as the younger son. In response to the younger son's request, the father "divided his property between them" (Lk 15:12). The elder son should have publicly refused this distribution, which normally occurs only when the father is near death, but he remains silent. Oriental society would expect the elder son to adopt the role of a third-party mediator in conflict between his father and brother, but he remains silent. Further, while the village celebrates the son's return, the elder son's refusal to attend the party represents a public rebuke to the father. Bailey notes, "Middle Eastern customs and the Oriental high regard for the authority of the father make the older son's actions extremely insulting. . . . There is now a break in relationship between the older son and his father that is nearly as radical as the break between the father and the younger son at the beginning of the parable."[7]

When the father entreats him to join the party, the elder son proclaims, "All these years I've been slaving for you and never disobeyed your orders" (Lk 15:29). He viewed himself as ever obedient, in no need for repentance, although he publicly dishonored his father before the guests and chief persons of the village. Thus, both sons—each in his own way—only cared for the father in respect to his possessions, not his person. In his eloquent work

The Return of the Prodigal Son, Henri Nouwen's insights hit home.

The lostness of the elder son, however, is much harder to identify. After all, he did all the right things. . . . Outwardly, the elder son was faultless. But when confronted by his father's joy at the return of his younger brother, a dark power erupts in him and boils to the surface. Suddenly, there becomes glaringly visible a resentful, proud, unkind, selfish person, one that had remained deeply hidden, even though it had been growing stronger and more powerful over the years.[8]

Bailey notes that rather than being angry, "the father goes down and out of the house offering in *public humiliation* a demonstration of unexpected love."[9] The heart of the matter is whether pride or humility rules the course of one's life.

In a second parable of the Pharisee and the publican, Jesus explains that humility is for those "who were confident of their own righteousness and looked down on everybody else" (Lk 18:9).[10] Of course, the role of the arrogant one is again played by the esteemed Pharisee: "God, I thank you that I am not like other men—robbers, evildoers, adulterers—or even like this tax collector. I fast twice a week and give a tenth of all I get" (Lk 18:11). But the despised tax collector, Jesus claims, is the one who humbled himself before God and went home justified. With his head bowed and beating his breast, he prayed, "God, have mercy on me, a sinner" (Lk 18:13). Thus, "everyone who exalts himself will be humbled, and he who humbles himself will be exalted" (Lk 18:14). Even at the cross the Pharisees remained ignorant and arrogant. "He saved others . . . but he can't save himself! He's the King of Israel! Let him come down now from the cross, and we will believe in him" (Mt 27:42-43).

Paul, a Former Pharisee

Ironically, God draws one of these chief experts of pride, Saul of Tarsus, to become his humble servant. Consider his resume: "If anyone else thinks he has reasons to put confidence in the flesh, I have more: circumcised on the eighth day, of the people of Israel, of the tribe of Benjamin, a Hebrew of Hebrews; in regard to the law, a Pharisee" (Phil 3:4-5). "I was advancing in Judaism beyond many Jews of my own age and was extremely zealous for the traditions of my fathers" (Gal 1:14). This great arrogant heart bowed to God and became a humble slave of Jesus. "I consider [my prior accomplishments] rubbish" (Phil 3:8). Was it because of his previous grand arrogance that Paul called himself "the worst of sinners" (1 Tim 1:16)? God had the final laugh, to call a "Hebrew of Hebrews" to become the apostle to the Gentiles, people whom Jews looked down on as subhuman.

What does pride look like? Consider some vices of the Pharisees accompanying the "woes" of Jesus, from Matthew 23. Teaching and preaching was their stock in trade, but they did not practice what they preached (v. 3). Image was everything. They did their good deeds to be noticed by others (v. 5). For example, while engaged in seeking Jesus' death on trumped up charges, they would not enter Pilate's palace to avoid becoming ceremonially unclean, which would disqualify them from partaking of the Passover (Jn 18:28).

Pharisees loved the honor and respect accorded them by the people, and they loved being addressed as Doctor, Professor or Pastor (Mt 23:6-7). They deceptively used their expertise—theological terminology—to nullify previous agreements with others and justify exceptions of special privilege (Mt 23:16-22). German theologian Helmut Thielicke notes how theological knowledge can be used for the purposes of self-exaltation.

> Anyone who deals with truth . . . succumbs all too easily to the psychology of the possessor. But love is the opposite of the will to possess. It is self-giving. It boasteth not itself, but humbleth itself. Now it is almost a devilish thing that even in the case of the theologian the joy of possession can kill love. . . . In his reflective detachment the theologian feels himself superior to those who, in their personal relationship with Christ, completely pass over the problems of the historical Jesus or demythologizing or the objectivity of salvation. This disdain is a real *spiritual disease*. It lies in the conflict between truth and love. This conflict is precisely *the* disease of theologians. Like a child's disease, it is often especially acute. Even ordained pastors can still catch this disease without its power to do harm becoming diminished.[11]

For instance, the Pharisees harped and nitpicked about minor theological and ethical points, but were blind to the real issues of life—justice and mercy and faithfulness (Mt 23:23-24). They could put on a great show—an outward puffery of piety—but inside, all was putrid, hollow shells, full of hypocrisy and wickedness (Mt 23:25-28). Jesus' disgusting list hits much closer to home than we would like, especially for those in Christian leadership.

The Pioneer of Pride

For any position of leadership and responsibility, the greatest temptations are pride and self-exaltation. Even the angel of highest importance in God's hierarchy could not resist this subtle siren call to self. The apostle Paul notes that a church leader "must not be a recent convert, or he may become conceited and fall under the same judgment as the devil. He must also have a good reputation with outsiders, so that he will not fall into disgrace and into the devil's trap" (1 Tim 3:6-7). In moments of honesty we may be ready to admit that our prideful propensities developed naturally from our first "father"—the devil himself, the master of self-exaltation.

Arrogance reigns at the core of Satan's being: "I will ascend to heaven; / I will raise my throne / above the stars of God; / I will sit enthroned on the mount of assembly, / on the utmost heights of the sacred mountain. / I will ascend above the tops of the clouds; / I will make myself like the Most High" (Is 14:13-14).[12] Grabbing is what pride is all about, yet such devilish ambition always exceeds its grasp.

Additional features of pride become visible in the devil himself. He is a gossip, liar and deceiver, a manipulator (Jn 8:44)—having the gall to appear as if he really were a servant to others (2 Cor 11:13-15). He is puffed up with himself (Mt 4:8-9). He grasps for whatever he can steal, claiming it as his own (Mt 4:8-9; Rev 12:7-9, 13, 17). He uses and destroys people—enslaving and coercing Christian and non-Christian alike—to accomplish his own selfish ends (Jn 8:44; Eph 4:26-27; 2 Tim 2:26).

What Is Humility Like?

Like radiant light breaking forth in the midst of oppressive darkness, humility overpowers arrogance. Table 3.1 summarizes eight key scriptural principles of humility. As a guide to help us pursue this distinctive path within a world enslaved to arrogance, Dallas Willard offers this alliterative framework for ease of memory: In humility, "we refrain from *pretending* we are what we know we are not, from *presuming* a favorable position for ourselves in any respect, and from *pushing* or trying to override the will of others in our context."[13]

The commitment to humility is so crucial for successful living that God provides two contrasting examples for our learning benefit. There is no question where the path of pride leads. The depths and self-destruction of such hubris are of the devil. But Jesus our Lord represents the greatness, the magnificence and the beauty of divine humility.

1. Treating all people—regardless of race, nationality, class, age, occupation, intellectual acumen, accomplishments, wealth, even debauchery—with respect and dignity, as those created in the image of God and for whom Christ died (Rom 12:16).
2. Associating especially with those in the margins of life, of low status in society, whom other people tend to avoid (Rom 12:16).
3. Having an honest and accurate assessment of oneself (Rom 12:3, 16).
4. Honoring others as more important than oneself; serving and meeting the needs of other brothers and sisters in Christ before meeting one's own needs (Gal 6:10; Phil 2:3-4).
5. Serving others by sharing power and decision making, as fits the situation, rather than grasping onto power or position, or using coercion to get one's way (Mt 20:25-28; Lk 22:24-27; Phil 2:6-7; 1 Pet 5:1-4).
6. Doing menial tasks that might be considered below one's station of life (Jn 13:1-6).
7. Submitting oneself within all the appropriate contexts of authority and honor identified in the Bible (e.g., to other believers within the church, Eph 5:21; 1 Pet 3:8; 5:5; to family members, Eph 5:22—6:4; 1 Pet 3:1-7; to governing authorities, Rom 13:1-7; 1 Pet 2:13-17; within work relationships, 1 Pet 2:18-25 [by application]; to God himself, Jas 4:7, 10; 1 Pet 5:6).
8. Confessing one's sins to God (2 Chron 7:14; 1 Jn 1:8-10) and others (Mt 18:15-17; Jas 5:16).

Table 3.1. New Testament characteristics of humility

Jesus, the Humble One

Throughout history, examples of great hiding and disguises abound, from the legendary Trojan horse to notorious cases of spying and espionage during the wars in our own times. But if an award were presented for the best disguise ever in the history of the world, it would have to be given to our own Lord and Savior, Jesus Christ. For on this very earth walked *God*. The King of the universe visited this speck of a planet. Most were oblivious to this event unique in all of history.

Jesus is the foremost example of how to live in humility. Born to a poor family in a place where animals were housed, Jesus was raised as a blue-collar worker, a carpenter by trade—nothing that remarkable or spectacular. Jack Deere notes, "Another of the major lessons taught to us by the birth of Jesus is how utterly humble God is. . . . No one could have imagined that the Creator of the universe would stoop so low, could be so humble."[14] For thirty years, Jesus' life was hidden from the world, as he grew from childhood to adulthood in a small village. During his three-year public ministry, he associated with sinners and tax collectors, people of low position (Mt 11:19). He took a towel and washed his disciples' feet, a task each disciple considered beneath his station of life (Jn 13:1-17). Jesus humbly visited this planet, fully engaging his human nature, rubbing shoulders with insolent and clueless people. Then, being falsely accused, he humbly suffered and died a cruel and shameful death on a cross, taking the punishment deserved by all of humanity.

If he wanted to, Jesus could have displayed much more of his glory during the incarnation, a glory only partially evident for a moment in his transfiguration before Peter, James and John (Mt 17:2). Yet he walked this earth like us, humbling himself to show us how to be humble. Paul directs his readers in Philippi to this unusual example:

> Your attitude should be the same as that of Christ Jesus: / Who, being in very nature God, / did not consider equality with God something to be grasped, / but made himself nothing, / taking the very nature of a servant, / being made in human likeness. / And being found in appearance as a man, / he humbled himself / and became obedient to death—even death on a cross! / Therefore God exalted him to the highest place / and gave him the name that is above every name, / that at the name of Jesus every knee should bow, / in heaven and on earth and under the earth, / and every tongue confess that Jesus Christ is Lord, / to the glory of God the Father. (Phil 2:5-11)

Jesus did not need to grasp and retain the independent use of his divine functions, but was willing to take on human nature and live in this sin-infested world. His invitation is a continuing call to believers to become, in fuller measure, his disciples, "Come to me, all you who are weary and burdened, and I will give you rest. Take my yoke upon you and learn from me, for *I am gentle and humble in heart*, and you will find rest for your souls" (Mt 11:28-29, emphasis added).

In making the claim "I am gentle and humble in heart," was Jesus speaking only from his human side? Or was he speaking as one person, the unique God-man? May we entertain the possibility that God himself is humble, since most of the items of humility listed in table 3.1 are characteristic of God? Consider also the following unusual incidents in the Old Testament highlighting God's inherent humility. After God shared with Abraham what he intended to do about Sodom and Gomorrah, God waited patiently before Abraham, until Abraham formulated his petition (Gen 18:22).[15] With the reluctant and sulking prophet Jonah, God intimately shared his own feelings of care and concern for the Gentiles of Ninevah (Jon 4:10-11). Would it not require humility on God the Son's part, prior to the incarnation in eternity past, to be willing to take on human nature and die for us?

God's way of working is not always obvious or stunning. Much of the time, God is so subtle. Jack Deere explains, "God's humility is both a blessing and a very great problem. A blessing, because his humility leads him to fellowship with people as low as we are. A problem, because his humility leads him to come to us in ways that make it easy for us to reject him."[16] Pride is of the devil. Humility is of God.

God's School of Humility

Pride particularly pesters those in positions of power and of influence. Therefore God offers his assistance: "he gives grace to the humble" (Jas 4:6). Scripture records cases in which God humbled others whom he was preparing for important leadership roles in this life. For example, Joseph, sold into slavery as a teen, was jailed for many years on a false accusation. But God was preparing him to bear the weight and responsibility as second-in-command to Egypt's Pharaoh. Moses was groomed to become Israel's law giver through the humbling experience of leaving the privileges of Egypt to become a desert shepherd. To guard the apostle Paul from succumbing to pride, God offered support with a strange twist. Paul notes, "To keep me from becoming conceited because of these surpassingly great revelations, there was given me a thorn in my flesh, a messenger of Satan, to torment me" (2 Cor 12:7). Even arrogant Nebuchadnezzar, king of the empire of Babylon, finally bowed himself before God on high after God's unusual training. "At the end of that time, I, Nebuchadnezzar, raised my eyes toward heaven, and my sanity was restored. Then I praised the Most High; I honored and glorified him who lives forever. . . . And those who walk in pride he is able to humble" (Dan 4:34, 37).

From King David we learn some principles for how to respond in humility, first to those over us, and then to those under our care, those who may challenge our leadership. In two situations in which David could have taken the throne (from the reigning King Saul) or held on to it tightly (from his rebellious son Absalom), David let the moment pass, submitting himself to God's timing.

Although Saul was still king of Israel, he had forfeited this privilege through disobedience to God (1 Sam 15:22-23). As a result, God directed Samuel the prophet to anoint David as the next king (1 Sam 16:12-13), although his official installation as king would have to await Saul's death many years later.[17] Should David take matters into his own hand and expedite Saul's death, especially since Saul, aware of David's threat to the throne, sought to kill David? At an opportune time, David resisted the temptation to execute Saul and spared his life, persuading his own men to do the same: "The LORD forbid that I should do such a thing to my master, the LORD's anointed, or lift my hand against him; for he is the anointed of the LORD" (1 Sam 24:6).

In *A Tale of Three Kings* Gene Edwards imagines a conversation between a young man in Rehoboam's army (son of Solomon) and one of David's mighty men to illustrate David's heart of humility.

> My king [King David] has never threatened me as does yours [King Rehoboam]. Your new king has begun his reign with laws, rules, regulations, fear. The clearest memory I have of my king, when we lived in the caves, is that his was a life of *submission*. Yes, David showed me submission, *not* authority. He taught me, not the quick cures of rules and laws, but the art of patience. That is what changed my life. . . . As far as David's having authority: Men who don't have it talk about it all the time. Submit, submit, that's all you hear. David had authority, but I don't think that fact ever occurred to him![18]

Through the humbling experience of his exile and pursuit by Saul, David grew in humility and patience, awaiting the time God would exalt him as king.

In the second instance of humility, King David did not defend his throne against his own son but retreated, awaiting God's timing. As the consequence of David's sin with Bathsheba and the murder of Uriah, her husband, God judged David with a curse of future conflict within his family and his kingdom (2 Sam 12:10-12). Sadly, David's favored son Absalom became the one who challenged God's authority of David as king. With a strong following among many of the people and key leaders, Absalom arranged for himself to be declared king in Hebron (2 Sam 15:10-13). As the new king, he led an assault on Jerusalem to seize his father's throne. Rather than defend himself, David departed from the palace and, once again, was a fugitive.

Consider David's perspective as he learned of the rebellion while still in the palace, through an imaginary conversation with Zadok the priest, as created by Edwards.

> I shall do what I did under Saul. I shall leave the destiny of the Kingdom in God's hand alone. It may be that He is finished with me. Perhaps I have sinned too greatly and am no longer worthy to lead. Only God knows if that is true, and it seems he is not telling. . . . The throne is the Lord's. So is the kingdom. I will not hinder God. . . . If I am not to be King, our God will find no difficulties in making Absalom to be Israel's king. Now it is possible. God shall be God![19]

Pride in leadership grasps on to all it can, to exalt self whenever it can. The humble leader waits patiently for God to work his way, to be honored in God's timing.[20]

Yet even more important than any leadership role is our own relationship with God, as indicated from Israel's wilderness wanderings. "Remember how the LORD your God led you all the way in the desert these forty years, to humble you and to test you in order to know what was in your heart, whether or not you would keep his commands. He humbled you, causing you to hunger and then feeding you with manna. . . . Know then in your heart that as a man disciplines his son, so the LORD God disciplines you" (Deut 8:2-3, 5).

To prepare believers to reign with God in the future (Rev 22:3, 5), life on earth has been expressly designed as a boot camp, a tech course, to help us maximize our humility and minimize our pride—God's school of humility. The curriculum includes all our experiences of suffering, pains and the trials of life.[21] Even our own Lord Jesus Christ, who humbled himself to come to earth, "learned obedience from what he suffered" (Heb 5:8). Paul's perspective can become our own, "That is why, for Christ's sake, I delight in weaknesses, in insults, in hardships, in persecutions, in difficulties. For when I am weak, then I am strong [in God's grace]" (2 Cor 12:10). Every believer has the same opportunity to learn how to be humble, but not all learn from this golden opportunity.

Since pride and arrogance have been habituated deeply within our character as believers, God takes the initiative to offer opportunities to become aware of our pride and the need to exalt him, not self. Yet we also have our own responsibility to engage in this training project, for Scripture explicitly commands us, "Humble yourselves, therefore, under God's mighty hand, that he may lift you up in due time" (1 Pet 5:6; cf. Jas 4:7).

Our Initiative in Humbling Ourselves

Learning to be a servant is one important means to learn humility, especially for those in Christian leadership in today's world of power and manipulation. As noted previously, this sin is mentioned in a discussion of the qualifications for elders (1 Tim 3:6). The path to great leadership is learning how to live responsively and appropriately under the authority of another, to become a genuine servant to others.

Due to bouts of pride among his disciples, Jesus expounded his distinctive teaching about being a servant kind of leader, a manner of interacting with others that he himself practiced. On two particular occasions the Gospel writers record the disciples' disagreement over who was the greatest among themselves (Mt 18:1-4 and Lk 22:24). At another time, John and James attempted to garner the choice seats at his side in Jesus' future reign (Mt 20:20-24). By comparing parallel passages with the Matthew 18 episode, we note that

☐ the greatest in the kingdom are those who humble themselves like children (Mt 18:4)

☐ the one wishing to be first must be last of all and servant of all (Mk 9:35)

☐ the one who is greatest among them is the one who is least (Lk 9:48)

The opposing style of leadership is one of coercion, of manipulation, of oppression. "You know that the rulers of the Gentiles lord it over them, and their high officials exercise authority over them. Not so with you. Instead, whoever wants to become great among you must be your servant, and whoever wants to be first must be your slave—just as the Son of Man did not come to be served, but to serve, and to give his life a ransom for many" (Mt 20:25-28; cf. Lk 22:25-27). The apostle Peter adopted this same phrase in his exhortation to fellow leaders of the church, contrasting the mode of "lording it over those entrusted to you" with "being examples to the flock" (1 Pet 5:3). Peter's instructions to all: "Clothe yourselves with humility toward one another, because, 'God opposes the proud but gives grace to the humble' " (1 Pet 5:5).

To learn how to be a servant, God instituted a number of relational contexts for his saints to be under the authority of others, first in public life: submitting to the governing political authorities (1 Pet 2:13-17) and submitting to employers (by application, 1 Pet 2:18-25); and also among the body of believers: submitting to older believers (1 Pet 5:5), submitting to church leaders (Heb 13:17) and submitting to family members within certain functional roles, wives to husbands and children to parents (Eph 5:22—6:4).

Of course, these various functional roles of stewardship are temporary, for this life only, for we are essentially coequal heirs of God's grace for which there are no ultimate distinctions (Gal 3:28). Yet these relational contexts offer the opportunity to learn to trust each other and to submit to each other (Eph 5:21) as the outflow of our unity in the Spirit (Eph 4:2-3), since we have only one chief Shepherd (1 Pet 5:4) and Head of the church (Eph 1:18-20), the Lord Jesus Christ. Our growth in genuine love with other believers will yield greater experiences of mutual indwelling in one another and mutual submission toward each other. Increasing love and unity are important characteristics of Christ's body, as indicated by these words of Jesus: "By this all men will know that you are my disciples, if you love one another" (Jn 13:35). "I pray also for those who will believe in me through their message, that all of them may be one, Father, just as you are in me and I am in you. May they also be in us so that the world may believe that you have sent me" (Jn 17:20-21).

Consider the example of Paula, who exemplified this kind of servant leadership. A Christian leader of her day, she established a convent for women and a monastic community for men. Jerome (d. 420) wrote a letter of consolation to Eustochium when her mother, Paula, passed away. At the age of thirty-three Paula had left her wealthy Roman lifestyle to serve God in Bethlehem. Jerome explains:

> I am now free to describe at greater length the virtue which was her peculiar charm. . . . Humility is the first of Christian graces, and hers was so pronounced that one who had never seen her and who on account of her celebrity had desired to see her, would have believed that he saw not her but the lowest of her maids. When she was surrounded by companies of virgins she was always the least remarkable in dress, in speech, in gesture, and gait.[22]

The reward of humility is honor before God. The consequence of pride is destruction, for pride prevents the presence of God from being welcome in our hearts—the God whom we want to seek with all of our hearts.

Wasting Time with God: Confession

Regular confession of our sins, particularly thoughts and actions of pride, is at the heart of being a maturing Christian. Within his discussion of church reconciliation in Matthew 18:15-17, Jesus offers a measurable definition of a Christian. When confronted about a genuinely sinful practice, a genuine believer is willing to admit wrong and confess the sin. But a reluctant person reveals a heart ultimately set against God. If after an appropriate period of time and with multiple occasions of admonishment, a person is unwilling to confess his or her sin, the church must treat the unwilling confessor as a nonbeliever. "If he refuses to listen even to the church, treat him as you would a pagan" (Mt 18:17).

The traditional practice of confessing our sins is one important means of becoming humble, both before God and before others. When we do not confess our sins, we hide from God—as Adam and Eve did in the garden. Such a cover-up may even be worse than the actual sin itself. Of course, religious practices can only sustain our humility—they cannot guarantee it. As David sang so long ago, "You do not delight in sacrifice, or I would bring it; / you do not take pleasure in burnt offerings. / The sacrifices of God are a broken spirit; / a broken and a contrite heart, O God, you will not despise" (Ps 51:16-17).

Our heart can be very deceitful (Jer 17:9). Here are some of the sign-posts that pride may be lurking nearby: defending ourselves with various rationalizations[23] (a deluded form of omniscience), believing we can add another commitment on to our already busy schedule (a deluded form of omnipotence, "I can do all things"), comparing ourselves to others, judging others with contempt and sarcasm (a deluded form of perfection), pushing our way through without concern for others (a deluded need to demand special privileges).

How can we monitor the pride that arises in our heart—and agree with God about what he already knows? For example, I began examining an area of expertise, something I believe I do well. It is here that I find it hard to be patient with others less talented. Impatience may be a subtle indication of pride. David Harned suggests that "humility and patience are inseparable, just as are pride and impatience."[24] For me, pride and anger converged when I was driving on the road or freeway. In the past, my drive to work could defeat me and set a bad tone for the day. Finally I recognized the underlying problem: my contempt for these drivers who cut in front of me. I began to repeat Jesus' first words on the cross: "Father, forgive them, for they do not know what they are doing" (Lk 23:34), and genuinely began to develop a heart of pity for them instead of road rage. When my blood began to boil, I knew that something was amiss in my heart. The more I monitored my heart, the easier it got.[25]

Consider the following anonymous excerpts of journals after meditating on Isaiah 14:12-17, Philippians 2:5-11 and Psalms 139:23-24 for a period of about forty-five minutes:

> When I criticize others I am exalting myself. God searched my heart and made me realize that my attitude to my mother is sinful. . . . I have never liked her advice or her asking about my life.

> At first it wasn't easy for me to concentrate—my mind was wandering around after a few minutes. At the confession time, as I was praying, God brought to my attention my own anger that I didn't want to acknowledge. There is anger in my heart toward someone who didn't respond to me, and that anger was based on pride.

Through this exercise, I really was shown for the first time how these [past] humiliating experiences (which I believe were done in obedience to Him) may be part of His school of humility.

God can use his Word to offer insights for our consideration. Keeping our hearts open before God is an important practice for our spiritual health.

Furthermore, making it right with others is a high priority in God's kingdom. "If you are offering your gift at the altar and there remember that your brother has something against you, leave your gift there in front of the altar. First go and be reconciled to your brother; then come and offer your gift" (Mt 5:23-24). In this regard, I have difficulty admitting when I am wrong, mostly in my relationship with Beth, my wife. Do I presume omniscience? In writing these words, the matter is clear, but in the heat of a disagreement, I fall back on old learned habits to win and never give in. I am in the process of learning to exalt Beth more than myself, to listen to her insightful words, to let her help me become less full of pride. If I cannot be humble before Beth, God's companion for me, how can I claim that I am being humble before God?

We can also confess our sins to a trusted soul mate, to bare our innermost secrets (as encouraged by James 5:16, "confess your sins to each other") in order to counter the strong tendency to hide from ourselves, from others and from God. Willard explains the discipline of confession. "This will nourish . . . our humility before our brothers and sisters in Christ. Thus we let some friends in Christ know who we really are, not holding back anything important, but, ideally, allowing complete transparency. We lay down the burden of hiding and pretending, which normally takes up such a dreadful amount of energy."[26]

We desperately need others to help us become aware of our pride. Figure 3.1 portrays the Johari Window,[27] a common tool from human relations training, depicting areas of awareness regarding information about ourselves, with axes of "known" and "unknown." The "public" quadrant portrays what others know about us based on information we have shared. The "private" quadrant indicates that we keep a portion of our lives secret from others. The "blind spots" quadrant indicates what others know about us for which we are largely clueless (e.g., mannerisms, pride). The "unconscious" quadrant highlights what neither we nor others know about us, except God alone. This aspect of our life is tucked away in our unconscious until some event or experience brings it to light. The size of the space within each quadrant varies, depending on which particular relationship is in view. For example, with a next door neighbor the "public" quadrant may be rather small and the "private" area very large. With a deep friend the relative sizes would be reversed.

Confession is good for the soul and can prevent further sin. "He who conceals his sins does not prosper, / but whoever confesses and renounces them finds mercy. Blessed is the man who always fears the LORD, / but he who hardens his heart falls into trouble" (Prov 28:13-14). If we cannot be honest before our closest friends, can we truly know how to be honest before God?

	Known by Self	Not Known by Self
Known by Others	Public Self	Blind Spots
Not Known by Others	Private Self	Unconscious

Figure 3.1. Johari window

All believers have blind spots. Our frailties and faults are obvious to everyone except ourselves. This problem is compounded by the natural reluctance of believers to be completely honest with others. The Johari window could be a tool that might help friends, spouses, small groups and working teams (e.g., pastoral staff) initiate honest sharing and caring about the hidden aspects of our character for which we are clueless, particularly when our pride gives off its ugly odor. Only through the kindness of God and others can we ever become aware of this hidden side of our character.

Wasting Time with God: Service

Humility is the foundational virtue that issues in serving others. As Richard Foster affirms, "More than any other single way, the grace of humility is worked into our lives through the Discipline of service."[28] But humility will only take root in the heart to the degree that we are willing and ready to serve others. Jesus, the King of kings, easily picked up the servant's towel and water basin to wash the foul and dirt-covered feet of his disciples (Jn 13:4-16). This menial action so shocked Peter that he withdrew his feet to avoid seeing such abasement by the Lord he worshiped. The lesson was captured in Jesus' famous words, "You call me 'Teacher' and 'Lord,' and rightly so, for that is what I am. Now that I, your Lord and Teacher, have washed your feet, you also should wash one another's feet. I have set you an example that you should do as I have done for you" (Jn 13:13-15). Serving others' needs first, before meeting our own, is the expression of a humble heart. Furthermore, a spirit of submission pervades the encounter, as Foster notes: "We are at last free to value other people"[29] as fellow partners and equal heirs of God's kingdom.

The challenge for all believers, but especially Christian leaders, is to resist the lust for special privileges to make life more convenient. "Do nothing out of selfish ambition or vain conceit, but in humility consider others better than yourselves. Each of you should look not only to your own interests, but also to the interests of others" (Phil 2:3-4). For example, how do we treat little children in our midst, as a nuisance or as a gift from God? Are we willing to offer a helping hand for that task that seems below us? When someone criticizes us, are we ready to defend ourselves, or are we willing to listen and learn? Do we excuse moral shortcuts through the justification of a special privilege?

Facing pride and growing in humility may be one of the most difficult challenges for any leader, especially in the church and within Christian ministries. Consider the following specific suggestions as illustrations for how a servant leader might act, whether one is a pastor or an employer: Accept no special parking spaces. Ask those who report to you, "How can I help you be successful at your job today?" When getting together with subordinates, meet in their office space, not yours. Keep the office door open rather than closed. Avoid unilateral decisions. Work toward participative decision making and consensual agreement when and where appropriate.

Becoming more humble requires us to ask the question, How can we place our needs as secondary and seek to serve the needs of others first? Especially for those in leadership positions, we must become aware of the special privileges that tend to accompany leadership and to question whether or not these actually hinder leaders from becoming more humble.

Furthermore, Foster suggests that we must distinguish between self-righteous service and true service. Self-righteous service "centers in the glorification of the individual. Therefore it puts others into its debt and becomes one of the most subtle and destructive forms of manipulation known. True service builds community. It quietly and unpretentiously goes about caring for the needs of others."[30] We must be wary from which heart our service springs.

Conclusion

As we follow in Jesus' footsteps by serving others, by deferring to others, by being patient with others, we grow a humble heart that makes room for God. The decay and stench of sin and arrogance gives way to a beautiful fragrance that fills our soul with freshness and vitality of life. The fragrance of humility or the stench of pride. God wishes to draw us into his humble and sweet fellowship, to let him be God and run the universe while we are his servants, walking within his way of wisdom. My humbling encounter with God in that cabin has become another major turning point in my journey with God. I became convicted and convinced that the upward path to closeness with God requires a continual downward movement of humility within me. Metaphorically speaking, it means remaining on my knees or lying prostrate before God.

As David shows the way, we need to invite God's help in unearthing the dark recesses of our heart, to identify the pride that lurks in the shadows yet rules our life. "Search me, O God, and know my heart; / test me and know my anxious thoughts. / See if there is any offensive way in me, / and lead me in the way everlasting" (Ps 139:23-24). As we open up and reveal our hearts to God in honesty and in humility, he is able to reveal more of himself to us.

As we move forward in making room for God, a certain difficulty arises since visiting with God is not like having coffee with a good friend. In the latter case we can actually see him or her and notice a tone of voice and other nonverbal communication. But in meeting with God we must develop a perspective on approaching a God who is essentially invisible to our senses, the subject to which we turn in the next chapter.

4

FAITH

SEEING THE GOD
WHO IS INVISIBLE

"And without faith it is impossible to please God, because anyone who comes to him must believe that he exists and that he rewards those who earnestly seek him. . . . [Moses] persevered because he saw him who is invisible."

HEBREWS 11:6, 27

JESUS' EXAMPLE

"Let us run with endurance the race that is set before us, fixing our eyes on Jesus, the author and perfecter of faith."

HEBREWS 12:1-2 NASB

W hile his mother was on the phone, three-year-old Randy Scogin headed for the backdoor, pulling his toy dog behind him. He announced, "Bye, Mommy, I'm going to Bo-Bo's house."[1] Since Bo-Bo, Randy's grandmother, lived five miles away, Randy's mother, Marilyn, did not believe he was actually headed that direction but only playing make-believe. But fifteen minutes later Marilyn realized Randy was gone. She and her husband, Harold, scoured the house, backyard and immediate neighborhood, but no Randy. Marilyn called her mother, "Randy's lost. He left here half an hour ago, and he said he was going to your house."

"He'll never make it," responded the older woman. "Even if he knows the way, there's two busy streets between your house and mine. Marilyn, stay there. I'll leave right now and check every street on the way. Don't worry, we'll find him or I'll know the reason why."

"Thanks, Mom." Marilyn collapsed in a flood of tears. While Harold notified the police, Marilyn's mothering instincts took over. She grabbed the car keys, climbed into the family sedan and raced through their subdivision. *Please God. Please watch over Randy and lead me to him.* After a fruitless search, she returned home. In a few minutes her mother arrived but still with no news. While Harold stayed home with their six-year-old son, Marilyn and her mother ventured out once again and prayed as they drove. *Please God. He's only three years old.*

About a mile from their house—two hours after the disappearance—on a busy street, they came upon a threesome—a dark haired woman, a younger blond woman and a little one pulling a toy dog behind him. "Randy!" his mother shouted as they pulled up alongside the trio. *Thank you, God. Thank you.* Relieved and weeping, Marilyn fell to her knees and pulled Randy tightly to her, stroking his hair.

"Hi, Mommy. Hi, Bo-Bo!" Randy smiled easily, calm and unaffected by this perilous escapade.

"He's okay, ma'am," the older woman said softly. "He fell into a ditch back there a ways. There was a bit of water in it and we helped him out. We've been following him ever since so he wouldn't get hurt."

"Thank you so much," Marilyn responded, examining Randy and making sure he was all right. Marilyn then swept the boy into her arms, thanked the women and rushed off to share the good news. At home, once the rejoicing subsided, Marilyn realized she had forgotten to offer the women a ride after they had wandered out of their way following Randy. Marilyn and her mother quickly returned to the place of meeting. Although only a four-minute interval had elapsed, no one was in sight, despite the long stretch of road.

"That's strange," she muttered. "No one could walk that fast. I wonder where they went." But after a fifteen-minute search with no luck, they turned the car around. Back at home, the family gathered around Randy. Marilyn hugged him close once more and tousled his hair.

"We were worried about you, Randy," Marilyn said softly.

"I know, Mommy. I won't walk off anymore."

She took his hand in hers. "Listen, Randy, remember those ladies who helped you and stayed with you?"

The child nodded. "Yes, Mommy. They were strangers."

"But you weren't afraid of them, were you?"

"No, they were nice."

Harold nodded. "Yes, they looked after you. Did they tell you their names?"

"They told me they were from God," Randy simply said. The family got quiet, and curious expressions emerged on their faces.

Randy looked up at his mother, "What's an angel, Mommy?"

The adults stared at the child and then exchanged knowing glances. Harold directed his family to hold hands as he thanked God for his kindness and special care over "our little Randy."

An Additional Reality Beckons Our Attention

Now and then the supernatural—another reality beyond our physical sight—becomes noticeable in this natural world, as happened in Randy's circumstance with these apparent angels. This hidden, supernatural realm exists—a realm of angels and of God—even though it cannot be seen. A few decades ago, the word *angel* rarely surfaced, except in reference to a medieval academic dispute (How many angels could dance on the head of a pin?) or as roles in Christmas play scripts. But now, angelic beings have gained greater credibility due to bestselling books and popular television programs about angels, such as *Highway to Heaven* and *Touched by an Angel*. Angels are real beings (too numerous to count[2]) who are messengers sent by God to serve him and his people (Ps 103:20; Heb 1:14), including children (Mt 18:10). Because angels are invisible, the aid they offer may go unnoticed. But on occasion they might become visible to convey a message to people (see 2 Kings 6:15-17; Dan 10:1-21; Heb 13:2; Rev 22:8-9).

A few readers may have already received angelic help. "Some people have entertained angels without knowing it" (Heb 13:2) through encounters with strangers. May I pose a personal question? Do you believe angels exist? If it is difficult for contemporary Christians to believe in angels, then it will be problematic to sustain a deep belief in a God who regularly intervenes in the lives of believers. Jesus affirmed the need to believe without always seeing. "Because you have seen me, you have believed; blessed are those who have not seen and yet have believed" (Jn 20:29). If a deeper friendship with God is desired, Christians must become convinced that although God is invisible, he is more real than any material object, and he is ever present. Believers will need to acquire the worldview Jesus held during his life on this earth that "this is a God-bathed and God-permeated world."[3] The omnipresence of God must be personalized into the everyday experience that God is always near to each believer.

This chapter highlights realities accentuated in Scripture that cannot be discerned with the five senses: sight, sound, smell, taste and touch. "Now faith is being sure of what we hope for and certain of what we do not see" (Heb 11:1). In a sense, the window of Scripture permits us to poke our heads behind the veil into the heavens to explore further what God has revealed about this world in which we live. Conceptions of what is real and how the world operates significantly impacts whether or not there is room in our minds for the notion that an invisible God is real.

God is spirit (Jn 4:24), essentially immaterial, nonspatial, invisible. Yet the prevailing worldview of naturalism—that only objects accessible to the five senses actually exist—deletes God by definition. Consequently, when Christians are overtaken by such a narrow, naturalistic mindset— that existence requires physicality—it becomes very difficult to pursue further a closer relationship with God who is invisible. Thus, to expand our horizons of reality, our core beliefs must be strengthened by the Christian notion that existence does not necessarily require material substance.

Following in Jesus' Footsteps of Faith

In the first century it was primarily the disciples' lack of faith in God that prompted Jesus' rebuke (e.g., Mt 8:26; 14:31; 16:8; 17:20; 21:21). Was Jesus speaking from the posture of one who needed no faith himself?[4] Or rather, as the God-man who was also fully human, did Jesus need to grow in his faith in God also? Although some Bible translations have obscured the matter, the New Testament actually points to Jesus as the exemplar of one who learned to place his faith in God. For example, Hebrews 12:2 presents Jesus as the pioneer who became perfected in his faith and reliance on God during his earthly pilgrimage.[5] New Testament professor

William Lane offers this explanation:

> The poignant description as a whole points to Jesus as the perfect embodi-
> ment of faith, who exercised faith heroically. By bringing faith to complete
> expression, he enabled others to follow his example. The phrase reiterates
> and makes explicit what was affirmed with a quotation from Scripture in
> [Hebrews] 2:13, that Jesus in his earthly life was the perfect exemplar of
> trust in God.[6]

Furthermore, in Galatians 2:20, the apostle Paul expresses his own imitation of Christ's faith: "The life I live in the body, I live by the faith *of* the
Son of God, who loved me and gave himself for me" (author's translation).[7] The very attitude making it possible for Jesus to obey the Father on
earth is how Paul desired to live his life.

Jesus needed to grow in faith because he learned and grew in knowledge and in wisdom just as other humans do. This fact is mentioned twice
by Luke regarding Jesus' childhood (Lk 2:40) and his youth (Lk 2:52). If
Jesus was fully human, it can be no other way.[8] His concern over the lit-
tleness of faith in others (Mt 6:30; 8:26; Mk 9:19) would then indicate an
expression based on his own experience of a robust personal faith in
God. Thus when Jesus taught about faith, as Gerald O'Collins notes, "he
speaks about faith as an insider, one who knows personally what the life
of faith is."[9] Jesus exercised faith in God, and so must we.

Growing in our faith in God involves becoming convinced of three
pairs of contrasting features of God's plan to be explored in this chapter.
There are

☐ two coexisting realms of our world: a material and an immaterial reality (much of the chapter will be devoted to this topic)

☐ two kingdoms that compete for our allegiance: the kingdom of God
and the kingdom of Satan

☐ two sequential phases in the believers' journey: the "already" (life on
this planet) and the "not yet" (life beyond the grave)

In his book *Reaching for the Invisible God*, Philip Yancey observes that
"every creature on earth has a way to connect to the environment around
it."[10] For example, dogs use smell; bats use sonar. He continues, "At the
heart of the Christian story lies the promise of direct correspondence with
the unseen world, a link so profound as to be likened to a new birth, and

the key to life beyond organic death. . . . As the pathway into the unseen world, the Bible presents faith. . . . The Bible renders an account of another reality operating simultaneous to, but usually hidden from, the material reality of earth."[11] As we become more aware of and as we regularly live in light of these invisible realities, our confidence in God's daily existence will grow, an important ingredient to make progress in drawing closer to God.

Two Realms of Reality

Christians actually live in two kinds of reality—two coexisting realms—one visible and the other invisible. Note in 2 Corinthians 4:16, 18 the contrast the apostle Paul sets up between the outer, physical body and the inner, immaterial soul: "Though outwardly [physically] we are wasting away, yet inwardly we are being renewed day by day. . . . So we fix our eyes not on what is *seen*, but on what is *unseen*. For what is seen is *temporary*, but what is unseen is *eternal*" (emphasis added). Admittedly, it is hard to make sense of the immaterial realm since it is easy to be overwhelmed by the physical features of this world. Yet the immaterial can be discerned, for example, on occasions when time is forgotten, as in the company of good friends or when engaged in an exciting project. Here a little measure of eternity is experienced in those precious moments, where time will not be such a taskmaster anymore. "[God] has also set eternity in the hearts of men" (Eccles 3:11); humanity has an eternal yearning for another realm of reality.

Although thinking about God enjoyed a prominent place in human history—among peoples in different lands and languages and over many centuries—moderns dance to a different drumbeat. God's people now work, shop, talk and are entertained in a culture that believes God is as real as Santa Claus or the Easter Bunny, childish indulgences tolerated for seasonal celebrations. Thus, these enlightened ones conclude that God either does not exist, or if he does, he is irrelevant to the mainstream of life, just as if he did not exist. Note how few references to God and his perspectives emerge in the marketplace of valued ideas. Public discussion about God has landed on the politically incorrect list. To converse with neighbors or coworkers about God feels like swimming upstream. Generally speaking, two of the respected pillars of public life—the university and the mass media—take little thought of God and encourage believers to do the same.

The "Experts" Claim God Does Not Exist

University professors are the pied pipers of national intellectual life. Unfortunately, the majority of academicians conduct their research, write textbooks and offer their expert opinions on important policy matters from within a naturalistic perspective. These experts, and specifically the scientists, teach us that we live in a physical universe and nothing more. If it cannot be seen, touched, tasted, heard or smelled, then it does not exist.[12] Such a definition of science automatically excludes immaterial objects, thereby defining God out of existence.

Duke historian George Marsden laments the limitations imposed by this antisupernatural bias on the university classrooms of America: "One way to describe the current state of affairs, however, is that, in effect, the only points of view that are allowed full academic credence are those that presuppose purely naturalistic worldviews."[13] Berkeley law professor Phillip Johnson amplifies the point:

> It is practically impossible to discuss this important question [Are we created beings . . . or are we accidental products?] in any of our great secular universities, let alone in the public high schools. The reason is that modernist culture is ruled by a philosophy called *scientific naturalism*. . . . Naturalism is the doctrine that the cosmos has always been a closed system of natural causes and effects that can never be influenced by anything from "outside"—like God. It follows from such philosophical premises that "God" is an aspect of human subjectivity or a fantasy. . . . God is merely an entity in the minds of those who believe.[14]

Therefore, Christian university students who aspire to be intellectually respected within the academy are implicitly encouraged not to believe in God, or at least not to publicly acknowledge it.[15]

God as Irrelevant to Life in Mass Media

In the mainstream media, God does not get any better press. Portrayed in film, on TV and in the news is the pervasive, underlying philosophy that the good life can be fully enjoyed without recourse to a supreme being.

Rarely do main characters pray to God to help resolve tensions, problems and crises that emerge in the script. On occasion God and religion marginally come into view. Black-gowned clergy appear in typical wedding or funeral scenes, but usually as background props peripheral to the plot. A few religious events receive a sound bite or two, but the spin in the reporting reinforces the impression that God talk is viewed much like UFO and Elvis sightings—part of the bizarre and the peculiar. Based on the few religious news stories aired during one twelve-month period, L. Brent Bozzell, chairman of the Media Research Center conducting the study, claimed that "if network news was your sole source of information, you would have to conclude that religion is all but nonexistent in America today."[16]

The mass media play a powerful informational role in society. The public pores over newspapers and news magazines, devours TV news programs, and is entertained with offerings of movies and rental videos. And yet serious thinking about God is not displayed as a typical American experience. Rare occurrences of any genuine religious comments readily prompt viewer response. Tim Russert of NBC's *Meet the Press* closed an Easter Sunday segment with these lines, "It's a beautiful day in Washington. The sun is shining; the cherry blossoms are out. Christ is risen; Yahweh is coming. And the Orioles' opening day is tomorrow." He reflects, "I got more letters from people saying they had never heard that language on TV before."[17] Are Christians subconsciously imbibing this naturalistic mindset more—God is irrelevant to daily existence—and a supernatural outlook less?

Is God Really out There?

Imagine a world without God; what kind of world would it be? Some people do live as if God did not exist, but imagine what life would be like without God. It may be surprising to consider that if God did not exist, there would be no earth, no people, no animals, *nothing at all.* Everything in our world is dependent on "something else." Ultimately, all that exists, or ever has or will exist, is dependent on the limitless and unlimitable, self-existent God of the universe. Oxford philosopher Richard Swinburne surveyed the various reasons and evidence for and against God's existence, aside from any reference to the Bible, and offers this summary statement:

The conclusion of this book is that the existence, orderliness, and fine-tunedness of the world; the existence of conscious humans within it with providential opportunities for moulding themselves, each other, and the world; some historical evidence of miracles in connection with human needs and prayers, particularly in connection with the foundation of Christianity, topped up finally by the apparent experience by millions of his presence, all makes it significantly more probable than not that there is a God.[18]

If a dependent world exists, then God must exist.

God is the source of all created things. Until this basic truth permeates our soul, we will be hard-pressed to believe genuinely that God really exists. For if God is not necessary for our existence, then maybe God is not necessary to our daily living. Belief that God exists is a fundamental requirement in developing a relationship with God, as noted in Hebrews 11:6: "And without faith it is impossible to please God, because anyone who comes to him must believe that he exists and that he rewards those who earnestly seek him." Yet God's invisibility masks his presence everywhere to most people today.

A Brain Teaser

To explore the matter further, ponder the following brain teaser. Medical science continues to advance and conquer diseases of the body. For example, transplants can now be performed with the following major organs: kidneys, livers, lungs and even hearts. Imagine a time in the far future, due to fantastic technological breakthroughs, that doctors would be able to perform a brain transplant without complications. Perhaps victims of Alzheimer's disease might be worthy candidates for this futuristic complex surgery. In mulling over this thought experiment, what distinctly Christian response should be given? From a Christian perspective, might there be something morally wrong about this operation?

If memories reside in our brain, someone might reason, and the brain empowers thinking, as most neurologists report, how can a Christian ever endorse such an idea? Would this radical surgery not violate someone's very personhood? On the contrary, I have become convinced that thinking is not really done with the brain but rather done with the mind, implying that it is not necessary to have a brain in order to think. Note that God has no body nor brain—he is pure spirit—yet God thinks all the time. Thus, for

God, everything is a "no-brainer."[19] Angels and demons also have no brain, no physicality, and yet they can think. If this is the case and it were possible to perform a brain transplant, the brain could be regarded like any other human physical organ and available for a transplant.[20]

Ultimately the brain and the mind are not identical—the physical brain is not the same thing as the immaterial mind. Consider the following points. In examining the physical brain, any neuroscientist with the appropriate training and equipment can verify the same basic data about the human brain. Such scientific information constitutes a public kind of knowledge. It is accessible to any person who has acquired the scientific competencies and desires to study this gray matter. Yet the thoughts in my mind are accessible only to me (and to God). Thoughts can be categorized as private knowledge; no one can know my exact thoughts unless I reveal them. Furthermore, it is possible to weigh (measure) or stain (color) with a dye the cells of a brain. But there is no way to weigh or stain a thought. Thoughts belong to a different realm altogether. They belong to a realm beyond this natural reality, a supernatural reality.

The Bible points to a two-realms view of human persons, as comprised of a physical body and an immaterial soul or spirit, designed with capacities of relating within both of these differing realms, yet functioning in a seamless, integrated manner, for "the body without the spirit is dead" (Jas 2:26).[21] A human being is an embodied soul. Our material aspect, our brain and other body members, permits us to interact in this physical world, while our immaterial aspect, our soul or spirit, allows us to interact with God. Indeed, without our immaterial aspect, we could never interact with nor become friends of God, who is essentially immaterial.

Yet this conception flies against the commonly held notions of contemporary science that the human person is solely a material organism and that consciousness and thoughts are merely complex chemical reactions in the brain, as illustrated by recent movies. In *Bicentennial Man* (starring Robin Williams) a futuristic robot becomes a human being solely by replacing metal and mechanics with human skin and body parts. In *The Matrix* (starring Keanu Reeves and Laurence Fishburne), learning highly advanced martial arts skills is as easy as loading the appropriate software diskette into the brain. Yet, if a material reality is all there is, then God or angels cannot exist.

Research on Near-Death Experiences

The event of death forces the question of the essential composition of human nature. Research regarding near-death experiences (NDE) offers a measure of empirical evidence for some kind of consciousness after death. Consider the case of a young girl, Katie, who nearly drowned in a swimming pool. The following report was given by the attending physician based on his personal experience, with other details verified by testimony of medical staff and the family. Katie was resuscitated in the emergency room, although still profoundly comatose, and a CAT scan revealed swollen brain tissue. Furthermore, since a machine maintained her breathing, Dr. Morse estimated Katie had a 10 percent chance of living. Yet after three days she fully recovered, sharing the following account of her three-day ordeal. Although Katie's eyes were closed during the whole encounter, she could accurately describe details about the emergency room and her medical procedures. In addition, Katie had "followed" the family home and could recount specifics about the evening meal, her father's reaction to the accident, as well as the specific toys her brother and sister played with. She also reported meeting Jesus, the heavenly Father and an angel named Elizabeth.[22]

In an episode presented by Elizabeth Kubler-Ross, another young girl experienced an NDE during heart surgery. Afterward she reported having met her brother, although she had not known she had one. Her father revealed later there actually was a brother, but he had died prior to his daughter's birth.[23] After reviewing accounts of NDE during the 1970s and 1980s, psychology professor John Gibbs concludes:

> NDE research would suggest that the mind is sometimes capable at the point near bodily death of functioning without the normal (material) support of the brain and the sensory nervous system. . . . In general, then, although NDE findings do not prove theism, they would seem to be inconsistent with the materialistic ontology associated with the atheistic perspective.[24]

NDE research may help many to reconsider what lies behind the grave.[25]

When the Heavens Open

On a few occasions, the supernatural may intersect the routines of life and compel acknowledgment of a hidden realm. Two thousand years ago on that momentous evening in Bethlehem, a few shepherds on a late-night shift witnessed an angelic host bursting onto the horizon, lighting up the sky, singing joyful proclamations of the birth of our Lord Jesus (Lk 2:8-20). The first Christian martyr, Stephen, witnessed a glimpse of heaven prior to being stoned to death. Just before the stones flew, God momentarily removed the veil surrounding his realm and let Stephen gaze on unseen heavenly realities. " 'Look,' he said, 'I see heaven open and the Son of Man standing at the right hand of God' " (Acts 7:56).

A more dramatic instance occurred during Old Testament times of the kings, when Elisha the prophet helped Israel avert being ambushed by the Syrians (2 Kings 6:8-13). When the king of Syria discovered that Elisha was the culprit, he deployed the whole Syrian army to capture this one prophet. Early that morning Elisha's servant went outside and was horrified to see the city surrounded by a great army and quickly informed the prophet. But Elisha was already well acquainted with this unseen but very real world behind the veil—he saw that a far more powerful angelic host at that very moment outnumbered the Syrian army. " 'Don't be afraid,' the prophet answered. 'Those who are with us are more than those who are with them.' And Elisha prayed, 'O LORD, open his eyes so he may see.' Then the LORD opened the servant's eyes, and he looked and saw the hills full of horses and chariots of fire all around Elisha" (2 Kings 6:16-17). Much later in Israel's history, Ezekiel began his prophecy with this declaration: "In the thirtieth year, in the fourth month on the fifth day, while I was among the exiles by the Kebar river, the heavens were opened and I saw visions of God" (Ezek 1:1). Through the experience of others as recorded in the Bible, it is possible to peek into a realm that currently exists behind a "veil" (cf. Heb 6:19).

Yet the heavens need not remain closed for those in God's family. Believers are invited to live an abundant and supernatural lifestyle now, in which the heavens become increasingly open as God becomes more real in our experience. On some occasions, it will be necessary to stop and turn aside, as did Moses, to investigate a bush on fire that did not burn up (Ex 3:2-3). Or the supernatural may remain hidden until an ability to see this invisible reality with "eyes of faith" becomes more routine, as it was for Elisha. If we wish to know God more deeply, we must become convinced, at the core of our being, that this is a God-bathed world.

Shifting Our Confidence

All Christians enter earth as helpless infants. Through the passing of normal human development and maturation, we explore our surroundings and slowly gain confidence in the systematic stability of this physical world. Later in life, at the moment when God graciously regenerates each believer, God introduces another realm to the Christian's horizon that beckons further exploration with the requisite growth of faith. Of course, this reality was always there, since human nature was designed to exist within both realms, being made of both matter and spirit. But in becoming a member of God's family, a greater ability to discern this hidden realm of reality is acquired. Just as believers gain confidence in the physical realm, so God invites his children to live within this invisible realm, for example, as the apostle Peter did in walking on water for a stretch, until the physical circumstances overwhelmed him (Mt 14:29). Moreover, Christians must make a transition regarding where their primary confidence lies, shifting *from* a greater confidence in physical reality *to* a greater faith in the immaterial reality.

To sense more of God's presence, believers must become attuned to this invisible reality, where God is always near. "For since the creation of the world God's invisible qualities—his eternal power and divine nature—have been clearly seen, being understood from what has been made" (Rom 1:20). Despite the Russian cosmonaut's denial that he could not see God throughout his journey in outer space, God is everywhere present, although the degree of his presence may vary due to the situation. While God is not spatially located—he is immaterial—he is immediately accessible to those who sincerely call upon him (Ps 145:18; cf. 2 Chron 16:9). As Dallas Willard notes, "Every point in [the universe] is accessible to [God's] consciousness and will, and his manifest presence can be focused in any location as he sees fit. . . . So we should assume that space is anything but empty."[26] King David declared that it is impossible to escape from God's presence (Ps 139:7-12). Therefore, no physical barrier nor stretch of distance can prevent God from being present at any moment, within any situation, in our life. God is always near.

Furthermore, to draw believers into this different, immaterial reality—the realm in which God primarily exists—God himself remains largely hidden in the natural world. But he is there nonetheless. God partially veils his presence for our good. If God frequently showed up in a physical way, his children would never have the opportunity to explore the immaterial reality in which "we live and move and have our being" (Acts 17:28). This other reality typically does not impress itself upon the believer. It is rather *under*whelming but there to be discovered nonetheless. Willard posits that "the most important things in our human lives are nearly always things that are invisible. That is even true without special reference to God. People who cannot believe without seeing are desperately limited in all their relationships."[27] God hides himself to nurture in believers an increasing confidence in this invisible realm that offers the only sustaining resources for abundant living.

Christians are both material and spiritual beings who have now been regenerated to thrive in this eternal reality, although believers must grow in their ability to do so. Thus, during this earthly journey believers must progressively redirect the primary focus of their reliance from the visible world to the specific realities of the invisible world. Increasingly "we live [preeminently] by faith, not by sight" (2 Cor 5:7).[28]

Comparing Two Realms

Certain features of this invisible realm become more obvious when compared with known features of the physical world (see table 4.1; the regenerated Christian's experience of these realities is primarily in view). For the purposes of description, these features may be listed within separate columns; nevertheless God created both with his blessing, declaring them essentially both "very good" (Gen 1:31). They are coexisting, integrated realities. Believers, as integrated beings, live in both realms simultaneously during their earthly pilgrimage, and that is good. Of course, the physical world now exists under a curse (Gen 3:17-19; Rom 8:19-22) and awaits an exciting renewal in the future. Nonetheless, both material and immaterial realities have been created by God. Even in eternity future believers will experience both material and immaterial realities, for life within the new heaven and new earth (Rev 21:1) will not be exclusively a nonmaterial, spiritual experience.

Yet for this life now, a shift of confidence must take place. The purpose of the apostle Paul's remark about living by faith was to redirect the primary

Material Reality	Immaterial Reality
Visible	Invisible (Rom 1:20)
Matter	Spirit* (2 Cor 4:16-18)
Temporary	Everlasting (1 Cor 9:25)
Body—brain and five senses	Soul—mind and spiritual discernment (Jas 2:26)
Event cause-effect relations (natural causation)	Personal agency cause-effect relations (free will)** (Ps 32:8-9)
Living by sight	Living by faith (2 Cor 5:7)
Food and water	Word of God (Deut 8:3)
Partial hiddenness of God's glory	Fullness of God's glory (Col 3:3-4)

*Spirit here primarily refers to spirit beings: God, angels, demons and our own human spirits. In addition, there are nonphysical realities that exist which spirit beings either exhibit or employ, such as qualities, propositions, numbers and logical relations.

**Personal agency causation—free will—is the critical yet missing feature within most naturalistic worldviews and philosophies held in this modern, antisupernaturalistic world. Yet part of being created in the image of God is that we have free will, the ability to decide what to do and how to act, the power to lead and rule over God's creation. Some mention of free will is included in the final chapter on prayer.

Table 4.1. Contrasting features of material and immaterial realities

focus of the Christian's confidence for living. Believers must still live by sight in this essentially good world God has created, which still reflects much beauty God had intended—the sparkling colors, the permeating fragrances, the velvety textures. As we grow up in this world, we only see one realm—the physical. But as children of God we must become *bicultural*—fully reliant on resources within both the material and immaterial realms as God permits this side of eternity. Christians live within two differing realities, one material and the other immaterial.

Two Contrasting Kingdoms

Furthermore, two powerful kingdoms now vie for our allegiance—the kingdom of God, with Jesus Christ as its King, and the kingdom of Satan. This two-kingdom view of life was highlighted by Jesus during an encounter with the Pharisees, who falsely claimed that Jesus was in league with the devil by casting out demons. In response, Jesus pronounced the existence of two distinct realms of power and authority operating in this life. "If Satan drives out Satan, he is divided against himself. How then can his kingdom stand? . . . But if I drive out demons by the Spirit of God, then the kingdom of God has come upon you" (Mt 12:26, 28).

Life is not a bed of roses. Evil has invaded this planet. Why does God permit Satan to have an evil kingdom? That difficult issue is explored further in chapter seven of this book. Regardless, reality must be reckoned with—the devil and his minions are loose in this world. Satan is an angel, or at least was God's chief angel until pride surfaced (1 Tim 3:6) and he rebelled against God. Formerly an ally of God, he now is God's archenemy, spearheading a defiant and disobedient movement of evil on the earth. The Bible labels him as the god of this world (2 Cor 4:4) who can pose as an "angel of light" (2 Cor 11:14). Joining Satan's rebellion against God were some angels, usually referred to as "unclean" or "evil" spirits (Mk 1:23) or "demons" (Mk 1:34). The place of eternal punishment was expressly prepared for Satan and his angels (Mt 25:41).

Yet the official day of doom for Satan was at the resurrection of the Lord Jesus Christ, where "death has been swallowed up in victory" (1 Cor 15:54). Although Satan's destiny is fixed, he still attempts to drive a wedge between the saints and their God. At our physical birth all believers began life fully within Satan's dominion, and we learned to follow him willingly. "As for you, you were dead in your transgressions and sins, in which you used to live when you followed the ways of this world and of the ruler of the kingdom of the air, the spirit who is now at work in those who are disobedient" (Eph 2:1-2). In God's great mercy and love, he "rescued us from [Satan's] dominion of darkness and brought us into the kingdom of the Son he loves" (Col 1:13).

The Kingdom of God
During his earthly pilgrimage, Jesus' primary teaching topic was about the kingdom of God.[29] " 'The time has come,' he said. 'The kingdom of God is near. Repent and believe the good news!' " (Mk 1:15). Later, a whole series of Jesus' parables offered analogies to explain this kingdom (e.g., sower

and the seed, wheat and tares [Mt 13]). Prior to his ascension into heaven, Jesus remained with his disciples "over a period of forty days and spoke about the kingdom of God" (Acts 1:3). If this kingdom language is not as familiar, consider the terms which convey basically the same meaning: *eternal life* (in John's writings) and *salvation* (in Paul's writings).[30] Unfortunately, the commonly used phrase "being saved" does not conjure in the imagination the grandeur of all that the kingdom of God entails.

But what is a kingdom? Is it primarily a country—a geographical and political entity? Rather, consider a more fundamental definition. A kingdom is essentially the effective range of any monarch's will—his or her dominion, reign or rule over subjects. This basic notion also applies to anyone exercising some degree of freedom and authority over others, whether it be God in his kingdom or Satan in his. Furthermore, this conception applies to any human being who exercises some sort of responsibility, be it at home, within the church or at work. As Willard explains:

> Every last one of us has a "kingdom"—or a "queendom," or a "government"—a realm that is uniquely our own, where our choice determines what happens. . . . Whatever we genuinely have the say over is *in* our kingdom. And our having the say over something is precisely what places it within our kingdom. . . . Any being that has say over nothing at all is no person. . . . Now God's own "kingdom," or "rule," is the range of his effective will, where what he wants done is done.[31]

Two distinct senses of understanding the kingdom of God may be identified. Since God is the only self-existing supreme being, all that exists is dependent on God's power and sustenance, whether anyone is willing to bow to God or not. In this sense, God is the only sovereign over all creation— past, present or future—he is the supreme king and judge of all. Yet Scripture teaches a narrower sense that involves those empowered by the Holy Spirit who are willing to align themselves with God. It is this emerging kingdom that Jesus proclaims is now available for all to enter and become loyal citizens and subjects. Richard Longenecker draws such a distinction between these two senses.

> Primarily [the kingdom of God] refers to God's sovereign rule in human life and the affairs of history, and secondarily to the realm where that rule reigns. God's sovereignty is universal (cf. Ps. 103:19). But it was specifically

manifested in the life of the nation of Israel and among Jesus' disciples; it is expressed progressively in the church and through the lives of Christians; and it will be fully revealed throughout eternity.[32]

Jesus invited his followers to pray that God's "kingdom come, your will be done on earth as it is in heaven" (Mt 6:10), and we should seek God's kingdom as our highest priority: "But seek first his kingdom and his righteousness, and all these things will be given to you as well" (Mt 6:33). A proportional relationship exists between our daily priorities and the depth of our relationship with God. The more each of our kingdoms become aligned with God's kingdom, the closer our friendship with God can become.

Two Sequential Phases Within God's Kingdom

Thus far this chapter has outlined two differing realities that coexist now—one of the material world and another of the immaterial world. Second, two powerful kingdoms vie for our obedience. There is a third pair of contrasts: God's kingdom involves two distinct phases over time. An older TV commercial proclaimed, "You only go around once in this life, so grab all the gusto you can!" Is this all there is to life, some three score and ten years residing on this earthly space station orbiting the sun? The Bible teaches that this present world is but a temporary passageway toward arriving at the Christians' true home in the next phase of God's kingdom in heaven, the kind of world everyone dreams about: one of peace and love and goodness. "But in keeping with his promise we are looking forward to a new heaven and a new earth, the home of righteousness" (2 Pet 3:13).

The New Testament uses phrases like "the present life" and "the life to come" to depict the broader sweep of God's plan. For example, "Train yourself to be godly. For physical training is of some value, but godliness has value for all things, holding promise for both the *present life* and the *life to come*" (1 Tim 4:7-8, emphasis added; see also Mt 12:3; Mk 10:30; Lk 18:30). Similarly, these comforting words about the age to come appear in the final chapters of the book of Revelation: "He will wipe every tear from their eyes. There will be no more death or mourning or crying or pain, for the old order of things has passed away. . . . Nothing impure will ever enter it, nor will anyone who does what is shameful or deceitful, but only those whose names are written in the Lamb's book of life" (Rev 21:4, 27).

For Nancy Missler, heaven is more real now, due to the loss of her thirty-nine-year-old son to a sudden heart attack. "What Chip's death has done for me personally is to bring heaven and earth closer together. I now have one child in heaven waiting for all of us to come home. . . . The reason death is so difficult for so many of us, I believe, is because we are so preoccupied with the here and now."[33]

On the passing of their young son Jonathan to cancer, John and Brenda Bass sent the following e-mail to family and friends:

> Tonight—Jonathan accepted the gracious invitation of our Lord and Savior Jesus Christ for an extended stay at a deluxe bed & breakfast in Heaven. His flight departed on Monday, May 29th, 2000 at 9:50 p.m. We stood at the gate and waved goodbye for awhile. There were tears of sorrow and tears of joy. We are fortunate that all the immediate family had the chance to see him off.[34]

Even for noted educator Jonathan Kozol, heaven is becoming an important factor. In light of his long-term work with inner-city children he muses, "I want to believe that there is something for the children after this [present life] because this isn't good enough."[35]

Believers must realize that God *is* in the process of creating that perfect world that we all dream about, only God has a different and better idea for how to get there. Nothing in this world compares to the excitement and surprises God has in store for his children in that new place. When believers know that life is even better beyond the grave, it makes it a little easier to put up with a lot of grief and anguish now. No ultimate fear need bother believers for what happens in this life—even with all of its troubles and pains—because God has promised eternal life.

There is an "already" and a "not yet" aspect of God's kingdom project, as the apostle Paul teaches, "For you died, and your life is now hidden with Christ in God. When Christ, who is your life, appears, then you also will appear with him in glory" (Col 3:3-4). As Peter O'Brien explains:

> For the moment their heavenly life remains hidden, secure with Christ in God. Their new life as Christians in Christ is not visible to others and, in some measure, is hidden from themselves. It will only be fully manifest when Christ, who embodies that life, appears at his Parousia. Indeed, the day of the revelation of the *Son* of God will be the day of the revelation of

the *sons* of God. That manifestation will take place 'in glory' for it will involve the sharing of Christ's likeness and the receiving of the glorious resurrection body.[36]

Christians are now living in the first "already" phrase of God's two-phase program. "We ourselves, who have the firstfruits of the Spirit, groan inwardly as we wait eagerly for our adoption as sons, the redemption of our bodies" (Rom 8:23). Soon, whether through death or at the Lord Jesus' second coming, all believers will move on to the world God really wants for us—the "not yet" phase of heaven.[37]

According to God's bountiful generosity, God awaits the day that all believers will experience what he has been dreaming about and designing for a long time. In one parable about the end times, Jesus offered this comment for all believers: "Then the King will say to those on his right, 'Come, you who are blessed by my Father; take your inheritance, the kingdom prepared for you since the creation of the world' " (Mt 25:34; cf. Dan 7:18, 27). God invites each believer now to align his or her individual and limited "kingdoms" and "queendoms" with his own grand kingdom project of righteous living for now and forever. Figure 4.1 summarizes the three sets of contrasting features developed in this chapter.

Through a college campus ministry, Steve Sawyer received Jesus Christ as his personal Savior. Sadly, a few years later, he was diagnosed with AIDS, the result of receiving a contaminated blood transfusion. During his last years on earth, he traveled for Campus Crusade for Christ, sharing his faith in Christ on a number of college campuses throughout the world. Yet his disease finally overtook him. On March 13, 1999, at 11:30 a.m., Steve left this earth. "His mother says that before Steve died, he sat up in bed and said, 'Wow'!"[38] Did Steve get a glimpse of this hidden reality in which God exists as he entered the next phase of eternal life with God?

Departing Empty-Handed?

Two friends were attending the funeral of a wealthy acquaintance. One leans over to his friend and whispers, "How much did old George leave behind?" The friend responds, "All of it." From God's vantage point, the fact is clear: everyone enters this life with nothing and leaves with nothing. Ultimately, all possessions are not permanent; nothing is carried to heaven, despite the hope of those ancient kings who hid their treasure in

#1 Putting Greater Confidence in the Invisible Reality than the Visible Reality

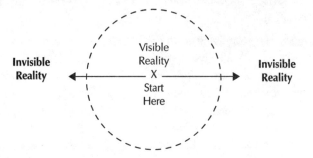

#2 Transferred to the Kingdom of God from Satan's Kingdom of Darkness

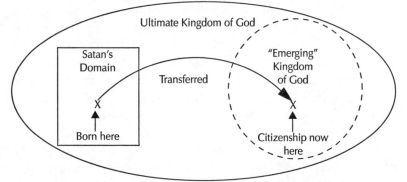

#3 Recognizing that Phase #1 Is a Temporary Passageway to Phase #2, Our Home

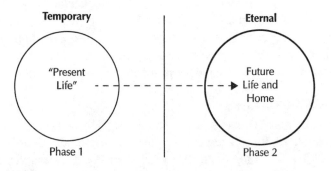

Figure 4.1. Three movements in nurturing our faith in God

their tombs for the afterlife. "For we brought nothing into the world, and we can take nothing out of it" (1 Tim 6:7; cf. Job 1:21; Eccles 5:15-16). Although believers enter eternity empty-handed—with no material possessions—they do not enter the next life empty-hearted. Consider these three permanent items from the immaterial realm of reality that Christians carry with them beyond the grave.

☐ Friendships

☐ Character

☐ Good deeds

In the first place, friendships are forever. There is a continuity of the relationships developed on this earth with God and with other members of God's family, as explored in chapter two. Growing in these relationships is part of God's long-term project of building his kingdom community. For the believer, friendships are of utmost importance.

Second, believers take along their character, the kind of person they are becoming. Learning begun on earth continues in the next life, developing further knowledge and wisdom, more skill and talent, deeper attitudes and desires.[39] Life on this earth contributes to the kingdom citizens Christians are becoming, the kind with which God desires to populate his eternal kingdom. "Godliness has value for . . . both the present life *and* the life to come" (1 Tim 4:8).

Finally, believers bring with them into the next life their good deeds, or at least the effects of such good deeds for others and themselves. During this life God's children can engage in kingdom work in doing good to overcome evil, to help other believers and to invite "outsiders" to become members of God's family and kingdom. How this life is spent and what good has been done will be reviewed at the Bema Seat of Jesus, and the Lord will honor believers for their labors there. "For we must all appear before the judgment seat of Christ, that each one may receive what is due him for the things done while in the body, whether good or bad" (2 Cor 5:10; see also 1 Cor 3:10-15).

These valuables that go with us to heaven must be included in our investment portfolio for eternity (Mt 6:19-21). As martyred missionary Jim Elliot so eloquently states, "He is no fool who gives up what he cannot keep, to gain what he cannot lose."[40] What God values highly has little to do with possessions owned, progress up the career ladder, other trophies collected, or with most anything physical in this world. In the midst of living in the "already" phase of God's kingdom believers must attend to what is of enduring value (Rom 14:17).

The Life of Faith in God

The challenge for believers who desire to know God more deeply is to keep God's grand kingdom project in mind so that this concept pervades how we think, how we feel, how we act. This permeation process involves growth and development of faith in God—that God is real, that God is near and that God is in the business of bringing his kingdom project to completion. If one lives only by sight, the naturalistic mindset of contemporary culture will continue to overwhelm one's worldview. Christians must live by faith. The apostle Paul urges all members of God's family, "Do not conform any longer to the pattern of this world, but be transformed by the renewing of your mind" (Rom 12:2).

The phrase "faith in God" is not clearly self-descriptive—conveying much meaning at first glance. How should this expression be defined or described? At its core, faith is primarily a relational term, a concept of trust one person has in another. For example, faith is that relational and affectional bond of trust experienced between deep friends or between a husband and wife who are committed companions. Likewise, our faith in God can increase as we grow in our realization that God is real, that God is near and that God can be relied upon to provide for our needs. The more we live moment by moment in light of God's present reality, the more our faith grows. Perhaps another way of understanding the phrase "having faith in God" is to focus on "learning to live in the presence of God, the God who is always near." If we genuinely believed that God is always near, how might we think or feel or act?

Children do not stuff their pockets with bread or rolls at the breakfast table because they have learned to trust that their parents will provide lunch at noon and dinner that evening. Just so, the children of God can grow in their ability to trust God for "daily bread" (Mt 6:11). The apostle Paul exemplified such a demeanor. "I have learned to be content whatever the circumstances. I know what it is to be in need, and I know what it is to have plenty. I have learned the secret of being content in any and every situation, whether well fed or hungry, whether living in plenty or in want. I can do everything through him who gives me strength" (Phil 4:11-13). Walking in God's presence will yield less worry and a greater sense of peace.

Growing in Belief

How do believers actually grow in faith? To answer this question, we need to explore the belief formation process to comprehend how our various beliefs about life—whether of God or about gravity or about proper moral action—become inculcated into our character. Core beliefs or convictions are not necessarily what one professes or claims to believe or what one may express at a Bible study or declare on a doctrinal statement. The convictions under discussion are the actual core values of a person that guide the automatic and reactive aspect of how we live. As J. P. Moreland notes, "Beliefs are the rails upon which our lives run. . . . When the rubber meets the road, we act out our actual beliefs most of the time. That is why behavior is such a good indicator of a person's beliefs."[41]

Furthermore, there is a general lack of reflection about these beliefs that so powerfully impact how we live. For example, a repairman may carefully walk on the roof of a house or at the ledge of some tall skyscraper in order not to trip and fall. But he does not specifically examine his thoughts about the law of gravity. It is just a core assumption of life that limits the scope of his actions. Everyone has myriads of these core convictions that form his or her character, but they never usually become the subject of thought.

Yet, on occasion we may become aware of a core belief by our agitation when a core assumption is challenged. Rising irritation may indicate a deep core belief has been touched. For example, this chapter presented two ideas that some readers may have heard for the first time, touching relevant core assumptions about these topics—that people think with their mind and not their brain, and that Jesus himself exercised faith during his incarnation. Regardless of whether or not I am right on these matters, we must still surface and examine our core assumptions about the important issues of life and of God if we wish to grow deeper in our walk with God. It may be, as mentioned above, that various core assumptions about God actually hinder a believer's attempt to grow in his or her faith. Christians need to be habitually in the process of affirming certain core beliefs and re-forming others regarding what is really true about God and his world.

Thus, contrary to popular belief, the ideas and convictions we hold dear do significantly affect our daily living, as Willard explains:

> But in our culture there is a severe illusion about faith, or belief. It is one that has been produced by many centuries of people professing, as a cultural identification, to believe things they do not really believe at all. . . . *Thus there arises the misunderstanding that human life is not really governed by belief.* This is a disastrous error. We often speak of people not living up to their faith. But the cases in which we say this are not really cases of people behaving otherwise than they believe. They are cases in which genuine beliefs are made obvious by what people do. We always live up to our beliefs—or down to them, as the case may be. Nothing else is possible. It is the nature of belief.[42]

Core beliefs direct our life walk whether we are aware of them or not.

Furthermore, core beliefs are formed in a very passive manner, according to Swinburne. "We believe our beliefs to be true because we know that we do not choose them, but we believe that they are forced upon us by evidence from the outside world."[43] Thus, it is not possible to change a core belief at will. We do not have direct control over our beliefs; one cannot believe in anything one wishes to. Beliefs are acquired passively over time, formed by the evidence about reality confronted in life. Consequently, beliefs cannot be changed in an instant of time just by wanting to believe differently. As Swinburne notes, "Beliefs are views about how the world is. . . . But a 'belief' would not be a belief if we could change it readily at will (and so realize we are doing so)."[44] We do not have direct control over our beliefs—we cannot believe in anything we want to.

Although beliefs cannot be changed *directly* at will (i.e., we lack "inner" freedom), we can *indirectly* influence our beliefs by our openness to consider new or additional evidence about God and reality (i.e., we have "outer" freedom).[45] Since the formation of beliefs involves a process of being convinced of truth over a period of time, believers can indirectly affect which beliefs are dearly held by directing their thought life through planned study.[46] For example, working through a book like this one offers an occasion to give more thought to beliefs about God and which beliefs may need revising. Of course, the belief formation process is not purely a cognitive venture. Actually, core beliefs affect attitudes, feelings and actions. It is a complex and holistic process that significantly impacts the core of character.[47] Thus, it makes sense, as the Bible urges, for minds to be continually renewed (Rom 12:2) by engaging in the regular study and meditation of God's Word (Ps 1). The corollary is that every claim in the marketplace of ideas must be examined so that believers "take captive every thought to make it obedient to Christ" (2 Cor 10:5).

Our ideas matter, particularly our ideas about God, if we wish to deepen our relationship with God. If I feel more at home in this physical world—with what I see and can touch—than I do with the invisible world that the Bible talks about, then it will be hard to believe that an invisible God is really relevant to my daily life in this material world. To draw near to God we must become convinced and be more comfortable with the fact that what we see and touch is not the rock bottom of reality. Only God is. Our faith must grow so we too can feel at home in the invisible realm in which we and God exist. "Though you have not seen him, you love him; and even though you do not see him now, you believe in him and are filled with an inexpressible and glorious joy, for you are receiving the goal of your faith, the salvation of your souls" (1 Pet 1:8-9).

Wasting Time with God: Watchfulness

If God is near and active now, then the effects of his activity will become evident to the discerning observer. We are encouraged to be alert regarding the coming of the Lord (e.g., "Therefore keep watch because you do not know when the owner of the house will come back. . . . Do not let him find you sleeping. What I say to you, I say to everyone: 'Watch!' " Mk 13:35-37) and to be vigilant against the diabolical assaults (e.g., "Watch and pray so that you will not fall into temptation. The spirit is willing, but the body is weak," Mt 26:41).

In the past I would complain about God's distance in my own experience, but then I began looking for "coincidences" in my life—those serendipitous and seemingly random acts of kindness for which I had no responsibility—not even an answer to my explicit prayer—but which I welcomed nonetheless. The examples I share are modest and mundane to encourage the belief that God is interested even in the minor and minute aspects of our daily experience. For instance, at a public library sale, I "happened" upon a few outstanding, out-of-print books—one I now use for a textbook for a class. In the same vein, the used book I came upon at a bookstore just "happened" to meet my needs at the moment.

I remember how my forgetfulness "happened" to rescue me. I was teaching a class across campus and usually drove my car there. This particular day I forgot my teaching binder—the only time it occurred that semester. So before class began, I went back to my office, and there was our dean of the faculty pacing the hallway looking for my class. I had invited him to observe my teaching and forgot to mention we had changed classrooms from the one listed in the registration booklet. I directed him to the right location.

Of course, there are more fantastic coincidences. Like the engagement ring lost off the west coast of Sweden and found two years later: "The ring was consumed by a mussel that turned up in shellfish caught by fisherman Peder Carlsson." He was able to trace the owner by the inscription in the ring.[48] Or what about the oil plug lost by missionary David Merkh on a dirt road in a rural region of Brazil? A mechanic had forgotten to tighten the plug, and apparently it fell off somewhere along the road. Eventually, without any oil, the engine coughed to a halt. After a long trek to the nearest village with an auto parts store, hope turned to disappointment. The manager apologized for not having a replacement plug. Back out on the street, David heard someone calling him. From out of the blue, a stranger produced the old, familiar plug. On his drive into town, the stranger "happened" to see the plug on the road. Without really knowing why, he stopped the car, threw the plug in the back and forgot about it, that is, until he overheard David talking with the parts manager. In the midst of a small village, in the interior of Brazil, God rescued a small oil plug for one of his children through the kindness of another.[49] What a coincidence.

Such coincidences abound for believers, but we are usually oblivious to the small instances of good in our lives. There are no accidental coincidences in God's plan when good comes our way.[50] Of course, these coincidences may be the answer to someone else's prayer for us. Or they may be direct interventions from God who would take the initiative to care for us in this small way. Be watchful and consider recording these important episodes in your life. Celebrate God's goodness in your life and share your stories with others. Encourage them to take their own "God walks" to recognize God's kindnesses in their daily experience and to share their stories with you. It may be amazing to note how much more God is involved in our lives than we previously thought. This truly is a God-bathed world; God really is near. Let us enter more fully into this realm of living.

Wasting Time with God: Fasting
Besides becoming more aware of our invisible God's involvement in daily circumstances, believers can become more attuned to the immaterial realm through temporarily de-emphasizing the material aspect of our being. A simple but profound spiritual discipline regarding the body is fasting from food. Although it is important to care appropriately for our physical body (Eph 5:29), we need not always pamper it. By not attending to our bodies for a set period of time, we remind ourselves of our immaterial, spiritual nature: "Even though our outer nature [physical body] is wasting away, our inner nature [spirit/soul] is being renewed day by day . . . because we look not at what can be seen but at what cannot be seen" (2 Cor 4:16, 18 NRSV).

Moses fasted (Ex 34:28), David fasted (2 Sam 12:16-23), Jesus fasted (Mt 4:2)[51] and Paul fasted (Acts 14:23). Fasting has a variety of purposes, for example, as a sign of repentance (1 Sam 7:6), as an aid in prayer to God (2 Sam 12:16-23), as a sign of grief or mourning (1 Sam 1:7-8), as a part of experiencing God's presence and help in spiritual warfare (Lk 4:2), as a part of public worship (Neh 9:1), or as a means of guarding against being mastered by the appetites of the physical body (1 Cor 9:24-27). This last category is the goal applied here.[52]

The usual fast is one with liquids only, eating no solid food. In an absolute fast one abstains from both liquids and food (e.g., Esther 4:16). Before engaging in a fast, believers with certain bodily imbalances may need to consult a physician regarding how to avoid damaging their bodies.[53] Another option is a partial fast, in which one skips one meal each day, for example, for a week or month or so. One may also target certain foods that involve greater temptations (e.g., chocolate, all desserts).

The concept of fasting as abstention can also be applied to other arenas of living, to target any lifestyle aspect in danger of becoming an addiction and distraction from being more aware of God. Mouthing the words *yes* and *no* is a simple task. But "learning when and how, to what, and to whom to give our yes and our no is a lifelong project. It is learning to live not merely in dull balance or tedious moderation but in passionate, disciplined choice and action," as Shawn Copeland notes.[54] For example, in a media fast, we would eliminate our contact with TV, movies, newspapers and magazines for a specified time. Believers could also fast from hobbies (e.g., golf fast), from work (only workaholics need apply here), married sex (e.g., 1 Cor 7:5), discretionary shopping, use of credit cards, driving a car as the main means of transportation (e.g., carpooling, using public transportation, walking). Experiment with different forms of fasting. As a spiritual discipline, the purpose is temporally abstaining from material aspects of our nature and lifestyle to become more attuned to the immaterial realm of God.

Conclusion

To get to know God better, believers must be convinced that God is more real than any physical object, that he is near each moment of the day, every day and night of the week. This chapter highlighted three sets of realities that are not visible but exist nonetheless. There are two realms of reality, the material and the physical. There are two kingdoms which now exist, the kingdom of God and of Satan. And there are two phases of God's kingdom project, the "already" and the "not yet" (see figure 4.1). If we wish to know God more and to seek first his kingdom priorities, we will need to shift our confidence toward these eternal and invisible realities.

Developing our faith in God along these lines involves a process of belief formation that is fairly passive. Yet Christians can indirectly influence the beliefs they acquire by directing their minds to consider and ponder God's description of reality over time. God graciously draws us into his own realm, an invisible realm just as real as our physical world. Spanish mystic John of the Cross (d. 1591) suggests that a limited faith perspective only yields restricted conceptions about God "based on the perceptions of our five fleshly senses, coupled with our mental calculations about God. This lower type of 'faith' has nothing to do with the ability to see with the eyes of the soul—which God himself must open up to us."[55] Although the heavens may be initially closed, they will open up as the ability to see with "eyes of faith" grows.

God's children must learn how to live and navigate in an immaterial realm by aligning their wills with God's within his kingdom. As C. S. Lewis (d. 1963) urges, "Aim at heaven and you get earth thrown in. Aim at earth and you will get neither."[56]

Unless we "waste time with God" little progress can be made in knowing God more. Sadly, believers often allow the busyness of life to dictate their schedule, passing up the opportunity to cultivate a deep relationship with God. Yet God patiently waits for us to "come near to God" (Jas 4:8). But what of the occasions that we do seek him earnestly and nothing happens? How should we understand such dryness in our soul? Are believers just not trying hard enough? Suggesting a way out of the time trap to seek God with all of our hearts and clarifying the confusion about such "dark nights of the soul" are topics treated in the next chapter.

PART 2

DEEPENING OUR FRIENDSHIP WITH GOD

5

COMMITMENT

SEEKING THE GOD WHO HIDES

"'Love the Lord your God with all your heart and with all your soul and with all your mind' This is the first and greatest commandment."

MATTHEW 22:37-38

JESUS' EXAMPLE

"Jesus often withdrew to lonely places and prayed."

LUKE 5:16

W hat kinds of things do we think about the most? Imagine that someone catalogued your most recurring thoughts. What would the top ten list look like? All Thomas Edison ever thought about was inventing anything that solved "the desperate needs of the world." Before he died in 1931 at age eighty-four, Edison patented 1,093 inventions, including the light bulb, motion-picture projector, mimeograph machine and record player, his favorite brainchild. Persevering to a fault, Edison performed about ten thousand experiments to make a successful storage battery. His progressive deafness never bothered him—Edison claimed that he could concentrate a lot more on his inventing.

Since he was eight years old, John Grunsfeld thought about outer space and dreamed of being an astronaut. Formerly a physics Ph.D. senior research fellow at Cal Tech, in 1992 at the age of thirty-three, Gruns-feld was culled from a pool of 2,054 qualified applicants along with eighteen others to become an astronaut candidate for the space shuttle program. Finally in March 1995, Grunsfeld fulfilled his dream by climbing into the space shuttle and participating in the longest flight up to that time: sixteen days in space.

Besides paying bills, selecting what clothes to wear and getting that pressing project completed, what grabs most of our attention? If someone had catalogued our recurring thoughts over this past month, would thinking about God appear on that top ten list? Of all the thoughts and ideas we mull over in our mind, if we wish to know God more deeply we must become much more conscious of God throughout the day.

The first theme to be explored in this chapter is the need for purposeful planning and commitment to make God the one recurring theme of the believer's thought life and lifestyle. A two-way dynamic always exists within any close relationship between two persons; each party must seek the other. For those in God's family, we must not think that our relationship with God is dependent on God's efforts alone. A deeper walk with God will never occur until we invest more effort to learn how to seek God with all of our heart. But first, we consider God's involvement in the dance of friendship with us, for it carries an unusual responsibility.

Meeting God for the First Time

What would it be like to be introduced to the God of the universe face to face for the very first time, especially if he showed up with thunder, lightning, fire, smoke and earth tremors as he did with the Israelites at Mount Sinai? Enter their experience and sense God's presence in this record from the Old Testament:

> On the morning of the third day there was thunder and lightning, with a thick cloud over the mountain, and a very loud trumpet blast. Everyone in the camp trembled. Then Moses led the people out of the camp to meet with God, and they stood at the foot of the mountain. Mount Sinai was covered with smoke, because the Lord descended on it in fire. The smoke billowed up from it like smoke from a furnace, the whole mountain trembled violently, and the sound of the trumpet grew louder and louder. . . . When the people saw the thunder and lightning and heard the trumpet and saw

the mountain in smoke, they trembled with fear. They stayed at a distance and said to Moses, "Speak to us yourself and we will listen. But do not have God speak to us or we will die." (Ex 19:16-19; 20:18-19)[1]

In the face of such terrifying manifestations, people usually run quickly away, not toward them. One day God will show up on this earth with such force that both the earth and sky will flee from his presence (Rev 20:11; see also Rev 6:15; 16:17-21). When the apostle John met the Lord of glory while on the Isle of Patmos, although he was Jesus' best friend during the incarnation, John reports, "When I saw him, I fell at his feet as though dead" (Rev 1:17). Even angelic messengers who suddenly appear must assure their human audience with words familiar from most Christmas plays: "Do not be afraid" (e.g., Lk 1:12-13, 26-30; 2:9-10).

But instead of such a grand entry, consider a subdued manner for a divine visitation, more like what might have happened in the Garden of Eden. Perhaps God walked up to Adam, and later Eve, appearing in some modest way—similar to our own human form—extended his hand and said, "Allow me to introduce myself; I'm your Creator." Did God tone down his full presence so as not to frighten Adam or Eve? In addition, after their sin, how was it possible for Adam and Eve to imagine they could hide from God unless God had manifested his presence in some visual manner that was perceived as being absent during their discussion with the serpent? Furthermore, would not God need to hold back a sense of his presence to allow Adam and Eve the actual experience of hiding from him? If it were our first meeting with God, we would feel much safer and more open to repeat visits from God if he came in a hidden form rather than some grand manifestation of glory.[2]

Can Christians admit that, in a sense, God is hidden now, that God has not fully revealed himself this side of heaven?[3] Hiddenness is not a word usually associated with God, for God is known as the one who reveals himself. But does he at the same time also intentionally conceal himself? Upon consideration, most would agree that God is not fully revealed now in this world. If God revealed more of himself, perhaps believers would never ignore his trademark. For example, maybe he could make a rainbow shine every morning to start the day, and end the day with a heavenly choir singing his praises to accompany the sunset. God could do much more, but he does not. Apparently God now conceals some of his glory—to hide himself to some extent—so that, among other purposes served, believers may be able to pursue a genuine and deeper relationship with him.

The Concept of Hiding

Among the various connections with the word *hiding,* one is related to a simple children's game of hide-and-seek. Sometimes we find ourselves in situations where it would be helpful to be hidden momentarily. Maybe it is in the classroom during recitation time; we were a little confused about the assignment and so hide from the teacher's summoning gaze by avoiding eye contact. Usually the telephone is our friend, but sometimes it invades our privacy; we can hide from telemarketers by screening those dinnertime sales calls with our answering machine. Or when that embarrassing moment occurs, would we not just like to sink into a black hole and be invisible? Then there is the kind of hiding a child engages in to avoid a parent after something is broken. Of course, thieves hide from the police. From these examples, we conclude that most meanings of *hiding* tend to be on the negative side—avoidance, embarrassment, shame, guilt.

Yet there are few situations when hiding takes another direction. For example, have you ever been to a masquerade party? For some party-goers, disguising themselves is a challenge, so no one will recognize them. And disguises are not just limited to parties. On occasion, famous persons move in our midst, but we are unaware. They appear incognito to permit more of a normal lifestyle for themselves. Even Billy Graham must use such a diversion on occasion. I know someone who recognized the evangelist traveling alone at an airport, despite his dark sunglasses, pulled-down hat, unshaven face and plain overcoat. At certain times there are benefits to being incognito. Do any of God's purposes call for these advantages?

The Challenge for God

Love is a powerful motive for creativity and kindness—love seems to know no boundaries. When love is in full bloom, no barrier is too high, no risk too great for love to conquer. But love—uncoerced love—must be freely given *and* freely received. Love cannot be forced or manufactured from without—it can only grow from within our heart. And it is precisely this fact of life that presents God with his greatest challenge. How does a majestic and infinite being develop a growing love relationship with believers who are frail and finite human beings? How can God initiate a mutually loving friendship with us without forcing us into it—without using divine strong-arm tactics?

Perhaps God could have designed humans so that our hardware and software programming would cause us to love him, so that we would automatically love God whether we wanted to or not. Yet what permeates a friendship relationship is a voluntary *and* mutual decision for each other. God could have a made a toy factory in which all believers mechanically proclaimed prerecorded praises. Pull the string and we chirp in unison, "I love you, God," "I thank you, God." But a genuine relationship must be entered into freely and not under coercion of will. For example, among family members, if you have to ask for a kiss, it is not the same as a kiss freely offered without a request.

Thus, God graciously cloaks his greatness for believers so he will not overwhelm us or coerce our loyalty. Such divine hiddenness provides sufficient room—a measure of "relational space"—for believers to respond to God's initiatives of love.[4] If we wish, we may remain at a surface level of acquaintance with God, or we can pursue a deeper friendship. Obedience to divine commandments is important to God, but God desires much more: the development of an ongoing and mutually willing relationship of love between God and each one of his children.

God Awaits Our Response
In two particular places in the Gospels, this manner of God's hiding—his humility and patience—is captured well, one from an incidental reference in Jesus' life and the other from a famous parable. One instance occurred following Jesus' resurrection when Jesus joined two disciples who were engaged in conversation on their way to Emmaus (Lk 24:13-32). Throughout the whole journey, Jesus' true identity was hidden, and he was comfortable with that. As the setting sun welcomed in the evening and the exciting conversation on the road came to a close, the trio arrived at the village. Despite being their Lord, Jesus did not presume upon his companions, but waited for their invitation of hospitality. Luke reports,

"As they approached the village to which they were going, *Jesus acted as though he were going farther*. But they urged him strongly, 'Stay with us, for it is nearly evening; the day is almost over.' So he went in to stay with them" (Lk 24:28-29, emphasis added). We witness no coercion or presumption. I. Howard Marshall notes, "The stranger [Jesus] made as if to proceed further. . . . He is merely giving them the opportunity to invite him in, and will not force his presence on them."[5]

This episode reveals the kindness of God, who gives his followers the space we desire to relate with God as we wish. Physical space is important to us, especially in a group of strangers. Notice how we like to keep our distance in conversations with others. On a crowded elevator, when space becomes cramped, we maintain a relational distance by all facing the same way, looking up at the floor-level indicator. Such distance and space play a role in any relationship. We do not like those who demand our time or who are overly possessive. On the other hand, within an intimate relationship the need for such space is drastically reduced. We desire to be as close as possible. The almighty and sovereign God, acting like a gentleman, waits patiently for our response.

God does not force his full presence on us; rather he partially hides himself to encourage a genuine response of friendship. It is as if God walks a precarious tightrope of giving enough clues about himself so that we could know he desires a deeper relationship, but not enough to overwhelm us or to coerce us toward him. God maintains a delicate tension between self-revelation and being hidden in order to assure that believers respond to his initiatives and pursue a relationship willingly. Ultimately God will fully live in our midst and show us his face (Rev 22:5). But now, God's invisibility poses a problem: it is easy for us to become distracted from seeking God.

Believers must not misinterpret God's intentions. The relational distance he offers never indicates any indifference toward us. Rather God's love is bountiful. For an eternity, God has been dreaming about cultivating a special relationship with each one of us. He has been willing to pay a great price to make this kind of relationship possible. Yet such a mutual love relationship with a majestic God requires a measure of distance in which God woos us to himself. One of the most famous stories Jesus told illustrates both God's willingness to give us all the space we need and his great desire for a love relationship with us.

Freedom to Wander

In response to a grumbling comment by the Pharisees, Jesus shared a series of three parables, all to communicate the heart of God: the lost coin, the lost sheep, and the lost or prodigal son (Lk 15). The heart of God is revealed in this famous story of the prodigal son told by Jesus, already discussed in chapter three. The younger son's request for his part of the inheritance while the father remained living was an arrogant rejection of his father. Kenneth Bailey explains the cultural significance from his study of Middle Eastern customs:

> For over fifteen years I have been asking people of all walks of life from Morocco to India and from Turkey to the Sudan about the implications of a son's request for his inheritance while the father is still living. The answer has always been emphatically the same. . . . The conversation runs as follows:
>
>> Has anyone ever made such a request in your village?
>> Never!
>> Could anyone ever make such a request?
>> Impossible!
>> If anyone ever did, what would happen?
>> His father would beat him, of course!
>> Why?
>> The request means—he wants his father to die.[6]

The son not only asks for his part of the inheritance, but also intends to spend it as he wishes. Bailey explains the implications. "After signing over his possessions to his son, the father still has the right to live off the proceeds . . . as long as he is alive. Here the younger son gets, and thus is assumed to have demanded, disposition to which, even more explicitly, he has no right until the death of his father. The implication of 'Father, I cannot wait for you to die' underlies both requests."[7]

The father ignores the arrogant insult and permits his younger son the freedom to leave. After his debauchery, the son comes to his senses and returns home. While still a far way off, the father sees him and runs toward him—an unusual act for an elderly man in that culture—and lavishes his joy, comfort and love on this missing son. The parable offers a marvelous portrayal of the heart of God, whether toward those outside the faith or within. The parable shines the light on God's willingness to give us all the space we need to develop a close relationship with him—freedom to wander away and freedom to draw near.

Our Part in Seeking God

One time I was offering some advice to a male friend about a relationship with a young woman: "Was this primarily a relationship of convenience or one of commitment?" Was he interested in her only when he happened to be with her, or was he willing to expend extra effort to demonstrate his love for her? The next day, these very words from my own lips returned to haunt me regarding my relationship with God. Was I interested in God only when it was convenient for me (e.g., at the regular church meetings and Bible studies), or was I really willing to pursue God no matter the cost—even if it would rearrange my priorities and lifestyle?

Is it time to ponder, "Is the honeymoon over in our relationship with God?" We who have been church members for many years must be alert here. Howard Hendricks shares an anecdote about the lawyer who announced to the marriage counselor, "I told my wife I loved her when I married her. That still applies until I revoke it!"[8] Just as some husbands may stop courting their mates after the wedding, do we adopt a business-as-usual relationship with God and become easily distracted from seeking God with all of our heart? Seeking God is never just a one-time affair or a passing fancy. Friends enjoy being in each other's company. The words of James are profoundly simple "*Come near to God* and he will come near to you." (Jas 4:8, emphasis added). Seeking God for believers requires commitment. It will not happen automatically just by attending church or reading the Bible or saying routine prayers. We must give effort to know how God can best be known.

In response to the question, "Which is the greatest commandment in the Law?" Jesus announced, "Love the Lord your God with all your heart and with all your soul and with all your mind" (Mt 22:37). What holds believers back from seeking God with all of their heart? How is it possible to recapture the romance in our relationship with God? One avenue of attack is to remind ourselves that "where your treasure is, there your heart will be also" (Lk 12:34). What do we treasure more than God? Or to rephrase the question with an Old Testament term, "What idols keep us from seeking God with all of our heart?" Consider that idols can relate to what we think about most, what goals and activities garner our greatest zeal and effort, and what objects we guard with our life (and lock and key). For example, time is one of our treasures to consider.

The Practical Problem

How do we find the time to waste time with God? In this day and age, busyness is the bane of the believer. The 1996 movie *Multiplicity* portrayed one way to solve the problem. Doug Kinney (played by Michael Keaton), a construction foreman, had just too many things to do. Work demanded all his attention, including evenings and weekends. Hardly any time was left for his children and his wife (played by Andie McDowell), and he had no time for himself to relax, to play golf. One day, his own pent-up anger and frustration about life erupts, just like the broken water pipe at a job site.

In the next scene Doug meets the building owner, the serene and unhurried Dr. Leeds, who offers to solve Doug's time problem. Dr. Leeds claims, "I create time." How? By cloning human beings. He had already created his own double—two persons can do more than one—so that he had all the time he needed for enjoying life. So Doug submits himself to an operation. Along with the original Doug #1, there is now Doug #2. While Doug #1 goes out playing golf and spends more time with the family, Doug #2 works all day long. Later, to provide for Doug #2's need for companionship, Doug #3 is created. All seems OK until the clones themselves decide to have Doug #4 created to clean their apartment—except a copy of a copy turns out to yield an imbecile. Finally, Doug #1 realizes he has no life anymore: Doug #2 is doing all his work, Doug #3 is taking care of his family, and Doug #4 cannot even take care of himself. There is a happy ending, but to get there, Doug #1 has to send away the three clones and face the time problem on his own, without the help of science.

Science to the Rescue

Our technological advances appear to have created more time in our day. Cars reach destinations much faster than horse and buggy. Passing on information is only a phone call away. It takes less time to type a report, to prepare food, to wash clothes. But there is a downside to progress.

With more time on our hands, we have more expectations—we get used to getting more things done. Yet we do not have time to get all these new things done either. So the time problem will not easily let us go; there is too much to do and so little time. Is more time the answer to our woes? Even more money does not always offer the easy way out of financial woes; one must still live within a budget. The same is true for time; one brute fact of life is that a day only lasts twenty-four hours, and everyone must come to terms with facing the time trap.

Of course, we can manage our time better by becoming more efficient. Time management systems and guidelines are useful here, but another problem may surface. Our to-do list may begin to take priority over quality time with people. We may start using people as means, rather than as ends, and not treat each person with respect and dignity. And that quandary may be compounded by its second cousin: being too busy. Thus, when push comes to shove, *work wins and relationships lose*— tasks become the trump card of life—robbing us of important time with the special people in our lives: family and friends. Furthermore, we rob ourselves of time for self-renewal. Ultimately, our relationship with God wastes away, squeezing God out of our schedule—not on purpose, but by default. Our most important relationship receives the leftovers of our life. How can we make room for God in the midst of the modern pace of life?

Overcoming Our Busyness

If we are going to make more room for God in our lives, we must move beyond our busyness and our preoccupation with lesser matters. Deadlines, commitments, meetings, appointments. Life is full of things to be done, promises to keep, schedules to follow. "It is a strange kind of Christian marathon we run in North America," muses one missionary after returning stateside.[9] But our busyness can desensitize us to the needs of our inner life and our communion with God.[10] Yes, now and then, God may give us a wake-up call—a lingering illness, an accident, maybe terminal cancer, or even a loved one's sudden death—to get off the merry-go-round of life and reconsider what our life is all about. But why must we wait for such tragedies to strike to clear our minds and clarify our priorities?

Perhaps reflecting on God's appointed cycles in nature may offer some insight about discerning the rhythms of life. Consider God's "natural" appointments with the following regular cycles:

☐ day and night (rotation of the earth)

☐ monthly (cycles of the moon)

☐ quarterly and annual seasons of the year (e.g., movement of the earth around the sun) linked with weather appropriate for each: winter, spring, summer, fall

Nature compels our observance of these particular rhythms. But the week of seven days is not nature-bound. It was imposed by God himself—the pattern he set as he created the world: six days of creation and one day of rest (Gen 2:1-3). Much later God incorporated this sabbath concept into the Mosaic law as the fourth commandment:

> Remember the Sabbath day by keeping it holy. Six days you shall labor and do all your work, but the seventh day is a Sabbath to the Lord your God. On it you shall not do any work, neither you, nor your son or daughter, nor your manservant or maidservant, nor your animals, nor the alien within your gates. For in six days the LORD made the heavens and the earth, the sea, and all that is in them, but he rested on the seventh day. Therefore the Lord blessed the Sabbath day and made it holy. (Ex 20:8-11)

All of the Ten Commandments are explicitly reaffirmed in the New Testament in some form, except for this sabbath day command. Paul expressly states that as believers in Christ, we do not need to regard one day as any holier than any other (Rom 14:4-10) and that the ceremonies of the Mosaic law were but shadows of future realities (Col 2:16-17). Yet God first set up a pattern for a day of rest at the beginning of creation, prior to any Mosaic code. The concept of rest is treated in the New Testament extensively in Hebrews 3—4 as a metaphor for the whole of Christian living. We err by not recognizing a broader sabbath principle, a principle of renewal for our contemporary lifestyle as New Testament believers.

Were these natural regularities created by God to inform us of underlying eternal truths? The physical body has been expressly designed by God to require regular periods of rest and renewal, with one-third of life devoted to sleep. Although we are unconscious as we sleep, our body is engaged in a form of renewal. If our bodies need renewal, what of our souls? Some form of a principle of rest and renewal is crucial in Christian living. It is the starting place to make room in our lives for God.

What does a principle of renewal imply? The main point is that we engage in certain activities, or cease to engage in certain activities, to bring renewal to our inner life, our mind and heart, and to make a place for communing with God. How we practice the principle will vary for each believer, due to age, circumstances and needs. But that we each attend to the renewal of our souls is imperative. Other words that capture a sense of renewal and rest include *refreshment, celebration, recreation, retreat, leisure, enjoyment, relaxation* and *play.* Simon Chan observes:

> Play may be understood as the ability to suspend temporarily the usual course of life to enter a different world, a world in which another dimension of relationship opens up to reveal a more profound meaning of life. . . . If the [Christian] community does not learn to enjoy each other at play, it is doubtful that it truly understands what it means to "enjoy God forever," which is "man's chief end."[11]

We need to take a break *from* our routines *for* times of communion with God, for being alone and for being with others, for times of deep fellowship as well as group recreation and play; for times of learning and for times of the aesthetic appreciation of the beauty, art and music of life from God.

Of Old Testament Feasts and Festivals

Instruction about renewal primarily comes from the various Old Testament feasts and festivals of ancient Israel, as recorded mainly in Leviticus 23 and Numbers 28—29. The recurring theme throughout the directions is to do no regular work (Lev 23:7-8, 21, 25, 28, 31, 35-36). All work and no play make Jack and Jill dull people. There is much more to life than work and fulfilling the basic routines of life (e.g., balancing a checkbook, cleaning dishes, mowing the lawn, doing laundry). For too many of us, work and routines have become the trump card of life—they supersede the values of all other concerns. When this trump card is played, work wins and everything important loses: family, friends, inner life, relationship with God.

What exactly constitutes work from which we must take a break? Consider the following illustrative contrasts:

☐ In work, we earn our living; for renewal activities, no remuneration is needed.

☐ In work, we attend to clock time; for renewal activities, we remove our watch and enjoy unstructured and unhurried time.

☐ In work, we report to others (e.g., boss or customers); for renewal activities, we do them for their own sake.

☐ In work, the goal or product is all-important (taking precedence over the process); for renewal activities, the process itself is all-important, with no tangible outcome needed.

Rest as a Component of Balanced Living
This rest or renewal theme is one component among others that contributes to balanced Christian living with God. The following model proposes a concerted focus on four broad themes, thus offering a foundational blueprint for what it means to live abundantly, to experience great joy and the deep sense of satisfaction about life as God meant it to be (see figure 5.1).[12] The four themes appear to stand the test of time in that they seem valid to guide living in any period of history, whether before the Fall in the garden, after the Fall, this side of salvation by grace, or even during the eternal state. As the themes are briefly explained, the reader may wish to validate whether or not these themes ring true.

Of course, the main purpose of life is growing into an obedient and deep relationship with God. But how do we practically live each day in light of this central purpose and relationship? Three subordinate yet essential themes shed light on what human flourishing encompasses—the three R's: relating, reigning and renewing—each theme highlighting specifically what it means to be created in the image of God. *Relating* signifies that we are social creatures made to live in community with others and with God, mirroring the eternal fellowship existing within our trinitarian God. *Reigning* involves our desire and ability to function and accomplish various tasks as commissioned by our Creator and Sovereign. Finally, *renewing* primarily points to the need to attend to our inner life so we can fully realize all of our potential—to love God, to love others and to be successful in our work—and become the kind of persons who echo God's own character. Thus, the more we attend to and engage in the appropriate values and opportunities of each theme, the more we can experience balanced and abundant living and fully enter into a life lived in relationship with God.

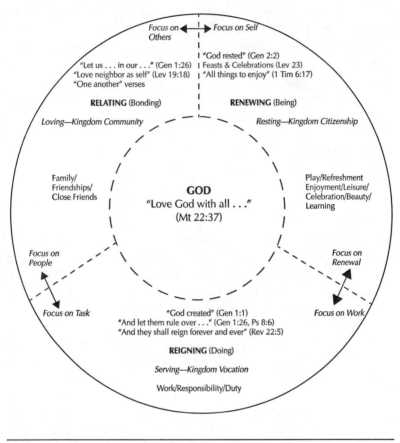

Figure 5.1. Enduring themes of kingdom living

Relating, Unity and Community

It should be no surprise that these themes emerge from God himself, from his statements and activity in the first two chapters of Genesis. God has made us very much like himself, and thus he shows us how to live. The theme of relating is introduced in a subtle manner in Genesis 1:26, "Let *us* make man in *our* image, in *our* likeness" (emphasis added). This enigmatic use of the plural pronoun is finally explained in the New Testament. We learn that God himself is an eternal being-in-fellowship, a trinitarian God—Father, Son and Holy Spirit. John Sailhamer comments, "In a similar way the one God . . . created man through an expression of his plurality. . . . Following this clue the divine plurality expressed in v. 26 is seen as an anticipation of the human plurality of the man and woman, thus casting the human relationship between man and woman in the role of reflecting God's own personal relationship with himself."[13]

Interdependence is the preeminent value of Christian living, not independence. Accordingly, God has made humanity as a duality, consisting of male and female (Gen 1:27-28). In Genesis 2, God declares, "It is not good for the man to be alone" (v. 18). Further, the marital command of Genesis 2:24 that "the two will become one" anticipates the more comprehensive version enunciated in our Lord's high priestly prayer for all New Testament believers, "that all of them may be one, Father, just as you are in me and I am in you" (Jn 17:21), an important issue developed in chapter two of this book. The New Testament concept of unity characterizes God's own community of relationships and mutual indwelling within the Trinity.

Reigning, Working and Serving

The theme of reigning permeates the creation chapters of Genesis 1 and 2—"all the work of creating that [God] had done" (Gen 2:3). The creation of the world marks a new aspect of God's own reigning and working. During each day of creation, God praised his work and called it "good" (Gen 1:4, 10, 12, 18, 21, 25, 31 "very good"). God then commissioned Adam and Eve to reign over his creation, "Be fruitful and increase in number; fill the earth and subdue it. Rule over the fish of the sea and the birds of the air and over every living creature that moves on the ground" (Gen 1:28). David's psalm points back to this directive, "You made him ruler over the works of your hands" (Ps 8:6). Before Eve was fashioned, God placed Adam in the Garden of Eden "to work it and take care of it" (Gen 2:15, literally, "to worship and to obey" in the garden). Even after the Fall, work is part of life, yet now the ground is cursed and work will not be as easy as before: "through painful toil you will eat of it" and "by the sweat of your brow you will eat your food until you return to the ground" (Gen 3:17, 19). In the wisdom literature, work is affirmed as good: "Then I realized that it is good and proper for a man to eat and drink, and to find satisfaction in his toilsome labor under the sun during the few days of life

God has given him—for this is his lot" (Eccles 5:18).

Our Lord sets a pattern for how we should reign and do our work. Our Lord prays to the Father at the end of his sojourn on earth, announcing that he has completed "the work you gave me to do" (Jn 17:4). Jesus demonstrates throughout the New Testament that leadership should be carried out through serving and with humility, an issue developed in chapter three of the book. "But do not use your freedom to indulge in the sinful nature; rather, serve one another in love" (Gal 5:13). Ultimately, in eternity, we "his servants will serve him," and with God we "will reign for ever and ever" (Rev 22:3, 5).

Renewing and Rest

The main idea underlying the final theme of renewing is related to the biblical words *rest* and *sabbath*. From a strange announcement in Genesis 2:2-3, we learn that on the seventh day of creation God himself "rested from all his work." William Lane notes, "The expression [as quoted in Hebrews 4:4] 'my rest' in Ps 95:11 called to mind God's primordial rest announced in Gen 2:2. The state of completion and harmony experienced by God after his creative labor is the archetype and goal of all subsequent experiences of rest."[14] What is clear is the specific pattern established by God related to work and rest. Terence Fretheim clarifies, "The divine act of blessing the sabbath is an unspoken report of God's act of giving power and potentiality to a particular temporal order, in the sense that human honoring of the work-rest rhythm has the capacity of deeply affecting life itself (as does its neglect)."[15] As noted above, this work-rest rhythm is further clarified in the explanation of Israel's feasts and festivals with the recurring phrase "hold a sacred assembly and do no regular work" (Num 28:26; 29:1, 7, 12, 35).

The primary emphasis in renewal is setting apart special times from the routines of life to focus on one's relationship with God. And in this "activity" we receive rest for our souls. Just as we give time to renew our physical bodies, so we must give time to renew our souls—to engage in any and all activities that contribute to renewing our inner person. Of course, this involves meditating on God's Word (Ps 1:1-3), which facilitates the renewing of our mind (Rom 12:2). We must take a break from the routines and work schedule of life to attend to the sustenance of our walk with

God and the care and nurturing of our own souls. Times of retreat for solitude and prayer, engaging in avocational activities and hobbies, taking opportunities to appreciate inspiring beauty, learning new ideas and skills, engaging in athletic exercise, healing our emotions and fears. All these can contribute to the enhancement and maturing of our inner life. Throughout our marriage, Beth and I have taken time to read books to each other. I was introduced to C. S. Lewis's Chronicles of Narnia and J. R. R. Tolkien's Fellowship of the Rings this way, since I tend to read only nonfiction myself.

At a more general level, the whole of life with God can be characterized as entering "God's rest" (Heb 4:10). Our busyness and workaholism will only destroy our inner life and our walk with God if we do not become intentional about making time for renewal and rest. The church community—particularly older couples and single adults—may need to step in with child care assistance to make such renewal times possible for members squeezed by family responsibilities, such as couples and single parents with young children.

Toward Balance
The configuration of the three outer themes in figure 5.1 also suggests certain tensions that may hinder balanced Christian living. We must manage lifelong tensions
☐ between task and people
☐ between work and renewal
☐ between a focus on others and a focus on self
As one sustains a relationship with God, it involves giving attention to these three subordinate themes as a checklist and prod, not as a rigid guide to be emphasized one-third of the time.
☐ How well am I seeking and loving God with all of my heart?
☐ How well am I growing in my relationships with others?
☐ How well am I getting the job done and using my expertise, talents and gifts in work and in serving the needs of others?
☐ How well am I attending to the need for renewal of my inner life?

Consider Richard Swenson's proposal that the healthiest lifestyle, like a car's engine equipped with four gears, employs each gear appropriately, rather than always running on overdrive.[16] "Park" represents the contemplative mode for renewal of the soul, appreciating nature, relating to God. "Low gear" is for cultivating the relationships of family and friends, for holding a child on our lap and reading a story. We can be engrossed in conversation without to-do lists distracting our attention. "Drive" is the third gear, the standard mode for work (and rigorous recreation as well), requiring more energy but yielding progress and achievement. Finally, we may shift into "overdrive" for our emergencies, the times the extra push is needed to meet the pressing deadlines or to care for loved ones who are ill or in life-threatening situations. Swenson notes, "Unfortunately, many in our society do not shift down from overdrive. Our cars are not meant to race at high speeds continuously—the engine would burn up. Neither are our bodies or spirits."[17] The issue is one of intentionality—purposeful planning and effort to make God the predominant recurring theme and driving force of our thought life and lifestyle.

What Did Jesus Do?

Of course, Jesus himself offers an example to follow in this area, particularly as he took time aside from his ministry to be alone by himself and talk with God. Consider the following episodes that depict his commitment for communion and rest and renewal.

Jesus began his public ministry alone in the desert with a forty-day fast to prepare himself for the battle with Satan (Mt 4:1-2; also Mk 1:12-13; Lk 4:1-2). Note the contrast between the busy days of public ministry, and the private times of solitude and prayer in the following passage.[18]

> That evening after sunset the people brought to Jesus all the sick and demon-possessed. The whole town gathered at the door, and Jesus healed many who had various diseases. He also drove out many demons. . . . Very early in the morning, while it was still dark, Jesus got up, left the house and went off to a solitary place, where he prayed. (Mk 1:32-35)

> Yet the news about him spread all the more, so that crowds of people came to hear him and to be healed of their sicknesses. *But Jesus often withdrew to lonely places and prayed.* (Lk 5:15-16, emphasis added)

Prior to making the important decision of selecting the twelve disciples, Jesus devoted himself to solitude and prayer. "One of those days Jesus went out to a mountainside to pray, and spent the night praying to God. When morning came, he called his disciples to him and chose twelve of them" (Lk 6:12-13). And before his arrest in the Garden of Geth-semane, Jesus was alone and praying. "Jesus went out as usual to the Mount of Olives, and his disciples followed him. On reaching the place, he said to them, 'Pray that you will not fall into temptation.' He withdrew about a stone's throw beyond them, knelt down and prayed" (Lk 22:39-41). If Jesus realized his own need to take a break from his public routines to attend to his inner life, then we can do no less. Since Jesus gave us an example to follow, we must give serious attention to marking off periods of rest and renewal in contemporary life.

Wasting Time with God: Personal Retreat

A difficult battle rages in our lives over the matter of a tenacity to seek God with *all* of our hearts. Believers must engage the enemy within and without by destroying footholds of Satan that hinder us (see Eph 4:27). Our use of time with overcommitted calendars and busy routines all bor-der on becoming genuine addictions—we cannot live without them. To gain any ground of mastery over time, we must take breaks from the rou-tines of life to visit and vacation with God; there is no other cure. We must press the pause button of life now and then.

We can use the phrase "wasting time with God" to justify these special occasions—especially if we are a fairly driven kind of person. This kind of "wasting" is of high value in God's economy. Having no agenda is all right; in fact, it is preferred. Anything we do that truly nurtures our soul and relationship with God is worth the effort and time. Some believers have become so accustomed to a busy pace of life that being alone for any length of time will initially involve discomfort and withdrawal pains.

Many occasions can become brief retreats for rest and renewal.[19] We can designate some of our normal alone times for such purposes. While driving, turn off the radio now and then, and be quiet and listen to your own mind and to God. While showering or taking a bath, remember to connect with God. There are times to commune with God while lying in bed before sleep, when awake in the night or just after the alarm clock rings, before getting out of bed. Almost all meal times, whether alone or with others, can become moments of refreshment in a busy day. When at the doctor's office waiting for an appointment, we can leave the magazine on the table so we can sit, reflect, commune with God and enjoy the special moment.

One simple but powerful form of rest I have found helpful is taking one-minute breaks at various times during the day, when I just sit alone and do nothing. Not only will our body thank us, but our inner self will have time to connect with the immaterial reality in which God lives. Taking such brief breaks may be more difficult than we think, but it is well worth developing this simple habit of brief periods of daily rest. Persevere in consistency before increasing the number of breaks taken (or increasing the length of the breaks). We can find a place of refreshment, a change of scenario—whether for a lunch break at work or home—to get our mind off routines and on to other important matters of life.[20]

At some point, we may consider taking thirty minutes or an hour once a week to sit and do nothing but listen to the inner life and commune with God. Furthermore, it would be worthwhile to plan an extended time away, a Saturday morning, an overnight or a whole weekend, to focus on seeking God and waiting before him. Whenever taking breaks from our routines, it is always appropriate to waste time with God. John Wijngaards notes, "The essence of a retreat is our withdrawal from everyday life and all its involvements for a considerable amount of time. We go for a number of days to some other place where we shall not be distracted from our main task in hand: sorting ourselves out in the face of God."[21] At a later point, Wijngaards continues, "We should not put ourselves under any kind of pressure. . . . Much of our time will be spent in leisure, walking around in a park or doing something else that sets our mind free."[22]

Waiting is a fact of life—the doctor's office, the grocery supermarket, even at Disneyland we will gladly endure a forty-five-minute wait for a two-minute thrill ride. Yet in waiting for God, we get bothered and agitated. But the act of shutting ourselves away from the hustle and bustle of life opens the door of opportunity for God to speak in his "still small voice."

☐ "Wait for the LORD; / be strong and take heart / and wait for the LORD" (Ps 27:14; cf. Ps 37:7; 40:1).

☐ "I wait for the LORD, my soul waits, / and in his word I put my hope. / My soul waits for the Lord / more than watchmen wait for the morning" (Ps 130:5-6).

There might be many times we are alone. But in times of solitude, we intentionally set our minds to seek God and renew our souls. Henri Nouwen warns, "Without solitude it is virtually impossible to live a spiritual life. . . . We do not take the spiritual life seriously if we do not set aside some time to be with God and listen to him."[23] Dallas Willard suggests that solitude is the foundational spiritual discipline. "Solitude frees us. . . . The normal course of day-to-day human interactions locks us into patterns of feeling, thought, and action that are geared to a world set against God. Nothing but solitude can allow the development of freedom from the ingrained behaviors that hinder our integration into God's order."[24]

Moving toward an enjoyment of solitude may take time and training, for a battle rages in the mind. The following account from the early church illustrates the struggle and change that takes place: "The first stage of solitary prayer [is like] the experience of a man who, after years of living with open doors, suddenly decides to shut them. The visitors who used to come and enter his home start pounding on his doors, wondering why they are not allowed to enter. Only when they realize that they are not welcome do they gradually stop coming."[25]

One traditional format for spending extended time with God may offer some guidance: ACTS—Adoration and worship, Confession and humbling, Thanksgiving and praise, and Supplication, with prayer requests for others and yourself.[26] In times of retreat, we listen to God, we talk to him, we sing to him.[27]

Yet what about times when we do seek God intentionally, but he seems distant? From the accounts of those who have known God we learn there are seasons of our lives when God is silent and chooses not to speak.

The Lingering Silence of God: The Dark Night of the Soul

Occasionally God hides from us to impose a time of solitude in our relationship with him, what some refer to as a dark night of the soul. The Christian life regularly cycles through times of intimacy and joy with God and times when God withholds his communication for a season of spiritual dryness. From the early Christian literature, Louis Bouyer identifies "alternations of drynesses and illuminations constitut[ing] as it were a rhythm of trials and strengthening inherent in spiritual progress."[28]

One definition, suggested by John Coe, outlines God's distinct purposes: "The Dark Night is God's work to move us into a place of painful self-awareness regarding the truth about ourselves, which we would not (and could not) do on our own, with the intent to dissuade us and cure us from trusting in ourselves or trusting in the feelings of spirituality."[29] What does the experience feel like? Richard Foster shares about such at time while he was in demand as a speaker and writer.

> Through a series of events it seemed clear to me that God wanted me to retreat from public activity. In essence God said, 'Keep quiet!' And so I did. I stopped all public speaking, I stopped all writing, and I waited. At the time this began, I did not know if I would ever speak or write again—I rather thought I would not. As it turned out, this fast from public life lasted about eighteen months. I waited in silence. And God was silent too. I joined in the Psalmist's query: 'How long will you hide your face from me?' (Ps 13:1). The answer I got: nothing. Absolutely nothing! There were no sudden revelations. No penetrating insights. Not even gentle assurances. Nothing. . . . It ended finally and simply with gentle assurances that it was time to reenter the public square.[30]

Upon looking back over that time, Foster notes the initially imperceptible growth that occurred, "It was a little like when you do not realize that a child has grown at all until you measure her against the mark on the hallway doorjamb from last year."[31]

To understand this kind of experience, we must sit at the feet of the Spanish mystic John of the Cross (d. 1591), who offers intriguing clues.[32] The period of dryness encompasses two basic purifications that occur in the dark night of the soul.[33] In this first kind we are stripped of dependence upon exterior results, whether that be "big buildings, big budgets, big productions, big miracles" or impressive acts of devotion. There is nothing wrong with these in and of themselves, but we can become less enamored with them. And "we become less in control of our destiny and more at the mercy of others."[34] But the second kind of purification strips us of dependence on interior results, as Foster clarifies.

> This is more disturbing and painful than the first purification because it threatens us at the root of all we believe in and have given ourselves to. . . . We discover that the workings of faith, hope, and love become themselves subject to doubt. Our personal motivations become suspect. We worry whether this act or that thought is inspired by fear, vanity, and arrogance rather than faith, hope, and love. . . . Through all this, paradoxically, God

is purifying our faith by threatening to destroy it. . . . We know more deeply than ever before our capacity for infinite self-deception. . . . Our trust in all exterior and interior results is being shattered so that we can learn faith in God alone. Through our barrenness of soul God is producing detachment, humility, patience, perseverance. Most surprising of all, our very dryness produces the habit of prayer in us. All distractions are gone. . . . The soul is parched. And thirsty. And this thirst can lead us to prayer. I say "can" because it can also lead us to despair or simply to abandon the search.[35]

In the depths of our sorrow, we must not consider that God has completely abandoned us, although it may feel that way.

The most famous biblical account of such an experience appears in the book of Job.[36] Although God regarded Job as a man of integrity, Satan was permitted to torment this righteous man. The outcome was a purifying of Job's faith in God. "My ears had heard of you but now my eyes have seen you. Therefore I despise myself and repent in dust and ashes" (Job 42:5-6). Job's experience of God's silence yielded the fruit of a deeper faith in God.

In July 1990, Chuck and Nancy Missler began the journey they call their "night season" of seven years of travail. It involved bankruptcy of Chuck's company, an IRS bill of millions of dollars, the loss of a dream house and possessions, the sudden death of their thirty-nine-year old son, the loss of sentimental mementos through an earthquake and the loss of many so-called Christian friends. Nancy explains:

We not only were experiencing the bankruptcy, the IRS mess and the loss of our homes, cars and insurance, but also at the this same time, many of our close friends had turned their backs on us. As soon as the local media began broadcasting news of our bankruptcy, the rumor mills began. . . . For me, the loss of my Christian brothers and sisters was the most agonizing part of the whole ordeal. When we had millions of dollars, our friends were too numerous to count. But when we owed millions and were in desperate straits, many of these "friends" quickly disappeared. If it hadn't been for the encouragement of a few faithful families and a couple of people we barely knew, Chuck and I would have felt completely abandoned by the Body of Christ! It was an absolutely crushing experience.

Nancy describes what she felt in the midst of this darkness:

No one is able to comfort our intense suffering, because it's like our soul has been literally cast off and flung out in to space. We find ourselves in a whirl-pool of despair and loneliness. There is a deep bitterness within us that cries out like David in Psalm 51:18, "Oh, God, You have broken all my bones." We feel dismembered, in anguish, in a state of numbness and lifelessness, like we are in a dark dungeon. In fact, we sometimes feel "death" would be a relief because what is happening is in our eyes cruel. Formerly we found God in solitude, prayer and mediation, but now *none* of these things brings us peace. Thus, because God's voice is silent, our sense of meaning and purpose is lost.[37]

Madame Jeanne Guyon (d. 1717) weathered a series of trials of her own. Her work on *Final Steps in Christian Maturity* clarifies what happens at the bottom of the experience: "When a Christian has reached this wilderness, this desolate place, this dark night of the senses, this time that touches the very experience of Christ when He cried out 'Why??' [Mt 27:46] . . . it is only at *that* time, when the believer walks by naked faith, that he begins to become truly established and well founded in his Lord."[38]

For Nancy Missler, the trial brought a winnowing that yielded greater intimacy with God, as she notes:

Since I have tasted what it's like to dwell in God's presence, it's easier for me to choose to get back there—because I know what I am missing! Before I experienced intimacy with Him, I wasn't sure what I was striving for or working towards, as I had never really been there. It's difficult to choose to do something when you have never experienced it before. But now that I know what intimacy with Jesus is like, I can hardly wait to "turnaround" and get back there. And praise God, it seems my "turnaround time" is getting shorter and shorter.[39]

The psalmist reveals the aftermath of the dark night, "You turned my wailing into dancing; / you removed my sackcloth and clothed me with joy, / that my heart may sing to you and not be silent. / O Lord my God, I will give you thanks forever" (Ps 30:11-12).

It is important to note that this journey into the darkness, into the dessert, into the abyss is at *God's own choosing.* By extending such an invitation, God considers us ready for a new and deeper level of intimacy with him. By means of such periods of dryness, God purifies our faith, and in the process he dislodges what we hold dear, including our false fixed ideas about God. Paradoxically, God desires to draw us closer to himself by being temporarily distant and hidden.

Millie de Beers shares her gleanings of a dark night. After having lived all their lives in South Africa, Piet and Millie left family and friends to move across the ocean to the island of Jamaica.

> I thought I could only be happy surrounded by friends and family. However, after some time I came to understand that God had brought me to Jamaica to isolate me from all the things I used to fill the gaps of my life. I needed to get my direction and peace from him and nothing else. Waiting on him in solitude from that time, I spent hours drinking in his Word and learning to depend on him. I needed to break away from all the noises and disturbances of my busy life, so God could begin to touch my inner core and satisfy my deepest needs.[40]

The Double Knowledge

These testimonies confirm that a genuine pursuit of God cannot occur without personally becoming open before God at the same time. "Search me, O God, and know my heart; test me and know my anxious thoughts. See if there is any offensive way in me, and lead me in the way everlasting" (Ps 139:23-24). Hiding and personal detachment prevent relational engagement with God. Seeking God is indeed unique and cannot be accomplished without simultaneously being willing to know oneself—what is referred to as the "double knowledge": knowledge of God and knowledge of self.[41] John Calvin (d. 1564) opened his magisterial *Institutes of the Christian Religion* within this guiding framework: "Without knowledge of self there is no knowledge of God. . . . Without knowledge of God there is no knowledge of self."[42] The concept is evident in other writers, for example:

☐ Augustine: "God, always the same, let me know myself, let me know Thee, I have prayed."[43]

☐ Blaise Pascal (d. 1662): "Knowing God without knowing our wretchedness leads to pride. Knowing our wretchedness without knowing God leads to despair."[44]

Genuine intimacy within any personal relationship can never flourish in an atmosphere of distance or deception. Especially is this true in a relationship with God.

We are beloved by God (Rom 8:35-39; Eph 3:14-19; 1 Jn 4:7-21). He cares enough for us that he will not leave us as we are. He is committed to the project of helping us enter into a life without any lack (Ps 23:1; Jas 1:2-4), to a life filled with the richness of himself in intimacy and deep mutual friendship.

Wasting Time with God: Journaling/Reflection
One means of holding an honest conversation with God is through journaling, recording our musings about life and thoughts about God. A journal is a tool to help us voice our thoughts and feelings to God. It may take any form that suits us, such as a letter to God, a poem or a psalm. Whatever form is used, the purpose is to be honest with God. For Morton Kelsey, an investment in the time and effort to maintain a journal paid significant dividends.

> For thirty years my journal has been my constant companion. My daily writing in its pages has been a most helpful practice in my attempt to grow into the fullness of Christ. The journal sustained me in darkness and has given me a thread to find my way back into the light. It has provided a place where I could come to clarity and insight. It has recorded and stimulated my journey toward the loving God. It has opened the door for me to see the hand of the . . . Father outreached to me, allowed me to come to his forgiving embrace.[45]

The privacy afforded by a journal permits honest reflection on our experiences, particularly our feelings about our day. Although Scripture talks a lot about feelings, only late in life have I recognized the importance, beauty and goodness of feelings. Jesus experienced a full range of emotions (e.g., weeping, Lk 19:41; compassion, Mk 6:34; righteous anger, Mk 3:5; frustration, Mt 17:17; and being troubled in spirit, Mt 26:37).[46] The apostle Paul prays that believers experience the deep love of Christ that "surpasses knowledge" (Eph 3:19) and the peace of God that "transcends all understanding" (Phil 4:7). God's love and peace fit into a nonrational (not irrational) category—a supracognitive aspect of our nature.

Feelings are essential aspects of our nature created in God's image. Emotions just appear and are indicators of the current state of our soul. Deryck Sheriffs explains that "emotions are like colours. The spectrum arranges them in adjacent gradations but they also come in odd mixtures. Emotions are first felt before they can be named. They present themselves with a startling immediacy ahead of our ability to describe them in words."[47]

We must ponder the inner recesses of our soul. What are our yearnings, our longings? We reflect on any spontaneous reactions to events or words or thoughts. What does that sighing indicate? Is there a lack of God's peace (Phil 4:7)? This four-step process may help us monitor the inner mutterings of our heart:[48]

1. How do I feel? For example, am I glad? sad? mad? What do I dread? What are my dreams for the future? We enter the experience of these feelings and stay with them.

2. Can I tell God how I feel? Let us share with him honestly how we feel.

3. God, what is the root cause of my feelings?

4. God, how can I address the problem that is the root cause of my feelings?

Since I have been attending more to my feelings in comparison to past years, I am able to cooperate more with God's inner work in my heart and receive the blessing of God's peace on a more regular basis.

Kelsey writes daily in his journal; I write weekly in mine. We pick a schedule that works well. Occasionally, I read past entries to remember God's presence in past times and to discern patterns that may offer insight for my journey ahead. A journal is but a catalyst to deepen our normal conversation with God, to nurture our frankness and honesty with him.

Conclusion

John of the Cross raises this challenge: "Determine in your heart that you want to reach the highest place in God. By that, I mean, learning how to live each day in pure, loving oneness with Him. And once you have set your heart on this upward path, you will have to choose it every day, and many times during each day. For indeed your desire to rise to higher places in spirit will face many obstacles."[49] To grow in our relationship with God, we must regularly "waste time" with God. Furthermore, we must be open to how God works in our life, especially during the spiritual dry seasons, through which God desires to take our friendship to a new level of intimacy.

Keeping communication lines open with God is of utmost importance. We must become more frank and honest with God if we wish to deepen the friendship. But how does God communicate with us? Is the Bible God's sole means of providing guidance for his children today? What if we wish to know God's mind about a matter not explicitly discussed in Scripture? Does God speak today to offer specific counsel in our time of need? The next chapter explores these important questions.

6

COMMUNICATION

HEARING THE GOD WHO SPEAKS

"If any of you lacks wisdom, he should ask God, who gives generously to all without finding fault, and it will be given to him."

JAMES 1:5

JESUS' EXAMPLE

"I wrote about all that Jesus began to do and to teach until the day he was taken up to heaven, after giving instructions through the Holy Spirit to the apostles he had chosen."

ACTS 1:1-2

D oes God speak to us today? In his autobiography the famous British preacher Charles Spurgeon (d. 1892) recounts a noteworthy instance. While in the midst of a sermon, a word from the Spirit was given him for one of his listeners.

> While preaching in the hall, on one occasion, I deliberately pointed to a man in the midst of the crowd and said, "There is a man sitting there, who is a shoemaker; he keeps his shop open on Sundays, it was open last Sabbath morning, he took ninepence, and there was a fourpence profit out of it; his soul is sold to Satan for fourpence!"[1]

Later that month a city missionary happened upon this man while reading one of Spurgeon's sermons. The missionary asked if he knew Mr. Spurgeon. The shopkeeper answered in the affirmative and explained his side of that surprising encounter.

> I went to the Music Hall, and took a seat in the middle of the place; Mr. Spurgeon looked at me as if he knew me, and in his sermon he pointed to me, and told the congregation that I was a shoemaker, and that I kept my shop open on Sundays; and I did, sir. I should not have minded that; but he also said that I took ninepence the Sunday before, and that there was a fourpence profit; but how he should know that, I could not tell. Then it struck me that it was God who had spoken to my soul through him, so I shut up my shop the next Sunday. At first, I was afraid to go again to hear him, lest he should tell the people more about me; but afterwards I went, and the Lord met with me, and saved my soul.[2]

What does Scripture say about such divine communication?

James 1:5 articulates the Christian's expectation for God's guidance when facing a bewildering trial: "If any of you lacks wisdom, he should ask God, who gives generously to all without finding fault, and it will be given to him." From the Shepherd Psalm, we know that God "*leads* me beside quiet waters" and "*guides* me in paths of righteousness" (Ps 23:2-3, emphasis added). But *how* does God communicate to believers today? Through his written Word only? Or does God also offer situation-specific and person-specific counsel?

A Personal Journey

Intimacy with God. Is it not our deepest longing to experience the kind of friendship with God portrayed in the Gospels, of walking with Jesus, of sharing our problems and getting his guidance, of making known our requests and seeing answers to prayer? We long for a lifestyle where God actively involves himself personally with us on a daily basis. As an old hymn sings, "He walks with me, and He talks with me, And He tells me I am His own."[3] Yet my experience seemed fairly two-dimensional in contrast to the vibrant three-dimensional dynamic relationship with God portrayed in the pages of Scripture.

Although God seemed more active with people during biblical times—

God spoke to them and intervened supernaturally in their lives—I thought that today it was not necessary for God to work that way. I believed that since during Bible times God's people did not have access to the full record of God's Word, they required a more direct means of communication from God until the Bible was completely written. But now that God had furnished his full counsel in the Bible, I thought that believers were expected to seek divine direction solely through the Bible. Here was the "God-breathed" Word "useful for teaching, rebuking, correcting and training in righteousness, so that the man of God may be thoroughly equipped for every good work" (2 Tim 3:16-17). My main task was to study the Bible faithfully, to do my best at applying it in every situation.

Yet does God offer something more? If God is personal, would there not be continuing communication, as Dallas Willard suggests?

> It is simply beyond belief that two persons so intimately related [as Jesus indicates in John 14:23] . . . would not explicitly speak with each other. The Spirit who inhabits us is not mute, restricting himself to an occasional nudge, a hot flash, a brilliant image or a case of goose bumps. . . . How could there be a personal relationship, a personal walk with God—or with anyone else—*without* individualized communication?"[4]

A relationship with God has many similarities to friendship on the human plane, involving some form of give-and-take communication. Although I was aware that people in Bible times could be on such intimate terms with God, I never thought God offered believers that same kind of lifestyle today. The main point of this chapter is that every child of God can enjoy a full-flowering three-dimensional relationship with God, similar to what God displays for us in Scripture. We will explore a model of divine guidance as an aspect of personal communication with God. In discerning God's direction, the believer's posture is one of being alert and receptive to however and whenever God chooses to communicate.

The Spirit of the Age

As Jesus anticipated his death, resurrection and ascension to the Father, our Lord promised not to leave his disciples—and us—as orphans. "I will ask the Father, and he will give you another Counselor to be with you forever—the Spirit of truth. The world cannot accept him, because it neither sees him nor knows him. But you know him, for he lives with you, and will be in you. I will not leave you as orphans" (Jn 14:16-18). From Pentecost on, believers now live in the age of the Holy Spirit as God's empowering presence in our lives and in the world.

This miraculous divine association was promised by God about twenty-five hundred years ago as a key component of new covenant blessings. "And I will put my Spirit in you and move you to follow my decrees and be careful to keep my laws" (Ezek 36:27). Our Lord Jesus Christ inaugurated this new covenant (cf. Lk 22:20; 2 Cor 3:6; Heb 9:15). Post-Pentecost believers are beneficiaries of this special blessing. In a mysterious way, Jesus' departure from this earth made available to the disciples and to us the ministry of the Spirit that he experienced. "But I tell you the truth: It is for your good that I am going away. Unless I go away, the Counselor will not come to you; but if I go, I will send him to you" (Jn 16:7).

Thus, within this age, the Holy Spirit, the author of Scripture, assumes the distinctive role in divine guidance for filling and leading believers, "Those who are led by the Spirit of God are the sons of God" (Rom 8:14; Eph 5:18). Each believer has been eternally paired with God's Spirit as roommate and potential soul mate forever (Jn 14:16). God takes up his residence within each of us—through the person of the Holy Spirit—so believers can experience the outflow of the eternal friendship of deep intertrinitarian love. The indwelling Spirit is our divine mentor, our *doctor internus*—the Inner Teacher.[5]

Unfortunately, whenever the Holy Spirit is mentioned, a range of reactions spring up. There is fear of controversy and disunity. Local churches have divided over discussions about the person and work of the Holy Spirit—regarding matters of doctrine and of experience. There is fear of the excesses that seem to be associated with those who talk about the Holy Spirit. Gary Badcock suggests three distinct periods within church history when emphasis was placed on the ministry of the Holy Spirit, and certain extremes followed suit: "The one sidedness of ecclesial life that can arise from a priority of pneumatology over christology is well documented in the excesses of the Montanists [3rd century], for example, or of the radical reformation and [within the twentieth century] the charismatic and pentecostal movements."[6] But in attempting to eliminate the smoke that may arise now and then, do we tend to put the fire out as well?[7]

Consider the testimony of Daniel Wallace, professor of New Testament and Greek: "The last few years have shown me that my spiritual life has gotten off track—that somehow I, along with many in my theological tradition, have learned to do without the third person of the Trinity. This has not hindered my academic work. Mine has become a cognitive faith—a Christianity from the neck up."[8] In our practice, have we come to believe that the holy Trinity consists of Father, Son and Holy Scriptures?[9] Have we overemphasized the written Word to the neglect of the Spirit, the divine author of Scripture? Wallace thinks so.

When Wallace's son contracted a rare disease from which he almost died, their family was thrown into a whirlwind of medical procedures—a "summer from hell." Although an accomplished New Testament professor, Wallace was confronted with the need to sense God's presence more than ever before.

> Through this experience I found that the Bible was not adequate. I needed God in a personal way—not as an object of my study, but as friend, guide, comforter. I needed an existential experience of the Holy One. Quite frankly, I found that the Bible was not the answer. . . . I found a longing to get closer to God, but found myself unable to do so through my normal means: exegesis, Scripture reading, more exegesis. I believe that I depersonalized God so much that when I really needed him I didn't know how to relate. I longed for him. . . . I found a suffocation of the Spirit in my evangelical tradition as well as in my own heart.[10]

The problem is not with the Bible—it is God's revelation to us, the vibrant and living Word of God, inspired by the Spirit of God. The problem stems from approaching the Bible only at a cognitive or historical level. Scripture must be studied within the context of a dynamic and growing relationship with the God who is personal and who is intimately and supernaturally involved in the everyday aspects of his children. We skew our perception of God by reading Scripture as essentially a historical account of how God acted in the past, rather than a divine record about people just like us who experienced a normal friendship with God available to contemporary believers as well. As Dallas Willard warns, unless we identify with these biblical folk, "we will not genuinely be able to believe the Bible or find its contents to be real, because it will have no experiential substance to us. . . . [The Bible] becomes simply a book of doctrine, of abstract truth about God, which one can search endlessly without encountering God himself or hearing his voice."[11] Such divine guidance requires many of us to color outside the lines from our customary view of God, to permit him to impact our experience as he so chooses.[12]

I must confess my own complicity in this sin of a cerebral faith, of a cool orthodoxy, of a substitution of Bible study for a dynamic relationship with God. Although indwelt by the Spirit and sustained in many ways by the Spirit, I never acknowledged the Spirit's ministry in my life by thanking him for his faithfulness. As mentioned in an earlier chapter, on a spiritual retreat of solitude and seeking God, I met the Spirit personally. Graciously but firmly, God the Spirit enlightened my mind and heart of attitudes of pride. For almost two hours I wept in the Spirit's presence in this time of confession and healing. That life-changing event set me on a new dynamic in my personal relationship with God, mediated through the indwelling of the Holy Spirit.

Sadly, Christians have little practical working knowledge about the Holy Spirit for cultivating their relationship with God and for sustaining daily Christian living. In comparison to other major doctrines treated in systematic theology textbooks, relatively little space is given to the Spirit, the third person of the Trinity.[13]

God Is Personal

In discussing matters of the Holy Spirit, coming to terms with the personal nature of the Holy Spirit is of utmost importance. Theologian Wayne Grudem notes, "After Jesus ascended into heaven, and continuing through the entire church age, the Holy Spirit is now the *primary* manifestation of the presence of the Trinity among us. He is the one who is most prominently *present* with us now."[14] Today, God the Spirit mediates the very presence of God to us.

One stumbling block continues to be the Spirit's nonpersonal name. The words *Father* and *Son* can stir up affectionate images in our mind while *Spirit* engenders little more than an empty question mark. To Nicodemus, Jesus spoke of the Spirit and the wind, offering this play on words, since both words come from the same Greek term *pneuma*. "The wind blows wherever it pleases. You hear its sound, but you cannot tell where it comes from or where it is going. So it is with everyone born of the Spirit" (Jn 3:8; cf. Eccles 11:5). On a few occasions, *pneuma* is also translated in the New Testament as "breath": "a breath of life from God entered them" (Rev 11:11).[15] From the bestselling fiction series At Home In Mitford, such a metaphor was employed by the beloved Episcopal priest Father Tim as he preached to his parish at St. John's: "What some believers still can't believe is that it is God's passion to be as near to us *as our very breath.*"[16] Moreover, J. I. Packer suggests that Augustine and other theologians "had in mind the Holy Spirit when they spoke of God's 'grace.' "[17] May we then place "a face" on the active agent of God's grace, that of the Holy Spirit? After working through this material on the Holy Spirit, one student responded, "This leads to the conclusion that I should be capable of so much more—that truly walking with the Spirit has the potential to open up a whole new realm of righteousness and intimacy with God!"[18]

The Spirit is not a silent partner in the Trinity, for he speaks (see Acts 10:19) and may be grieved by us (Eph 4:30). All members of the triune God—the Father, Son and Holy Spirit—are coequal persons. Therefore, just as believers interact with the Father and the Son, we can interact with the Spirit—in conversation and prayer, in worship and thanksgiving. If we avoid any interaction with the Spirit, practically speaking, we perpetuate the ancient heresy of regarding the Holy Spirit as some kind of impersonal force. Packer affirms that "prayer to the Spirit is equally proper when what we seek from him is closer communion with Jesus and fuller Jesuslikeness in our lives."[19] It is the Spirit who gives life and renews life.

Some confusion may arise as to which trinitarian person actually abides in believers. For example, what of Jesus' comment using the pronoun *I*? "I will not leave you as orphans; I will come to you" (Jn 14:18). "I am with you always" (Mt 28:20). Scripture teaches that *each* person of the Trinity abides in us: God the Father abides in us (e.g., Jn 14:23; 1 Jn 4:15); God the Son abides in us (e.g., Jn 14:23; 15:4); God the Spirit abides in us (e.g., Jn 14:16-17). Moreover, the third person of the Godhead is called both the "Spirit of God" and the "Spirit of Christ" in Romans 8:9-11. Peter Toon explains:

Apparently Paul is teaching that the risen and exalted Lord Jesus Christ is now experienced in and through the Spirit. . . . We are not to think that the Spirit and Christ are one and the same; rather, the "Spirit indwelling" and "Christ in you" are synonymous. Thus the lordship of Jesus Christ over his own is exercised by the presence and activity of the Spirit in their lives. On earth now Jesus is known only through the Spirit.[20]

Fee notes, "Some mystery is involved here, because finally we are dealing with divine mysteries. There can be little question that Paul sees the Spirit as distinct from God [the Father]; yet at the same time the Spirit is both the interior expression and the visible manifestation of God's activity in the world."[21] In light of the Trinity's mutual indwelling in each other (*perichoresis,* "You are in me, and I am in you," Jn 17:21), in some way God's trinitarian presence ("We will come to him and make our home with him," Jn 14:23) is mysteriously and uniquely mediated through the person of the Holy Spirit (e.g., 1 Cor 2:12; Eph 3:16; 1 Jn 3:24; 4:13).

The Holy Spirit as Our Roommate and Copilot

What happens when we have guests living at our dormitory, apartment or house? It is hard not to ignore visitors under foot. Normal living arrangements are disrupted a bit. Some quote the old proverb, "Fish and visitors smell after three days." But despite the reality that God the Holy Spirit lives in every genuine believer forever (Jn 14:16), some believers simply ignore the Spirit throughout the day. Like a fire extinguisher, he is left alone until an emergency arises. Perhaps exploring certain metaphors can help us gain a perspective regarding the kind of working relationship that is available between the Spirit and believers.

Imagine your mind being like a desktop computer. Technological advances continue to make personal computers capable of greater functions, for example, for project management and graphic design. Yet as powerful as they are, when connected to the Internet, personal computers access a vast array of resources that no single computer could ever store. When connected to the World Wide Web, there is no limit to what can be done. Likewise, when we remain in regular communion with God the Spirit, we can supersede the limitations of relying solely on our own human power.

Or by combining two biblical word pictures, the Spirit as wind and the believer as a soaring eagle (e.g., "they will soar on wings like eagles," Is 40:31), a dynamic image takes shape, depicting how supernatural assistance helps believers rise above human limitations. Eagles were made for soaring, having long wingspans with powerful pinions. They soar great distances for hours at a time when the wind carries them.

From his experience of living near an eagle's hollow, Terry Fulham explains how eagles mount up.[22] As a child of nine or ten he would visit the hollow for hours and sit and watch eagles circling and soaring overhead. On one occasion, he remembered observing an eagle standing at the edge of its nest, high up on the crags of a cliff. It just stood there, wings spread out wide open. And it stood and stood. Terry became impatient and started to throw rocks at the eagle to make it fly (of course, the nest was much higher than his stone's reach). All of a sudden, the eagle slowly lifted off the nest and began soaring—*without any movement of its wings.* It had waited for the wind to carry it aloft. We learn that apart from the wind there is no soaring, only weary flapping. We were made for soaring with the Spirit, to soar above the heights as well as through storms.

Perhaps a metaphor related to air travel might also be helpful. Imagine your relationship with the Spirit to be like that of a pilot and copilot flying a multimillion-dollar passenger airplane through the friendly skies. Similar to an airplane, human life, a priceless and miraculous creation of God, is expressly designed to be a two-pilot arrangement. God has so fashioned human nature that both a human person and a divine person can occupy the pilot's quarters together. Yet the Holy Spirit does not become the senior pilot in this arrangement, although he is the superior expert. The Spirit is our divine mentor, our flight instructor as it were, to help us live our lives to the glory of God. We desperately need a copilot of greater power, of greater wisdom, to guide us in navigating through the turbulence toward the important destinations of life. Flying solo through life portends an accident waiting to happen. Most of us have learned this truth through the countless "crashes" in our lives, disasters of our own doing.

To change the metaphor, the Spirit is like a permanent driving instructor, sitting in the passenger seat of the car of your life. The Divine Mentor goes with us wherever we go and is always ready to offer counsel, encouragement and admonishment—if we are ready to listen. Jesus' promise of "another helper" is just what we need.[23] God the Spirit makes available to us all the resources to help us become the kind of persons who love God and serve him (2 Pet 1:3-4). Christian living is a cooperative or synergistic venture.[24] Only then is abundant living possible.

The particular ministry of sanctification and empowerment for ministry is the work of the Holy Spirit. Regarding the process of sanctification, although the Holy Spirit has promised its completion (Rom 8:29-30), this side of death and heaven the believers' growth is never complete. And neither is it automatic or monergistic (i.e., in which God alone works). Jesus noted that believers tend to be clueless about "blind spots" (Mt 7:3). Would it not meet a great need to have access to a wise counselor who is able, with love and grace, to point out our foibles and frailties in a confidential manner? For this very purpose, the indwelling Spirit willingly mucks about in the cesspool of the unconscious and conscious aspects of our being to facilitate the transformation of our lives toward holiness.

The Spirit offers a comprehensive and pervasive ministry for believers.[25] The New Testament records at least four significant areas for which the Spirit's assistance is needed for living well within God's kingdom:

☐ empowerment in deepening our relationship with God ("fellowship of the Spirit," Phil 2:1; 2 Cor 13:14)

☐ empowerment for Christlike living ("fruit of the Spirit," Gal 5:22)

☐ empowerment for growing together into a healthy and mature Christian community (the "unity of the Spirit," Eph 4:3)

☐ empowerment for ministry to others ("spiritual gifts," 1 Cor 12:1) and for evangelism ("filled with the Holy Spirit and spoke the word of God with boldness," Acts 4:31; see also Acts 1:8)

Wasting Time with God: Orienting Prayer

How can we become more aware, more conscious of the presence of God the Spirit each moment of the day? Consider the example of missionary Frank Laubach (d. 1970) known for his work in literacy. In 1937 he decided to increase the time he thought about God each day with a "game of keeping Thee in mind every second."[26] On certain days he recorded what percentage of the day he was conscious of God. Some percentages that appear: April 2, 35 percent; April 3, 50 percent; April 4,

75 percent; April 5, 80 percent; April 6, 25 percent. On June 16, Laubach listed 96 percent and wrote, "This day, a higher percentage than any before it, is so rich I could write pages."[27] The diary concludes on June 30, "The last morning of the best six months inwardly and outwardly of my life, up to this time."[28] The goal is to be mindful of God throughout the day: "pray without ceasing" (1 Thess 5:17 NASB). Brother Lawrence (d. 1691), author of *Practicing the Presence of God*, maintained a focus on God while working in the monastery kitchen cleaning pots and pans.

Mindfulness is the key. A practical question: What do we tend to think about? What do we regularly place before our minds? One important human ability is the power to focus our minds on something. Peter Toon suggests that "the place of the Holy Spirit in the renewal of the mind and transformation of the soul is crucial."[29] In a significant discussion of the ministry of the Holy Spirit throughout Romans 8, the major contrast is articulated in verses 5-7: "For those who live according to the flesh set their minds on the things of the flesh, but those who live according to the Spirit set their minds on the things of the Spirit. To set the mind on the flesh is death, but to set the mind on the Spirit is life and peace. For this reason the mind that is set on the flesh is hostile to God" (NRSV; cf. Rom 12:2; Phil 4:8).

The goal of orienting prayer as a discipline is to increase our focus on God throughout the day.[30] Human nature is so constituted that we can do more than one thing at the same time (e.g., driving a car and listening to the radio or talking on a cell phone). We have the power to place our minds wherever we wish. Through practice, we can become continually mindful of God, whether he is in the center of our consciousness or at the periphery of it. But it will take practice.

For example, identify some meaningful verses or brief scriptural phrases (or phrases from hymns or choruses) for use as orienting prayers:

"The LORD is my shepherd, I shall not be in want" (Ps 23:1).

"Praise the LORD, O my soul" (Ps 103:1; 104:1).

I have used the Jesus Prayer,[31] a practice from the Orthodox tradition: "Lord Jesus Christ, Son of God, have mercy on me" (an adaptation of Mk 10:47). These ten words convey good theology, a good request and a reference to our humble posture. The purpose is to repeat this orienting prayer slowly and meditatively over and over both as an end, as a prayer to Jesus for his mercy, and as a means of focusing the mind on things above.

At the beginning of the day or at an early point of our day, meditate on the verse to orient your thoughts toward God. Repetition is the key to this orienting process. The verse must be repeated several times (e.g., begin with twenty times and increase the repetition to one hundred or more times a day). Whenever events in the day turn sour, when stress starts mounting, the orienting prayer should be used. By connecting with God, our soul begins to take on a whole new orientation to God's resources, and his peace can again pervade our being, as he promises (Phil 4:6-7; 2 Thess 3:16), even within the present turmoil. Whenever we catch our mind wandering, even within a church service or in personal times of prayer, the orienting prayer is an aid to refocus on God. In this way we train our mind to connect with God moment by moment.

An important component to incorporate in this project is your body. We are embodied beings, and any lifestyle change must involve our bodies in some way. Exclusively focusing on mental activities will yield limited results. We must literally "offer the parts of [our] body to him as instruments of righteousness" (Rom 6:13). Scripture records various body postures in prayer. King Solomon dedicated the new temple praying on his knees with his arms spread toward heaven (1 Kings 8:54). Ezra prayed lying face down (Ezra 10:1). Consider taking short "knee breaks" throughout the day (thirty seconds to five minutes in length) and kneel in your bedroom, your office, between TV commercials, at lunchtime. Kneeling is a posture of humility before God. Placing of hands may also contribute to the discipline (e.g., palms down during confession, palms up while making requests to God). Singing favorite Christian choruses or hymns has the same effect. In this discipline we regularly offer our mouths, our arms, our knees to God. When body and mind work together, change takes place at a quicker rate (e.g., memorizing a group of numbers is easier by repeating the sequence out loud).

Finally, at the beginning of the day and throughout the day as I think of it, I regularly and explicitly invite God the Spirit to walk with me because God does not presume upon our friendship. When my brother lived nearby, we met almost every week for breakfast. Yet we still made a courtesy call earlier in the week to confirm our time together. I am also reminded of the German prayer my brother, sister and I recited hundreds of times at the table during our growing up years: "Come, Lord Jesus, *be our guest.* And may this food to us be blessed. Amen" (English translation, emphasis added). Only now can I fully appreciate the significance and weight of this prayer that was so glibly uttered long ago. Just like you and me, God does not like to show up where he is not welcome. God awaits our regular and personal invitation to join us each day. To become aware of God on a moment-by-moment basis, we need to develop the habit of turning our mind regularly toward God.

Listening to God the Spirit

Through the permanent indwelling ministry of the Spirit, believers have a unique mode of living available for the first time in history for all of God's people. The other alternative is to rely on one's own resources as Adam and Eve did and failed. Along the same lines, when God gave the law to the Israelites, they naively claimed, "We will do everything the Lord has said" (Ex 19:8; 24:3). Jesus, the "Adam" of a new God-oriented human race (1 Cor 15:45-49), shows us we can only live the abundant life God designed for us by walking in the Spirit (e.g., Mt 12:28; Lk 2:40; 4:1-2, 14, 18-21; Jn 3:34; Acts 1:2).[32] This supernaturally assisted lifestyle was promised by God through the prophets (Jer 31:31-34; Ezek 36:22-27) and has been inaugurated in the life and death of Jesus (Lk 22:20).

Klaus Bockmuehl notes, "The Holy Spirit is the teacher who *speaks, rebukes, reminds,* and *guides.* In Christian circles, he is far too often represented merely as the enabler, and thus is reduced to a mute 'force' or impersonal agent. . . . Only the pagan idols are mute, and Christians have been liberated from their service."[33] The verbs employed to describe the ministry of the Spirit are communication terms.

> The Holy Spirit, whom the Father will send in my name, will *teach* you all things and will *remind* you of everything I have said to you. (Jn 14:26, emphasis added)

> The Spirit of truth . . . will *guide* you into all truth. He will not *speak* on his own; he will *speak* only what he hears. (Jn 16:13, emphasis added)

Although we can never fathom everything about the Spirit's working,

believers must attend to two dynamic processes characteristic of a supernaturally assisted lifestyle: (1) divine guidance—becoming increasingly
aware of the Spirit's promptings in our lives—and (2) divine empowerment—initiating new steps of faith in which we leave room for God to
work. Some comments about the second component are offered before
devoting the rest of the chapter to a discussion of divine guidance.

Leaving Room for Divine Aid

Taking new steps of faith may involve an action on our part or it may
involve doing nothing and waiting on God's timing. For example, in the
Old Testament, priests carrying the ark of God were explicitly instructed
by God to walk forward—literally taking a step of faith—and place their
feet in the Jordan River. At the moment of contact, God would dry up the
waters for the Israelites to pass through on dry ground (Josh 3:13-17). But
nothing happened until their feet actually touched the water.

Similarly, during the times of the kings, Jonathan and his armor bearer
stepped out in faith to engage a company of Philistines in battle. "Perhaps
the LORD will act in our behalf. Nothing can hinder the LORD from saving,
whether by many or by few" (1 Sam 14:6). Due to Jonathan's initiative,
with God's help, these two routed twenty soldiers, and subsequently God
brought a panic on the whole Philistine army (1 Sam 14:15). "The Philistines [were] in total confusion, striking each other with their swords" (1
Sam 14:20).

Yet at other times taking new steps of faith may mean doing nothing
about a problem but waiting for God's timing and solution (cf. Phil 4:6-7).
For example, the prophet Samuel instructed King Saul to wait until Samuel
arrived to offer the appropriate sacrifices. But King Saul was more anxious
about the approaching enemy than entrusting himself to God's provision so
he did not wait; for this pattern of disobedience, God removed the kingdom
from Saul's heirs (1 Sam 13:5-14). Contrast the differing mindsets of King
Saul and his son Jonathan in their actions. Saul was anxious and fearful
about the enemy (1 Sam 13:11-12), yet Jonathan was explicitly conscious
that he was leaving room for God to work (1 Sam 14:6). Whether we wait
or act, it must be with an awareness of a dependence on divine resources.
Walking with the Spirit is an intentional endeavor involving the paradox of
grace; we work and God works—both are necessary.[34]

The Critical Point of Divine Guidance

How best to capture the gist of divine guidance? Consider a phrase often used regarding research with human subjects. Anyone participating in a study must do so with "informed and willing consent." This concept helps clarify the process of divine guidance. God informs us about a matter, and then we can willingly respond. Any person-to-person encounter conducted within an ongoing healthy and loving relationship always involves information and voluntary cooperation, never manipulation nor coercion. People are not like animals led on a leash.

For example, in Psalm 32:8-9, a contrast is proposed between guiding a person with the mind and physically leading an animal: "I will instruct you and teach you in the way you should go; / I will counsel you and watch over you. / Do not be like the horse or the mule, / which have no understanding / but must be controlled by bit and bridle." Derek Kidner explains, "This vivid picture brings out, by its contrasts, the emphasis in verse 8 on intelligent co-operation, which God has set His heart on eliciting from us (cf. Jn 15:15); for whatever else one can do with a horse one can hardly *counsel* it (8), or control it without bringing pressure on it."[35] We have been created in God's image, with a full array of capacities that permit us to choose intelligently how we will speak and act. Such communication from God is necessary if a personal relationship with God is to be cultivated.

This kind of give-and-take process of informed and willing consent runs through many of the stories of the Old Testament, especially during the times of the monarchy. Although God's written revelation was available at the time, a prophet would nonetheless be sent to the king of Israel or Judah with a specific message from God of potential blessing (e.g., 2 Chron 15:1-8) or impending doom (2 Chron 18:16). On some occasions the king responded positively to God (e.g., Asa in 2 Chron 15:8-19; Jehoshaphat in 2 Chron 19:2—20:30), but usually the king continued the pattern of disobedience, even placing the prophet in jail (e.g., Asa in 2 Chron 16:7-10; Ahab in 2 Chron 18:25-27).

Informed and willing consent is also depicted in the New Testament. In the Acts 10 account of Peter and Cornelius, a Gentile centurion, Peter first became aware of God's guidance through a strange vision of a sheet of clean and unclean animals, a vision to raise questions in Peter's mind.

While he was perplexed about the vision, the Spirit specifically commanded him to accompany some messengers, "Do not hesitate to go with them, for I have sent them" (Acts 10:20). For up to that moment in his life, Peter had never associated with or visited any non-Jews (Acts 10:28).

Geography plays a role in this episode. Peter was in the port town of Joppa at the time, the same location in which Jonah had boarded a ship to run away from the Lord. Peter could have followed Jonah's path of disobedience, but he probably figured God knew best, and it was not worth the discipline Jonah went through. Despite his inner hesitations, Peter stepped out in obedience, inviting in the messengers, later accompanying them to Cornelius' house and finally presenting the gospel and welcoming Gentiles into the household of faith.

In divine guidance, God the Spirit attempts to make us aware of a need or a new direction we might take by using a variety of divine and human means, to be surveyed in the following order. We can attend to

☐ Scripture as the primary and objective means of discerning God's moral will

☐ the voices of others (e.g., sermons, conversations, written material, even our own words to others may prove helpful to us)

☐ the inner voice of the Spirit (being alert both to our thoughts and feelings)[36]

Our awareness is essential to the process if we wish to make any progress in deepening our relationship with God. One cannot change one's life direction without making a choice to alter course.

Listening to the Written Word of God

Only Scripture presents the authoritative and normative guide about what is real and how to really live. Against this standard, we test all other propositions about life. As we consider the matter of Scripture, the doctrine of illumination comes into play, which encompasses a narrower focus than the doctrine of guidance. Illumination is the Spirit's ministry to assist us in discerning the *significance* and practical import of the Bible's particular message for personal living (1 Cor 2:9-16). This divine tutoring does not replace our need to study and discover the *meaning* of the Scriptures. As Walt Russell notes, "While sometimes debated, the basic thrust of the Holy Spirit's illuminating or enlightening work relates primarily to our *welcoming of the truths of Scripture* rather than to our *understanding* of them. . . . The Holy Spirit aids us in appraising or assessing the significance of the passages we are reading."[37] Consider these two cases of illumination.

Walt and Marty Russell, good friends of ours, were engulfed in grief over the loss of their eighteen-month-old son Christopher, who died suddenly while asleep when the Russells were away vacationing with friends. This is what Walt experienced at the graveside service:

> It is an unspeakably painful moment in my life. If I could muster any more tears, I would be uncontrollably weeping as I watch four men struggle to lower a steel vault lid to cover the grave vault holding Christopher's little casket. I will see his little smiling face no more. . . . And as I stand there looking into what feels like the abyss, I realize that this could be the most despairing, skeptical, and faithless moment of my life.[38]

In that time of sorrow, the Spirit directed his thought to a passage about the coming of the Lord, on which he had recently been meditating: 1 Thessalonians 4:13-18. Russell continues, "Not only did God bring them to mind, but I was overwhelmingly comforted and encouraged about seeing our little son again when Jesus comes to raise His people. . . . I began to experience profound, soulish comfort in the deepest recesses of my being as God used His Word to renew hope and courage in me."[39]

Illumination may also come in a rather tangential manner in which the Spirit uses his Word based on an underlying thrust of the passage. Following a church service, Pastor Jack Deere was about to rebuke an older women regarding her conversation with a younger women, when Isaiah 42:3 came to his mind, "A bruised reed he will not break, and a smoldering wick he will not snuff out." Although a prophecy about the coming of Jesus and his gentle character, this verse was used to turn Deere's heart from irritation at the woman to compassion for her. "All it would take was one rebuke from her pastor to break her and snuff her out. . . . The Lord was telling me that this was not the day to rebuke her, that he would handle her correction in another way, at another time."[40] Regardless of how central or peripheral the significance, the more Scripture we study and memorize—becoming familiar with the very tone and texture of God's Word—the more the Spirit can illuminate his Word for us.

Illumination and Guidance

But does God offer any kind of communication not specifically connected with the Scriptures? For example, is God only interested that we tell the truth, that we are regular members of a fellowship of believers? Or is he also interested in helping us choose which car to buy, which neighborhood to live in, what kind of vacation we might take? Does God provide particular words to guide specific choices we make that no Scripture passage addresses explicitly? I became convinced that God offered just this, as did Charles Swindoll.

> For years I embraced a limited view of that statement ['he will guide you into all truth' (Jn 16:13)], even though Jesus specifically used the word, "all." I felt He was referring only to the truth of Scripture. . . . If one of the Spirit's tasks is to guide us into and disclose the truth, who says that means only the truth of Scripture? Why couldn't it include the truth of His will? Or the truth about another person? Or the truth regarding both sides of a tough decision?[41]

Although Scripture offers sufficient and comprehensive authoritative guidance for Christian living, it never claims to be exhaustive, encompassing all the truth that can be known. As suggested by the apostle John, that would take many more pages and books (Jn 21:25).

The Bible itself teaches us to look outside of Scripture for God's wisdom—"Go to the ant, you sluggard; consider its ways and be wise!" (Prov 6:6)—as well as listening to the counsel of others: "The way of a fool seems right to him, but a wise man listens to advice" (Prov 12:15). There is more wisdom to gain from God, and this is accessible within a dynamic relationship with God the Spirit. Sometimes this wisdom will come through Scripture; other times it will arrive by other means.

To summarize, illumination is the particular ministry of the Spirit geared to helping us discern the significance or practical implications of Scripture for daily living. In receiving direction in our lives from a Bible passage, this is illumination or biblical guidance. Furthermore, the Spirit may give counsel unrelated to any particular passage—what might be called extrabiblical guidance—that offers situation-specific direction. Thus, divine guidance may involve a particular biblical passage, or it may not.

Should believers value situation-specific guidance from God as inspired, on par with Scripture? It is important to note a distinction between the doctrine of inspiration and the doctrine of guidance, between God's *universal* revelation in Scripture and his *particular* communication to individuals. With *inspiration*, the human authors were uniquely inspired with God's message in a clear and accurate manner so that no error would take place, since the very words would be recorded in the Bible for all time.[42] But a certain message offered by God in *guidance* to a particular individual never carries any normative, universal authority for all times, as the Bible does. Furthermore, any guidance must always be tested against the final standard of the Bible to discern whether or not the particular message fits within or contradicts the plain teaching of Scripture (1 Thess 5:19-21; 1 Jn 4:1).

Let us then consider further such extrabiblical, situation-specific guidance. The Bible records varying ways in which God has communicated to his people in the past. The more spectacular experiences have included angelic messengers (e.g., to the shepherds at the birth of Jesus, Lk 2:13-14), dreams[43] and visions (e.g., Peter's vision of a sheet with clean and unclean animals, Acts 10:11-12), and unusual phenomena that accompany an audible voice (e.g., the light from heaven flashing around Paul on the road to Damascus, Acts 9:3). In the following pages, I focus on the less spectacular but more common modes of divine communication—the voice of others and the inner voice.

Listening to the Voice of Others

In addition to seeking divine guidance through God's Word, we must also be alert for God's message spoken through the words of others. As King David took flight from Jerusalem during Absalom's rebellion, the king encountered Shimei, a man throwing sticks and mud at him, with shrill curses: "Get out, get out, you man of blood, you scoundrel!" (2 Sam 16:7). David did not permit Abishai to lop off Shimei's head for such disrespect because the king was conscious of God's potential involvement. "If he is cursing because the LORD said to him, 'Curse David,' who can ask, 'Why do you do this?' " (2 Sam 16:10).

During the days of the exodus, Moses' father-in-law, Jethro, offered an idea to Moses about decentralizing the system for judging cases for the people. "If you do this and God so commands, you will be able to stand the strain, and all these people will go home satisfied. Moses listened to his father-in-law and did everything he said" (Ex 18:23-24).

Prior to Augustine's conversion, after which he became one of the influential theologians of the Church, his mother, Monica, was overwrought with concern that her son would ever be enmeshed in a cult of that day and never come to faith in God. She pleaded with a church leader to visit her son and persuade Augustine of the merits of Christianity. This leader wisely declined, knowing the barrier was not primarily intellectual. Yet Monica persisted with tears and pleadings. Finally the church leader conveyed these comforting words: "As you live, it is impossible that the son of such tears should perish."[44] Augustine recounts his mother's perception of this counsel: "As she was often wont to recall in her conversations with me, she took this as if it had sounded forth from heaven."[45]

Missionary Frank Laubach devoted the year 1937 to "learning the language of God": "I shall try to learn Your language as it was taught by Jesus and by all others through whom you speak—in beauty and singing birds and cool breezes, in radiant Christlike faces, in sacrifices and in tears."[46] Two journal entries offer examples of his experience: "As my hostess read the Bible and prayed, I heard You speaking this morning. She was the channel broadcasting Your words. I shall try to listen for Your speaking through the language of men, especially men who are trying to do Your will" (Monday, Jan. 4). "This seeking to learn Your vocabulary seems to be the clue! Every hour is new evidence that You are trying to speak. This morning the prayer calendar asked, 'How many messages have you had from God?' *That* was a message from God! You speak from the pages of books" (Wed, Jan. 6).

Chip Missler, although in excellent health with no prior medical problems, suddenly died at the age of thirty-nine of a heart attack while out jogging one summer Saturday evening. His parents, Chuck and Nancy Missler, were stunned, grief overflowing with many tears. Halfway around the globe in Australia, at that very moment, a close friend of Nancy was in a church service and felt that Nancy was in great need. She penned this letter, excerpted here:

> So, sister, what is going on in your life? Seems like the Lord has given me a

heavy burden on my heart for you. I know these are not my own thoughts. When the Lord spoke to me this morning, I heard three words: lonely, hurting and uplifted. I wrote them on my pad during the sermon. I truly was trying to listen [to the sermon], but it seems the Holy Spirit was having His own agenda with me. Even though we are 8000 miles apart, I feel very close to you right now and am writing this letter from my heart, not my head. . . . I don't know what is wrong, but I know you are hurting, and I just want to uplift you.[47]

In light of the comfort she received from this correspondence, Nancy Missler advises, "Remember this story next time God lays someone on your heart to pray for or to write a love note to."[48]

Have you ever heard someone speak words that somehow caught your attention more than usual? I regard these times as God speaking to me. For example, on one occasion during a chapel message on campus, I was distinctly prompted to begin a weekly time of resting and wasting time with God. On another occasion my own words of advice to a friend came back to haunt me a few days later and convict me of the need to strengthen my relationship with my wife, Beth. I am learning to be more attentive to listening to others to discern when it is that God speaks to me through others.

Repetition of a message can usually signify a confirmation of God's point on the matter. For example, Pharaoh's dreams came as a related pair, though with different imagery (Gen 41:1-9). J. P. Moreland shared with me an occasion where the same message, in relation to a parenting task, was repeated within a three-hour span by two different people. The first time the idea was spoken, he did not take much notice. But when the same message was repeated a few hours later from another person in an altogether different context, his ears perked up. Similarly, one occasion I was struck by the primary thrust of an article in *Christianity Today*, regarding the futility of seeking acclaim through research and writing. Later that week, a faculty colleague shared a new commitment to reduce his research and writing agenda, which had been prolific, to spend more time with his family. Now I pay more attention for God's words as I converse with others, hear a sermon or read a book.

Seeking out the counsel of wise believers—especially the elderly—is a component of how the Spirit guides us. "Plans fail for lack of counsel, but with many advisers they succeed" (Prov 15:22). I am learning to ask others for advice, in order to avoid self-inflicted pains stemming from stupid decisions. Although at times the words are difficult to receive—the truth hurts—I am learning to heed such "wounds from a friend" (Prov 27:6) and enjoy smoother sailing. In difficult situations when a believer goes astray, seemingly unaware that the path is off course, Scripture commands fellow believers to come alongside and offer encouragement and admonishment to return to God's path (e.g., Mt 18:15-20; Gal 6:1-2; Jas 5:19-20). If we cannot listen to words of admonishment from those who know us well, how can we ever hear the inner voice of God (see 1 Jn 4:20)?

Listening to the Inner Voice

The most difficult form to discern but most common type of God's communication is through the inner or "still small voice." Willard explains:

> That is, of all the ways in which the message comes from *within* the experience of the person addressed (such as dreams and visions or other mental states), for those who are living in harmony with God it most commonly comes in the form of their own thoughts and attendant feelings. Of all the possible subjective routes, this mode is best suited to the redemptive purposes of God because, once again, *it most engages the faculties of free, intelligent beings in the work of God as his colaborers and friends.*[49]

The process of informed and willing consent consists of information in a propositional form—the kind that could be written out as a sentence. As Laubach clarifies, "God, you talk to us through our best thoughts. Lovely ideas are your whispers, even though we may never suspect that they come from You. I am sure that every step forward in my life came as an idea while I was looking up with the eyes of my soul, waiting to be 'stirred by the invisible.' "[50]

Stephen, one of the deacons in the early church, astounded the Jews of his day with such help from the Spirit. "These men began to argue with Stephen, but they could not stand up against his wisdom or the Spirit by whom he spoke" (Acts 6:9-10). A professor of mine, Dr. Haddon Robinson, recounted a dramatic occasion of such divine guidance while participating in a public debate regarding the creation-evolution issue in Dallas, Texas. In his closing comments at the debate, although he had ably prepared for his role, words just came to him—from where, he knew not—that clearly marked out the distinctions of the issue.

Have you ever wondered where that good idea came from? Could it have been God the Spirit himself offering a word of guidance? I remember an occasion at a professional conference when I was stymied as to how to respond to a question following my presentation. My mind went blank. After what seemed like an eternity, all of a sudden an answer "came" to me. I shared the idea, and it was a great response to the question. Now I realize it was the Spirit's kindness to bail me out instead of my own sudden genius. By reflecting on past experiences—times where thoughts came to us at just the right moment—and mulling over the particulars of these encounters, we can be more alert and discerning when such guidance comes in the future.

Is not this the kind of experience Jesus said could happen in tight spots, that God the Spirit would speak? "Whenever you are arrested and brought to trial, do not worry beforehand about what to say. Just say whatever is given you at the time, for it is not you speaking, but the Holy Spirit" (Mk 13:11).[51] I. Howard Marshall comments that "the Spirit gives guidance regarding both the general form of a speech and the actual content."[52] It is likely that this particular teaching was based on Jesus' own experience, for he always listened to God (Jn 5:30; 8:26-28; 12:49-50). Is not this John's point—that the Spirit is ready to teach us as well? "But you have an anointing from the Holy One. . . . The anointing you received from him remains in you, and you do not need anyone to teach you. But as his anointing teaches you about all things and as that anointing is real, not counterfeit—just as it has taught you, remain in him" (1 Jn 2:20, 27). The Spirit, who indwells us, is ready to offer assistance and perceptive thoughts for the moment at hand.

Pastor Swindoll shares an account of God's guidance in the midst of a difficult counseling session. The counselee, sitting next to his wife, was deeply troubled, anxious, overcome with panic, weeping and shaking uncontrollably. Swindoll shares, "Then, seemingly out of nowhere, I got a flash of insight, sparked by something [the wife] said. It tied in beautifully with a scriptural principle I had spoken on several days earlier."[53] Surprisingly, Swindoll's comment struck home so quickly that the man regained his composure, made a brief comment, got up, shook Swindoll's hand

and walked out of the office with his smiling wife! Swindoll pondered, "What happened? I am convinced the Spirit who surprises guided us into that moment of truth and with surgical precision revealed the statement that needed to be said and heard."[54]

Not only is God concerned about saving marriages, but he also cares about the minor domestic aspects of life. At our house, we began to have problems with our fifteen-year-old refrigerator. Now and then it would stop running and then start up again. While my wife was out of town, it went on the blink again. Since I did not want to replace it without Beth's input, I prayed earnestly that God would keep it running until she returned. During that same time, a couple of our electric plugs went out in the living room. A fleeting thought went through my mind that the two problems were related. I considered trying the refrigerator's electrical cord on another plug, but for some reason dropped the matter. Later, while in our bedroom, a thought came to mind, "Try the other plug." Immediately I went to the kitchen, and it worked. The problem was not a defective refrigerator, but a malfunctioning electrical circuit and socket.

For our daughter Ruth, the Spirit helped her get to an event on time. While in her college dorm room preoccupied with another activity, she was suddenly "reminded" at 6:27 p.m. of her need to be at the gym nearby by 6:30 p.m. to keep score for the upcoming women's volleyball game. Believers may have such occurrences over their lifetime, but may never recognize the source of the thought as coming from God the Spirit because their view of God does not yet include a God who communicates directly with believers about mundane matters.

Yet even small children can hear the Spirit's voice. Through a bizarre set of circumstances, Anita was left behind at the gas station while her husband drove off down the road with daughter Leah (age three) and son Lucas (age eleven months). Anita first laughed until she cried, imagining her husband's expression when he realized she was not in the car. Then she got frightened when he did not return right away. Anita prayed, "Lord, please let Leah say, 'Papa, where's Mama?' before the next exit."[55] About twenty minutes later, the car pulled into the gas station with a humiliated driver. Anita learned that about two miles before the exit, Leah had asked, "Papa, where's Mama?"

A speaker at our church recently related how Margie, eighty-five years old, always considered any name suddenly popping into her mind as a nudge from the Lord to pray for that person.[56] One morning I was stepping out of my office on the way to class, having decided not to use a particular handout. But before I got out the door, I was "reminded" of the benefit for students and so took the handouts along with me.

Spirit Moves in Our Feelings

The Spirit may also prompt us within the affective realm through our feelings. Swindoll explains how feelings have become more important to him. "I have found that my feelings often represent some of the most sensitive areas in my life touched by the Spirit of God. Not infrequently do my emotions play a vital role in how and where the Spirit is guiding me, giving me reasons to make significant decisions, cautioning me to back off, and reproving me for something in my life that needs immediate attention."[57] The proper response to feelings is not to repress or deny them, but to let our emotions come and learn from what they teach us about how we are coping in life.

When the peace of God overwhelms our soul, it is the Spirit's practical internal indicator that we have given all of our concerns and worries over to him (Phil 4:4-7). Swindoll shares a time when his daughter Charissa was severely injured during high school, falling from a cheerleading pyramid in which, as Charissa later described it, "Something snapped in my back, just below my neck."[58] She felt numb in her legs, arms and fingers. While Swindoll was driving to the school, along with praying for his daughter and the paramedics, he also prayed that God would prevent any panic by curing his soul with calmness. "As I drove and prayed, I sensed the most incredible realization of God's presence. It was almost eerie." Arriving amidst paramedics and a gathering crowd, he knelt beside Charissa, tightly wrapped on a stretcher with her neck in a brace. As he kissed her forehead she said, "I can't feel anything below my shoulders." Swindoll commented, "Normally, I would have been borderline out of control. I wasn't. Normally, I would have been shouting for the crowd to back away or for the ambulance driver to get her to the hospital immediately! I didn't."

Later they learned that the vertebrae in Charissa's back had been fractured. The following Sunday, although drained from the emotional roller

coaster ride of the past few days, Swindoll preached "one of the most requested sermons on tape" since coming to the church in 1971. "Amazing! God the Holy Spirit filled me, took full control, gave great grace,
calmed fears, and ultimately brought wonderful healing to Charissa's
back. Today she is a healthy, happy wife and mother of two, and the only
time her upper back hurts is when she sneezes!"[59] Supernaturally assisted
living can be a reality for all believers, whether in the midst of the stormy
or summer days of life.

Recognizing God's Voice

Whenever I answer the phone and someone speaks my name, I automatically go through my memory banks trying to match the familiar voice
with a name. The more you know a person, the easier it gets, and so it is
with God.

> His sheep follow him because they know his voice. (Jn 10:4)

> My sheep listen to my voice; I know them, and they follow me. (Jn 10:27)

> I have other sheep that are not of this sheep pen. I must bring them also.
> They too will listen to my voice. (Jn 10:16)

To make progress in hearing God's voice, we must overcome the hurdles
that prevent our receptivity. As already mentioned, believing that God
does speak to us today is the initial hurdle. Another problem is that we
may be too busy to hear. Willard notes, "Generally speaking, God will
not compete for our attention. Occasionally a Saul gets knocked to the
ground and so on, but we should expect that in most cases God will *not*
run over us."[60] As mentioned in chapter five, the cure for busyness is taking appropriate breaks from the routines of life for rest and renewal in
which we cultivate a listening ear to hear God speak.

Finally, we will need to grow in our ability to recognize whatever way
God wishes to communicate with us. "Have you got your ears on?" a
phrase from the days of CB radios, is a another expression for Jesus' recurring phrase, "He who has ears, let him hear" (Mt 11:15; 13:43; Mk 8:18;
Lk 14:35). Each believer will need to learn through experience how to listen to God. Those with more experience will need to mentor others who
are in the early stages, as Willard notes:

And we may even have to help identify the voice of God for them and instruct them in how to respond. . . . How wonderful that Eli recognized what was happening to young Samuel and could tell him what to do to begin his lifelong conversational walk with God [1 Sam 3:1-9]! It might well have been years, in the prevailing circumstances, before Samuel would have found his way by himself. We must not mistakenly assume that if *God* speaks to someone, he or she automatically knows what is happening and who is talking.[61]

Not only must we learn the various methods he uses to speak to us, but we must also learn to discern his voice from other voices.

Is God Speaking or Another?

Scripture urges, "Dear friends, do not believe every spirit, but test the spirits to see whether they are from God, because many false prophets have gone out into the world" (1 Jn 4:1). Since many other voices may be speaking to us, we must assess whether or not the voice is of God. It might just be our own "self-talk" or voices from our past (e.g., old parental "tapes" being played in our mind) or even of demonic origin. As Willard outlines, believers need to develop a sensitivity to discern (a) the quality or "weight" of the voice, (b) the tone of the voice and (c) the content or message of the voice.

The *quality* of God's voice is discernible by its texture of authority and profundity. Second, the *tone* of God's voice is one of love, of joy, of peace. It is warm, uplifting, good—"what is helpful for building others up according to their needs, that it may benefit those who listen" (Eph 4:29). "But the wisdom that comes from heaven is first of all pure; then peace-loving, considerate, submissive, full of mercy and good fruit, impartial and sincere" (Jas 3:17). God never uses overtones of condemnation, oppressive demands and legalism—these come from other sources. Third, the *content* of the word from the Spirit will be consistent with his written revelation. The message will conform to the truths about God's character and with the truths and values of his kingdom as recorded in Scripture.[62] E. Stanley Jones (d. 1973) suggests, "Perhaps the rough distinction is this: The voice of the subconscious argues with you, tries to convince you; but the inner voice of God does not argue, does not try to convince you. It just speaks, and it is self-authenticating. It has the feel of the voice of God within it."[63]

Some church leaders may be concerned about the potential chaos and confusion such divine communication might bring into the life of the church. This main objection was raised by the Reformers, according to Klaus Bochmuehl: "The Lutheran and Calvinist versions of the Reformation both consisted of a rejection of and warning against the idea that God could—and would—speak to humans without an intermediary. . . . The Spirit works exclusively through Scripture and must be subjected to the interpretation of an ordained minister."[64] Of course, we cringe when someone attempts to convince us about a certain action by throwing down the gauntlet, "God told me that we should this and this" or "God told me you should do this and this."

Yet, there are checks and balances on situation-specific, person-specific guidance. Any alleged message must fit within scriptural principles. Furthermore, if God should speak about a matter for the Christian community, he will confirm this with others as well, as exemplified in the case before the first Jerusalem church council. "It seemed good to the Holy Spirit and to us" (Acts 15:28). The Christian community has an important role in assessing the wisdom of any espoused word from God.[65]

God's Purposes in Guidance

To review the matter of listening in divine guidance—a process of informed and willing consent—the Spirit attempts to make us aware of something (e.g., a need or new direction to take) by using a variety of divine and human means. After listening to such counsel, our part is to respond and act. "Do not merely listen to the word, and so deceive yourselves. Do what it says" (Jas 1:22). Whether guidance directly involves Scripture or comes from another source, we must still be good hearers first—discerning the message accurately—and then be obedient doers.

God desires that we intentionally tune him in and tune out other competing messages that travel through our mind in any given day. As we become comfortable with such communion, we get better at recognizing God's voice and his ways, as good friends do. There is always potential for error, for misreading a message God may have given—although we can get better at it. Being cautious and tentative in our "pronouncements" is appropriate. We are but feeble messengers with fallible capacities for discernment.

As children of God, we are important enough to God for him to speak to us, but just because God speaks to us does not make us more important than anyone else. Should we fall into this trap, we may be cut out of the loop of divine communication for a season. God is humble and desires to nurture his humility in us. We are never more righteous or "right" when we hear God, but we are more responsible. Such divine insight offers us a greater opportunity to do good for others as well as ourselves.

If God's goal is to grow us as adults, then on occasion, guidance may not come. In effect God is saying, "I trust you; decide for yourself." E. Stanley Jones explains:

> Obviously God must guide us in a way that will develop spontaneity in us. The development of character, rather than direction in this, that, and the other matter, must be the primary purpose of the Father. He will guide us, but He won't override us. That fact should make us use with caution the method of sitting down with a pencil and a blank sheet of paper to write down the instructions dictated by God for the day. Suppose a parent would dictate to the child minutely everything he is to do during the day. The child would be stunted under that regime. The parent must guide in such a manner, and to the degree, that autonomous character, capable of making right decisions for itself, is produced. God does the same.[66]

Becoming fully functioning adults is the goal, not children who must always be told exactly what to do.

By growing into a lifestyle of seeking God, we gain a familiarity in listening to God during the normal course of life events. But if we only seek God's counsel when desperate or anxious, we will remain novices to the nuances of how God speaks. Troubled souls have a difficulty in discerning with accuracy what God might be saying. It is better to develop our learning curve during less demanding times. After accumulating a track record of hearing God on varied occasions, we are in a better position to discern direction when trials arrive unwelcome on our doorstep. God may or may not offer guidance; if it comes, it will be in his timing, not ours. On occasions when no particular divine message is discerned, after listening to the other sources of guidance (Scripture, counsel of others), we step out in faith and act with wisdom.

As with any personal relationship, two-way communication is an essential feature in our relationship with God. God the Spirit speaks through his written Word and also through situation-specific guidance for the times we lack wisdom (Jas 1:5). During the early stages of listening for God, some may fear that nothing will happen or they may get it wrong. Mistakes are normal in the learning process. If we wish to deepen our relationship with God, we must grow in our ability to hear God's direct voice to us—in contrast to opposing voices—as it comes from within or in words others speak to us that are freighted with a heightened significance.

Wasting Time with God: Working with a Spiritual Mentor

Seeking advice from others is commonplace. Some today employ the services of a personal trainer to encourage better health and physical fitness. Why a not a trainer of the soul from whom we can receive help in discerning the experience of God in our lives? Spiritual mentoring is a contemplative process carried out within the context of a helping relationship in which the spiritual mentor assists the believer in paying attention, in recognizing God's speaking and activity in the believer's life and in attending to the believer's spontaneous reactions and responses to God's speaking and activity.[67]

Spiritual mentoring is different from pastoral counseling or psychological therapy in which problem solving, decision making and "fixing" the person are the major concerns. Furthermore, it is not purely a theological discussion of Christian doctrine or the nature of God. Rather, it is a dialogue about our relationship with God as evident in the experiences of our life. The mentor helps us learn how to discern God's movement within our life experiences. To what extent in this experience are we moving toward God or away from him? Where is God in this experience? What might God be saying in this experience? Or are we mostly self-absorbed about the matter? Mentoring involves a voluntary relationship of confidentiality and accountability, rather than one of authority over another.

We may wish to locate different spiritual mentors or guides to offer wise counsel at various points in our journey to seek God more. Kenneth Leech suggests five qualities of a spiritual mentor.[68] A primary and essential quality is that the guide be possessed by the Spirit, evidenced in "holiness of life, closeness of God." Second, the mentor should be a person of experience "who has struggled with the realities of prayer and life." Third, a spiritual guide should be one "steeped in the Scripture." Fourth, the spiritual mentor is a person of discernment, "of perception and insight, the man of vision, who can read the signs of times, the writing on the walls of the soul." Finally, he or she is one who "gives way to the Holy Spirit." Such a person is a fellow traveler on the journey to know God.[69] Of course, these wise and holy persons must never take the place of God in our life. Spiritual mentoring is but another means to assist our quest to know God.

Conclusion

The Christian life was not designed to be one lived alone within our own limited human resources, but one lived in cooperation with God the Holy Spirit, in the larger context of the community of believers. The key theme is supernaturally *assisted* living. Cultivating a personal relationship requires a dynamic, experiential communication between two persons. Thus, everyone indwelt by the Spirit must learn experientially how to walk with the Spirit. Because of this critical experiential component, a complete systematic written treatment of the doctrine of the Holy Spirit can never be complete. Much of this teaching about the Holy Spirit is lived out, by persons of differing gender, of differing personalities, of differing abilities and gifts, of differing cultures. Various "styles" of walking by the Spirit are possible and are available for our instruction as we observe other believers. Walking by the Spirit is a unique personal relationship between each believer and God the Spirit, and as with any other personal relationship, the growth of that friendship is specific to those two persons.

The biblical doctrine of guidance opens the way to deepen our relationship with God through two-way communication with God. When we are ready to listen, God the Spirit speaks to us, either giving us the significance of the scriptural passage we are contemplating, offering specific words of guidance for the matter at hand through others or a voice within, or letting a certain feeling overcome us. Either type of communication is distinctly relevant for us and can meet the need of the moment.

Of course, sometimes we may be clueless to any guidance from the Spirit and proceed on our merry way by grieving the Spirit (Eph 4:30).

Normally the Spirit first prompts our awareness (cognitively or emotion-
ally) of a specific need, problem or opportunity. Then we are in a position
to step out and trust God to help us move to the next stage of guidance.
The central point is that in order to listen to the Spirit, we must become
more aware of the Spirit's presence and promptings in our lives. As Bockmuehl notes, "When people listen, God speaks."[70]

  In chapter five, we began an inquiry into the hiddenness of God, into
God's lingering silence and the dark night of the soul. In the midst of suffering, God seems distant and hidden. We are puzzled why a loving God
would permit pain and suffering for his children. What good can come
from such evil? In the next chapter we take up this difficult and perplex-
ing problem.

7

APPRENTICESHIP

YIELDING TO THE GOD
WHO DISCIPLINES

"God disciplines us for our good, that we may share in his holiness. No discipline seems pleasant at the time, but painful. Later on, however, it produces a harvest of righteousness and peace for those who have been trained by it."

HEBREWS 12:10-11

JESUS' EXAMPLE

"Although [Jesus] was a son, he learned obedience from what he suffered."

HEBREWS 5:8

Rebecca had married a pastor known for his ability to facilitate retreats.[1] Only later did she become aware of his fascination with pornography and solicitation of prostitutes during these out-of-town engagements. On occasion he would admit his problem and ask her forgiveness. But eventually he left Rebecca for Julianne. This final abandonment was hard for Rebecca to handle. Furthermore, a few at church favorable to her husband considered that she was the cause of his problem. Regular calls to see her children forced Rebecca to maintain contact with him, painfully pricking her wounded heart with each visit.

But Rebecca was a wise woman, recognizing the two options open to her. Either she could slide down the path of revenge, conveying this bitterness to her children, or she could forgive him. After months of seeking God and wrestling with a wide array of emotions of hurt and pain, Rebecca gave in and released her former husband to God's care. Soon after, carried by God's strength, she phoned him. With a wavering voice she admitted, "I want you to know that I forgive you for what you've done to me. And I forgive Julianne too." With no remorse at all, he rebuffed this gracious gift. Yet Rebecca's public announcement paved the way for peace to grow in her own heart again.

But the story does not end there. After continuing his double life for a few more years, one evening her ex-husband was arrested by the police for prostitution solicitation while attending a ministerial conference. Now Julianne was the devastated woman. Whom did Julianne call to find solace in her own trial? Rebecca! Through tears of regret, Julianne confessed to Rebecca, "I kept telling myself that even if what you said was true, he had changed. And now this. I feel so ashamed, and hurt, and guilty. I have no one on earth who can understand. Then I remembered the night when you said you forgave us. I thought maybe you could understand what I'm going through. It's a terrible thing to ask, I know, but could I come talk to you?" Rebecca, a hero of God's grace, opened her home and her heart that evening to Julianne. And in that place Julianne became a new member of God's family.

Rebecca had wondered, "For a long time, I had felt foolish about forgiving my husband. But that night I realized the fruit of righteousness. Julianne was right. I could understand what she was going through. And because I had been there too, I could be on her side, instead of her enemy. We both had been betrayed by the same man. Now it was up to me to teach her how to overcome the hatred and revenge and guilt she was feeling." God's grace was being passed on to a fellow pilgrim moving through the valley of the shadow of death.

Pondering the Puzzle

"Why sin? Why suffering? Why the devil? These are questions I want to ask the Lord when I get to heaven."[2] Posed by evangelist Billy Graham in an interview with *U.S. News & World Report*, these questions probably echo many believers' bewilderment about God and his purposes. God is good, and a full flourishing of his kingdom of righteousness will certainly come (2 Pet 3:13). Yet suffering is a characteristic of this fallen world with such evils as betrayal, slander, outbursts of anger, disabilities, chronic disease and physical death.

At times, we wonder about the reasonableness of God's plan, for we desire a gentler, kinder world, not the one portrayed on the evening news. Surely God could prevent the tragedies of this life, but suffering continues. Reciting God's promise in Romans 8:28 may be easy: "all things God works for the good," but when the spotlight of suffering stares down on us and our loved ones, it is difficult to determine how any good will come our way. We may wonder if God really cares. Moreover, suffering could very well negatively affect our journey with God. Frances Young notes, "The outcome of suffering is in fact entirely ambiguous and unpredictable—it may ennoble but it often embitters; it may stimulate love and compassion, but it can equally well cause impatience, cruelty and rejection."[3] Why would God wish to endanger our relationship with him?

Questions, uncertainties, reservations. Suffering and evil are difficult topics involving complex issues for which many tomes have been written.[4] Why did God permit evil? Most likely God had a number of wise and complex purposes in mind.[5] My intent is not to offer a solution for the problem of evil, but rather to propose a perspective on suffering for believers that *engenders* rather than *endangers* deepening trust in God. Because while enrolled in God's school of suffering, regardless of the injustices experienced or the culpability of others for doing us harm, we are given an opportunity to deepen our faith and reliance on God. But to make progress, every believer must yield to God's fatherly role as he grows us to become "conformed to the likeness of his Son" (Rom 8:29). The point of this chapter, then, is that it may be easier to yield to God's supervision of our life if we know what good outcomes are possible through suffering.

Thus far in the book we have considered the ministries of two members of the Godhead: how Jesus our sympathetic high priest engaged in a God-oriented lifestyle for us to follow and how the Holy Spirit guides us. Regarding the topics of this chapter on suffering and the next on prayer, God the Father has a distinctive role among the persons of the Trinity. It is the Father who disciplines his children (Heb 12:9), which includes the permission of suffering in our lives (1 Pet 2:23; 4:19). In addition, it is the

Father who answers our prayers (Matt 6:9; Eph 3:14) and the prayers offered by the Son (Rom 8:34; Heb 7:25; 1 Jn 2:1) or the Spirit (Rom 8:26-
27), who petition the Father on our behalf. It is God the Father who initiates the divine decrees and eternal plan (Ps 2:7-9; Acts 1:7; Eph 1:3-14),
as Gordon Lewis and Bruce Demarest explain: the Father "creatively de-
signs and initiates relationships and activities. The point illustrated is not
a time of origin, but a distinctness of activity with sameness of nature. The
first person initiates and purposes."[6]

Being in Training

Every four years the Olympic games herald a showcase of dedication and
dexterity from champions of the world. We are inspired by their grace
and form, by their energy and endurance. Spectators from around the
globe cheer on their native sons and daughters in pursuit of excellence—
from the opening fanfare and entry of the athletes to the medal ceremonies with accompanying national anthems to the closing ceremony. But
our eyes only notice the ecstasy of victory and the agony of defeat. We
may be oblivious to the difficult journey each Olympian undertook to
qualify for the Games—the hours and years of preparation and practice,
of exercise and sacrifice.

Is it really worth all this effort—to get out of bed on a cold and rainy
morning for that daily workout, disrupting normal routines—for a chance
to earn a bronze, silver or gold medal? Is participating in the Olympics
worth the anguish and effort of such training and preparation? Of course,
each and every athlete would do it again—and maybe even train a little
harder. Certainly some questions and doubts may bubble up during a tir-
ing and discouraging workout. But the dedicated athlete eagerly anticipates what might become a reality—a place on the national Olympic
team and a winner's medal. Is it really worth it? That question can only be
answered after participating in the Games, not before.

Very much like these Olympic athletes, believers are also "in training"
during our time on earth. On four occasions in the New Testament, writers tap into such athletic imagery by using the Greek term from which we
get our words *gymnasium* and *gymnastics (gymnazo)*. In 1 Timothy 4:7-8,
this word appears twice within Paul's charge to Timothy: "*Train* yourself
to be godly. For physical *training* is of some value, but godliness has value

for all things, holding promise for both the present life and the life to come" (emphasis added).

The writer to the Hebrews employs the same term on two occasions to challenge his readers to regain their forward momentum in obedience to Christ. "Anyone who lives on milk, being still an infant, is not acquainted with the teaching about righteousness. But solid food is for the mature, who by constant use have *trained themselves* to distinguish good from evil" (Heb 5:13-14, emphasis added). "No discipline seems pleasant at the time, but painful. Later on, however, it produces a harvest of righteousness and peace for those who have been *trained* by it" (Heb 12:11, emphasis added). William Lane explains:

> As athletes engaged in a contest, for whom discipline is the key to their training and perseverance, the members of the house church are challenged to respond appropriately to the abuse and hardships they were experiencing and to remain steadfast. Their sufferings were disciplinary in character and were assigned by God for their benefit. They hold the prospect of joy and rest following painful suffering. . . . The benefits of divine discipline belong . . . "to those who have been trained by it."[7]

Only after the training is complete, can its full effects be best appreciated.

Similarly, the military trains its new recruits through a hellish type of boot camp—an experience one wishes to forget thereafter—in order to prepare for future assignments. In like manner, God is training us now— through this "hell on earth"—to prepare us to enjoy life to its fullest in the next age, when we will experience the richness of his presence and reign with him forever and ever (Rev 22:4-5).

Sharing in the Sufferings of Christ

Was God surprised when Adam and Eve sinned in the Garden of Eden? In his foreknowledge,[8] God planned for this problem prior to creation, as Gordon Lewis and Bruce Demarest note, "If the Father did not know that Adam and Eve would sin, why did he plan in eternity to atone for sin (Acts 2:23)?"[9] In eternity past, the only wise God considered all the worlds he could have made. God deemed that creating this particular world was worth it, despite the grief[10] that he and we would experience. God "reluctantly" employs evil for his varied purposes: "For he does not willingly bring affliction or grief to the children of men" (Lam 3:33).

Yet God did not remain an aloof spectator out of harm's way. Instead, God the Son took on human form and experienced the depth of suffering and shame, for "he himself suffered" (Heb 2:18).[11] "During the days of Jesus' life on earth . . . although he was a son, he learned obedience from what he suffered" (Heb 5:7-8). Apparently human nature is so constituted that suffering can be an aid in maximizing its full potentialities within God's kingdom. As the pioneer of a new kind of human race prepared to do God's will fully, Jesus himself suffered and set the example for us to follow:

> Dear friends, do not be surprised at the painful trial you are suffering, as though something strange were happening to you. But rejoice that you participate in the sufferings of Christ, so that you may be overjoyed when his glory is revealed. (1 Pet 4:12; cf. 2 Cor 1:5; Phil 1:29; 3:10; 1 Pet 2:21)

> Now if we are children, then we are heirs—heirs of God and co-heirs with Christ, if indeed we share in his sufferings in order that we may also share in his glory. (Rom 8:17)

Douglas Moo explains Romans 8:17: "Participation in Christ's glory can come only through participation in his sufferings. What Paul is doing is setting forth an unbreakable 'law of the kingdom' according to which glory can come only by way of suffering."[12] Jesus demonstrates that suffering is an important experience for all humans to accomplish God's purposes. Jesus our King set the pace, demonstrating how to suffer well— how to respond appropriately to trials. Yet for us, growing toward such a Christlike response will take time. Putting on a happy face misses the point, for there was no smile on Jesus' face while enduring agony on the cross. But Jesus was secure in God's sustenance: "Father, into your hands I commit my spirit" (Lk 23:46). It is now our opportunity and privilege to follow him in suffering so we can share in his glory.

As Thomas à Kempis (d. 1471) notes in *The Imitation of Christ*, "If there had been any better thing, and more profitable to the salvation [i.e., sanctification] of man, than suffering, surely Christ would have showed it by word and example. . . . So that when we have thoroughly read and searched all, let this be the final conclusion, 'that through many tribulations we must enter into the kingdom of God' [Acts 14:22]."[13]

Furthermore, during his lifetime the apostle Paul tasted a measure of both: the very heights of God's paradise through special "visions and revelations . . . caught up to the third heaven" (2 Cor 12:1-4 NRSV) and the very depths of pain and suffering:

> I have . . . been in prison more frequently, been flogged more severely, and been exposed to death again and again. Five times I received from the Jews the forty lashes minus one. Three times I was beaten with rods, once I was stoned, three times I was shipwrecked, I spent a night and day in the open sea. . . . I have been in danger from rivers, in danger from bandits . . . have often gone without sleep . . . have often gone without food; I have been cold and naked. Besides everything else, I face daily the pressure of my concern for all the churches. (2 Cor 11:23-28)

Having experienced both, Paul declares, "I consider that our present sufferings are not worth comparing with the glory that will be revealed in us" (Rom 8:18; cf. 2 Cor 4:17). Or as Hebrews 12:10-11 phrases it: "God disciplines us for our good, that we may share in his holiness. No discipline seems pleasant at the time, but painful. Later on, however, it produces a harvest of righteousness and peace for those who have been trained by it." Nothing can compare to the goodness and joy of being in God's full presence, experiencing what saints throughout the ages have longed for, the "beatific vision" of God (Rev 22:4).[14]

Good from Evil?

But surely there is a madness in God's method. That a high road can be taken in response to suffering was evident in Joseph's assurance of forgiveness to his brothers, "You intended to harm me, but God intended it for good" (Gen 50:20). Joseph's trials not only groomed him to become a great leader, but they also had a larger purpose in preparing a place in Egypt for Israel to prosper during a worldwide famine.

In permitting a particular evil in anyone's life, God may be pursuing a number of purposes. Most likely, multiple divine purposes, along with satanic intentions, impact why believers suffer; thus a single reason for suffering may never be the case (e.g., Job 1—2). Unless God offers a particular word of guidance on the matter—as the apostle Paul received (2 Cor 12:7-10)—the exact reason for God's permission of a specific episode of suffering may never be known. Job never received any explanation (Job 38—42). And although we may identify certain benefits from going through a trial, we will never know the full reasons, for "now we see in a mirror dimly" (1 Cor 13:12). As Richard Swinburne explains, "[God] will be so much greater than us in his understanding of which states are good and which are bad that we should expect there to be bad states for which . . . we do not see what greater good they would serve."[15] That is, we do not yet know the rest of the story.

What good might suffering bring for us, given that we are "destined" for trials (1 Thess 3:2-5)? In this chapter, five broad themes of potential benefits are developed.

☐ First and foremost, trials can become an important means to know God better.

☐ Through suffering we learn about the pros and cons of good and evil.

☐ Trials present an opportunity to engage in the cosmic battle with God against Satan and his demonic forces; by resisting Satan and exposing evil, we overcome evil with good through God's power.

☐ In suffering, our character can be formed toward Christlikeness.

☐ Believers can develop a closer unity and love for brothers and sisters as God forms his kingdom community; the caring ministry of God's family is a crucial indirect avenue for receiving God's comfort (2 Cor 1:3-5).

Any of these outcomes or others might be involved in a particular episode of suffering.

Yet, to grow in our friendship with God we must become deeply convinced that God is trustworthy to permit suffering that can serve wise and loving divine intentions. The challenge for believers then is—in the midst of suffering—to keep these good intentions in mind while in the classroom of God's school of suffering. In a manner of speaking, life in this present world of suffering is the closest experience of hell that God's people will ever have, and it is the closest experience of heaven that those opposed to God will ever have. Can we trust how God supervises our lives now to bring his kingdom project to completion in the next age?

The discussion in this chapter may touch more deeply if a particular episode of personal suffering, or that of a loved one, is kept in mind.

Working through the material may provide an opportunity for reflecting and assessing to what extent previous pains have been dealt with in relation to God. Let me share one of mine.

Roller Hockey and Me

My own world came to an abrupt halt in the midst of a friendly game of street roller hockey. At one moment I was enjoying the thrill of the challenge—a middle-aged man racing up and down the street going for a goal, that is, until I stopped the hockey ball with my left eye. The initial pain was immense. As I lay on the street, I tried to open my left eye for the first time, but I could see nothing. The thought crossed my mind: I may be permanently blind in that eye. It turned out I had an internally bleeding eye (hyphema).

The first twenty-four hours were unending pain as Beth and I visited the emergency room three times due to continued vomiting and the rising blood pressure in my eye. After my condition was finally stabilized, the doctor sequestered me to my bedroom, introducing me to a new phase of "living"— doing nothing. My experience did not match the yearning we have to do nothing. Lying in our darkened bedroom as if I were glued to my bed and stack of pillows, I could not move my head for fear my eye would begin to bleed again. The only variety in my day was when Beth drove me to my doctor's appointment every other day. I could listen to cassettes and sing and pray—but spending twenty-four hours, day after day, in the same room, with no physical activity was not a vacation. I had things to do, places to go. But there I was, laid up in bed, going zero miles an hour.

From this experience, I was given an opportunity for a lengthy time of solitude and silence before God—something I had wanted to do but had never taken the time to do. I learned how fruitful times of solitude can be, of taking a break from the routines of life to visit with God. I also experienced an important answer to prayer, which I describe in the next chapter. During those three weeks while being incapacitated, I grew closer to God.

Before moving to the discussion of potential benefits for believers, it may be helpful to clarify a few matters.

Natural and Moral Evil

Evil is usually classified as being either natural or moral. *Natural evil* encompasses the bad we experience from nature or the physical aspects of our world, such as floods, tornadoes and earthquakes; animal life may also be involved (e.g., being bitten by a dog). On the other hand, *moral evil* is that which we experience due to human actions, either by accident or by intention, encompassing such evils as murder, rape, a car accident with a drunken driver, devastation from civil unrest, riots or war. From a theological perspective, "sin against God" would be placed under the category of moral evil. The apostle John states that "sin is lawlessness" (1 Jn 3:4).[16] God defines what is right, what is moral and what is good by his own nature of holiness and righteousness.

One of God's unique endowments central to any discussion of evil is the exercise of free will by humans (and angels and demons)—the gift of decision making and agency.[17] This divine enablement of free will makes it possible for believers, ennobled by God's power, to fulfill certain purposes for which we were created, for example, to love God (Mt 22:37-38; Jn 17:3) and to reign with him (Gen 1:28; Ps 8:6; Rev 22:5). Genuine love is only possible if it is completely voluntary. God desires that in loving God and reigning with him, we learn freely how to choose good and resist evil.

Yet the good of such freedom also makes possible—from the hands of believers and nonbelievers alike—"the virtual inevitability of wrongdoing and suffering if humans are to have the great good of free and efficacious choice."[18] Alvin Plantinga concurs, "The price of creating a world in which [human beings freely] produce moral good is creating one in which they also produce moral evil."[19] In this world, God permits the existence of humans who often exercise their free will to bring about evil, suffering and pain on others.

God's Power and Forms of Divine Protection
Our God is able to bring good from evil. Otherwise we can assume he would not have permitted evil in the first place. As Thomas Aquinas (d. 1274) explains, by quoting Augustine, "Thus Augustine says (Enchir. ii): 'Almighty God would in no wise permit evil to exist in His works unless He were so almighty and so good as to produce good even from evil.' "[20] Furthermore, "if God is for us, who can be against us?" (Rom 8:31). No evil can separate us from God (Rom 8:35-39).

Our frustration about trials may be that we expect God to protect us in certain ways. Scripture suggests a variety of avenues God employs to sustain our journey through trouble. First, God restricts the duration of evil to this lifetime only; evil is not a permanent arrangement for believers. This too shall pass. Within the expansive range of everlasting time, God deemed it valuable to permit evil for the brief moment of a lifespan on this earth, "a mist that appears for a little while and then vanishes" (Jas 4:14). Our true home is with God in eternity, our final resting place.

Second, despite whatever pains we experience physically or psychologically, no evil can scar us forever—although our lives on this earth may involve much travail. God promises that in heaven "there will be no more death or mourning or crying or pain" (Rev 21:4). In the end, God will heal all of our hurts. No evil can or will ever permanently conquer and devastate God's children (cf. Ps 121:7-8; 2 Thess 3:3; 1 Jn 5:18).

Third, God limits the evil we experience in the sense that no evil need overwhelm us when we walk with God. "No temptation has seized you except what is common to man. And God is faithful; he will not let you be tempted beyond what you can bear. But when you are tempted, he will also provide a way out so that you can stand up under it" (1 Cor 10:13).[21] This divine hedge is alluded to by Satan regarding his temptation of Job. Following God's commendation of Job's uprightness, Satan complained about God's protection of Job, "Have you not put a hedge around him and his household and everything he has?" (Job 1:10). In response to the devil's request, God removed some of this protection and permitted Satan to bring harm to Job. Yet God placed distinct restrictions on Satan's evil activity. "Everything he has is in your hands, but on the man himself do not lay a finger" (Job 1:12). And again, "He is in your hands; but you must spare his life" (Job 2:6). This unusual record of an interaction between God and Satan indicates the kind of protection God provides for his children. With God's empowerment we can bear whatever evil that comes our way.

Furthermore, consider the differing ways God restricts the amount of evil believers encounter. Of course, God never guarantees continuing physical life on this planet. Eternal life is sure, yet our physical existence here is not.[22] Once we have received Jesus Christ as our personal Savior and have joined God's family, we could be called "home" at anytime through death—the final experience of evil. Some elderly saints long for that homeward journey, especially after their spouse has gone or when a debilitating illness leaves them significantly incapacitated (cf. 2 Cor 5:6-8). Thus, passage to new life in heaven through physical death is one avenue God uses for protecting believers from evil.

On some occasions God may prevent the effects of harm, although we are in harm's way. For example, the book of Daniel reports the case of three men being thrown into a fiery furnace—"heated seven times hotter than usual"—and yet surviving without even the smell of fire on them (Dan 3:27). Although Daniel stayed overnight in a lion's den, God supernaturally "shut the mouths of the lions" (Dan 6:22). Did not Satan allude to God's "hedge of protection" around Job (Job 1:10)?

For other occasions, God may offer us his special grace and presence in the midst of difficult suffering. As Stephen was being stoned, he had a vision of heaven and saw Jesus Christ standing at the right hand of the Father (Acts 7:55-56). Was it this extra help that made it possible for Stephen to utter these profound words, "Lord, do not hold this sin against them"(Acts 7:60). God's grace was sufficient for Paul, although tormented by "a messenger of Satan" (2 Cor 12:7). And while Paul was imprisoned in Rome, at his first trial, "no one came to my support, but everyone deserted me. . . . But the Lord stood at my side and gave me strength" (2 Tim 4:16-17).

Furthermore, is it possible we have no idea how many times God prevented past harms—that we were unaware of his loving care? Infrequently, a few may get a glimpse of such divine intervention. Was not Elisha's servant oblivious that—despite the encircling force of the Syrian army with horses and chariots—an angelic host of "horses and chariots of fire" surrounded the hills around Elisha (2 Kings 6:17)? But for the grace of God we would experience much greater evils than we actually do. Believers never need fear any evil. "Even though I walk through the valley of the shadow of death, I will fear no evil, for you are with me; your rod and your staff they comfort me" (Ps 23:4).

We consider now the various potential benefits that suffering can bring for believers.

Learning More About God as We Deepen Our Friendship with God

When push comes to shove we become aware of the need to rely on

God's resources and not our own. As we lean more and more on God our friendship flourishes.

1. Reminding us of our dependence. When all goes well, we tend to be forgetful of God's benevolence. Yet all good gifts and blessings come from God (Eph 1:3; Jas 1:17). "When you have eaten and are satisfied, praise the Lord your God for the good land he has given you. Be careful that you do not forget the Lord your God" (Deut 8:10-11). Our experience of evil reminds us that we are not self-sufficient beings, but ultimately dependent on God. We were designed for optimum living only when rightly related to God. How does God get our attention to consider seeking him further? In suffering, believers are placed in a humble position to look to God and listen to him.

2. Testing our friendship. God can use suffering to test our love for him. "Remember how the Lord your God led you all the way in the desert these forty years, to humble you and to test you in order to know what was in your heart, whether or not you would keep his commands" (Deut 8:2). Are we genuine friends who regularly seek each other's company or only fair-weather friends when the times are good? Satan's accusations about Job reiterate this point, "Does Job fear God for nothing? . . . But stretch out your hand and strike everything he has, and he will curse you to your face" (Job 1:9, 11). "Skin for skin! . . . A man will give all he has for his own life. But stretch out your hand and strike his flesh and bones, and he will surely curse you to your face" (Job 2:4-5). As Henry Blackaby and Claude King note, "When you face a crisis of belief, what you do next reveals what you really believe about God."[23] Our response to suffering reveals the quality of our friendship with God.

3. Appreciating more of God's majesty and beauty. God is infinite with varying attributes. One result of a world with evil is that we may see a side of God only evident in this kind of world. We learn the experiential depth of God's multifaceted love for us in challenging times: "But where sin increased, grace increased all the more" (Rom 5:20). As Abraham Kuyper notes, "The angels of God have no knowledge of sin, hence also they have no knowledge of forgiveness, hence again they have no knowledge of that tender love that is formed from forgiveness. Nor have they that richer knowledge of God which springs from this tenderer affection."[24]

Going through these taxing experiences together with God will mark us throughout eternity with a special kind of continuing effect. "And God raised us up with Christ and seated us with him in the heavenly realms in Christ Jesus, in order that in the coming ages *he might show the incomparable riches of his grace,* expressed in his kindness to us in Christ Jesus" (Eph 2:6-7, emphasis added; cf. Rom 9:22-23). In eternity we can share our distinctive stories of God's grace to us.

Learning Experientially That Good Is Best and Evil Is Destructive

A second potential benefit of suffering is that God deems it best that we discover for ourselves how evil, evil is and how good, good is. One of the key issues in the matter of good and evil is the battle for ideas. What is good? What is evil? What way is best? The evidence indicates that at one layer of analysis, God has permitted this world to become the ultimate experiment for exploring alternate ideas and alternate lifestyles—alternate to what God deems is good and true and beautiful. Moreover, if God had only permitted the world Adam and Eve experienced before the Fall, there would always be that lingering "what if?": Is God's way surely the best? Is there a better kind of world than this one? Or more pointedly, if I were God, could I make a better world? Thus, God offers the opportunity to Satan, demons and all human beings—within certain boundaries established by God—to try their hand at discovering what is the best kind of world to live in. Which foundational ideas survive intact the test of time? What kind of lifestyle brings the greatest joy, the greatest productivity, the greatest honor among others?

Moreover, to facilitate the learning process, God has so designed the physical world that it runs—generally speaking—on "autopilot," to yield the order and dependability of "the laws of nature" that scientists discover. Thus, through predictable consequences of events and actions, God offers a means to learn about good and evil, as Swinburne notes:

> If God is to allow us to acquire knowledge by learning from experience and above all to allow us to choose whether to acquire knowledge at all or even to allow us to have very well-justified knowledge of the consequences of our actions—knowledge which we need if we are to have a free and efficacious choice between good and bad—he needs to provide natural evils occurring in regular ways in consequence of natural processes.[25]

Although the physical elements are good (Gen 1:31), they can become dangerous to our health. Water has many good purposes, yet some people drown. Various natural disasters are a normal byproduct of how the world runs (e.g., forest fires from lightning, devastation from earthquakes around the fault lines). Some suffering results from animal predators (e.g., attacks by sharks and snakes). And in some cases, moral and natural evils intersect (e.g., flooding caused by faulty engineering, use of poor construction materials, procedures or neglected maintenance and care of equipment; a forest fire started by a cigarette; abuse of body in one generation passes on bad genes to the next).

But good can also come from evil, as reflected in the two following cases. Daniel Wallace now realizes that a bully's kick to his eight-year-old son's stomach (moral evil) actually saved his life from an undetected malady (natural evil). The son had contracted a rare disease that carries with it few distinctive symptoms and usually results in death. Due to that kick and a providential indiscretion—a bathroom door left open permitting Dan's wife to observe brown urine coming from their son—the Wallaces sought medical treatment that eventually led them out of the danger zone. During their difficult ordeal, Dan reflected on this insight: "In the midst of wondering, of confusion, of crying out to God, I could still see his hand in all this."[26] Or consider the unusual case of three fishermen lost at sea for fifteen days. Along with the destruction wrought by Hurricane Pauline, the winds blew their stranded boat closer to shore and within the vicinity of a vessel that happened to be near.[27]

Sometimes people tend to implicate God when the bad that happens is their own fault. Philip Yancey offers this list of supposed "acts of God":[28]

At the 1994 Winter Olympics, when speed skater Dan Jansen's hand scraped the ice, causing him to lose the 500-meter race, his wife, Robin, cried out, "Why, God, again? God can't be that cruel!" A young woman wrote James Dobson this letter: "Four years ago, I was dating a man and became pregnant. I was devastated! I asked God, "Why have You allowed this to happen to me?" In a professional bout, boxer Ray "Boom-Boom" Mancini slammed his Korean opponent with a hard right, causing a massive cerebral hemorrhage. At a press conference after the Korean's death, Mancini said, "Sometimes I wonder why God does the things he does." Susan Smith, who pushed her two sons into a lake to drown, then blamed a black

car-jacker for the deed, wrote in her official confession: "I dropped to the
lowest point when I allowed my children to go down that ramp into the
water without me. I took off running and screaming 'Oh God! Oh God, no!
What have I done? Why did you let this happen?' "

Yancey wonders, "Exactly what role did God play in a speed skater losing
control on a turn or a teenage couple losing control in a back seat, not to
mention the lethal effect of a boxer's punch or a mother's premeditated
act of violence?"[29] Some evils are preventable. Although accidents happen and honest mistakes are made, nonetheless, the effects of suffering
are not diminished. Regardless, God can bring ultimate good from our
tragedies.

God Uses Evil

Although God cannot be blamed for such evils, we should consider
God's relationship with natural and moral evils. Consider that God can be
involved *directly* with physical evils, but only *indirectly* with moral evils.
Regarding natural disaster, God may directly cause such events as sickness, famine and earthquakes for various purposes for believer and nonbeliever alike (e.g., 2 Sam 21:1; 24:21; 1 Cor 11:30) or to execute his
righteous judgment on nations (e.g., Num 16:33). Isaiah tells us that "I
form the light and create darkness, I bring prosperity and create disaster; I,
the LORD, do all these things" (Is 45:7).

On the other hand, God is never responsible for moral evil. "When
tempted, no one should say, 'God is tempting me.' For God cannot be
tempted by evil, nor does he tempt anyone" (Jas 1:13). Moral evil stems
from disobedience to God. God created very good things (Gen 1:31)
which then could develop a lack of good, thus introducing the potential
that evil could come to this world. It seems that God works indirectly in
moral evil both in a passive and active manner, somewhat similar to his
role in physical evils (e.g., passively: forest fires caused by lightning; actively: causing famines and plagues).

On the passive side, God indirectly brings about moral evil by removing degrees of his presence and gracious blessing, rather than by the creation or addition of any new elements. "But my people would not listen
to me; / Israel would not submit to me. / So I gave them over to their stub-
born hearts / to follow their own devices" (Ps 81:11-12; cf. Rom 1:26, 28).

Is not the primary torment of hell the complete removal of God's presence and the magnificent joy of heaven the full presence of God?

On the active side, God brings about his righteous judgment on peoples through the evil actions of demonic and human agents, whom he holds accountable for their sins. This recurring phrase appears in the prophetic literature: "sword, famine and plague" (e.g., Jer 21:9; 42:17; Ezek 6:11; 14:13-20). In some cases, God initiates the believer's potential encounter with Satan and evil, as indicated in the life of Job. "Have you considered my servant, Job?" (Job 1:8). The apostle Paul testified that "there was given me a thorn in the flesh, a messenger of Satan, to torment me—to keep me from exalting myself!" (2 Cor 12:7 NASB; cf. also 1 Cor 5:5). Satan's activity is also probably manifest, at God's behest, in the "deceiving spirit" from Micaiah's prophecy (1 Kings 22:19-23) and in the "evil spirit from the Lord" that terrorized King Saul after his disobedience (1 Sam 16:14).

Regarding the use of human agents, God appointed Nebuchadnezzar, king of Babylon to capture Judah and other rebellious nations in order to serve Babylon: "I will punish that nation with sword, famine and plague, declares the Lord, until I destroy it by [Nebuchadnezzar's] hand" (Jer 27:8). Yet God would then punish Nebuchadnezzar and the Babylonians for their guilt (Jer 25:12-14). The important distinction is that God permits moral evil but never himself perpetrates it. God uses the evil intentions and actions of human and demonic agents to bring about his good ends.

God's great display of power and wonders in judgment—whether it be the plagues in Egypt or the destruction of nations during the times of the prophets—is offered to demonstrate there is only one God, that all the nations will know that "I am the LORD" (Ex 7:17; Ezek 35:9; 36:38). Benjamin Musyoka explains, "The Western mind looks for evidence; the African mind looks for demonstration of power. The power of the Almighty—this is what leads to submission and worship of God."[30] C. S. Lewis notes the strategic role suffering can play to get our attention: "God whispers to us in our pleasures, speaks in our conscience, *but shouts in our pains:* it is His megaphone to rouse a deaf world."[31]

Why do we never take a pencil and poke it in our eye? Because it is stupid and destructive. Eventually believers will gain this same insight for each of our evil practices that inflict harm on ourselves and others and that dishonor God. As a continuing lesson for believers throughout eternity, might the example of this current evil age be a continuing historical reminder of the destruction of evil?[32] God's ways are best. Through experiencing physical and moral evils—whether from God's passive or active involvement in each—believers can learn that evil truly is a stupid idea (Prov 14:12).

Partnering with God to Defeat Satan and Evil

Besides learning more about God and learning how bad evil is, a third potential benefit of suffering is that engaging in the fight against evil is also good for us. We have the opportunity to join God's battle to crush Satan and evil (Eph 6:10). Until Satan is finally cast into hell by God (Rev 20:10), God permits Satan a range of authority within his own diabolical dominion of darkness (Mt 12:26; Col 1:13; 1 Jn 5:19). The devil gives all his energies to thwart God's purposes and defeat believers. The battle metaphor taps into an important theme within God's grand project.[33] As John Feinberg reminds us, "Yes, we are engaged in a spiritual war. But did you think you could go to war, even be in the front lines of the battle, and never get wounded?"[34]

The expert in evil. Satan is the grand master of evil and the prime mover behind much of the evils of this world, as illustrated in the first chapters of the book of Job. The devil is full of revenge and gets even with those who cross his will (Rev 13:12-17). He is the ultimate whiner (Job 1:9-11; 2:4-5) and faultfinder (Rev 12:10), and will trip up a Christian using any means possible (Eph 6:11-13; 1 Pet 5:8). He opposes what is good—everything for which God stands (Jas 3:14-16).

Rather than banishing Satan to hell (Mt 25:41), God has permitted Satan's existence as part of God's plan for a specified period of time (Mt 8:29; 25:19), along with the angels that followed him (demons, Mt 10:8; evil or unclean spirits, Mt 8:16; 10:1; 2 Pet 2:4). For purposes beyond our ken, God has given Satan a sphere of influence, a kingdom in this world (Mt 12:26), and apparently grants certain requests of Satan (e.g., Job 1—2; Lk 22:31-32).

The devil has the ability to effect natural disasters (e.g., fires and great winds, Job 1:16, 19) and to perpetrate moral evil (e.g., thievery, Job 1:15, 17). His influence is enhanced by those who willingly open themselves to his influence (Mt 8:28-31; 17:15). The apostle Paul describes those who have not experienced God's repentance as being in "the trap of the devil, who has taken them captive to do his will" (2 Tim 2:26). Christians make their own contribution to such moral evil when we sin against God and offer Satan a "foothold" in our lives (Eph 4:27). Moral evil results from the choices and actions of created beings, not God. Yet, in the person of Jesus Christ, God permitted himself to be subjected to the evil of Satan to achieve the ultimate victory over Satan.

The victor. Jesus came to earth "to destroy the devil's work" (1 Jn 3:8), disarm "the powers and authorities" (Col 2:15) and set people free from sin (Rom 8:3-4). But to do so, he personally had to engage in battle with Satan within his humanity—as vulnerable as you and me—to face and overcome the best temptations Satan could ever concoct. In the power of the Holy Spirit, Jesus assaulted the kingdom of evil. He triumphed in his first major devilish skirmish (Mt 4:1-11)—possibly the first time Satan had ever been so resolutely rebuffed. Later in the ministry, after the seventy had returned from their mission and reported how "demons submit to us in your name, . . . [Jesus] replied, 'I saw Satan fall like lightening from heaven' " (Lk 10:17-18).[35] When the Pharisees accused him of being in league with the devil, Jesus proclaimed, "But if I drive out demons by the Spirit of God, then the kingdom of God has come upon you" (Mt 12:28).

The beginning of the end for Satan came at the death and resurrection of our Lord, for "death has been swallowed up in victory" (1 Cor 15:54). Although Satan was doomed at the cross, he now wreaks his havoc on all of God's people. In his high priestly prayer, Jesus asked for our protection, "My prayer is not that you take them out of the world but that you protect them from the evil one. They are not of the world, even as I am not of it" (Jn 17:15-16; cf. 2 Thess 3:3). Jesus, our Lord and King, knows deeply what suffering and temptation is like, demonstrating for all history that it is possible to persevere in temptation and resist Satan in God's power, although it will not be easy. We can follow his footsteps (1 Pet 1:21; 4:13) and defeat Satan and evil.

Engaging in the battle. God may permit Satan to work his evil on us temporarily, as indicated in the life of Job. Victory is achievable when believers keep both of these parties in view: God and Satan. Their differing purposes are evident in the use of the same Greek term, *peirazo*, translated into English as "test," "try," "tempt" or "entice" (cf. Jas 1:2, 13). For example, when Ford Motor Company tests its own cars, the purpose is to improve each car's performance. Yet if another car company were testing Ford's cars, their purpose might be to locate and magnify the weak points with no intent of helping to correct them. The psalmist's insights are helpful to bear in mind (Ps 119): "Before I was afflicted I went astray, / but now I obey your word" (v. 67). "It was good for me to be afflicted / so that I might learn your decrees" (v. 71). "I know, O LORD, that your laws are righteous, / and in faithfulness you have afflicted me" (v. 75).

Yet within any trial there is a potential to fall, which is Satan's primary goal.[36] Although people are responsible for their actions, ultimately people are not the real enemy. For behind any evil action—directly or indirectly—Satan is loitering. "For our struggle is not against [people] flesh and blood, but against [demonic] rulers, against the authorities, against the powers of this dark world and against the spiritual forces of evil in the heavenly realms" (Eph 6:12). The believers' primary battle is not with people—whether they are Christian or not—but rather with these evil principalities (Eph 6:10-13). They can be resisted in the power of the Spirit, as Jesus showed (Jas 4:7; 1 Pet 5:8-9),[37] resulting in the peace of the pilgrim: "Even though I walk / through the valley of the shadow of death, / I will fear no evil, / for you are with me" (Ps 23:4). Unassisted resistance fails, as demonstrated by Adam in the garden—he did not seek God's help to resist Satan—but supernaturally assisted resistance yields victory, as Jesus exemplified in the Garden and on the cross.

As God prepares us to reign with him, we contribute to the enlargement of God's kingdom on this earth by defeating evil as we sin less, resist Satan (1 Pet 5:9), "overcome evil with good" (Rom 12:21) and "expose the [fruitless deeds of darkness]" (Eph 5:11). There are cosmic consequences in each act of resistance to temptation for believers, thus limiting the scope of Satan's kingdom on this earth. God's reign is manifested as we cultivate beauty in the midst of ugliness, offer uplifting music in the midst of a cacophony of noises and proclaim truth that liberates captives held hostage by false ideas.

Forming Christian Character

The fourth potential benefit of suffering affects our character. Just as parents train their children for growth toward maturity, so God the Father "disciplines" believers "for our good, that we may share in his holiness" (Heb 12:10; cf. Job 5:17-18; Ps 119:67, 71, 75; Prov 3:12; Lam 3:33). James tells us that we can grow through trials: "The testing of your faith develops perseverance. Perseverance must finish its work so that you may be mature and complete, not lacking anything" (Jas 1:3-4). Certain character traits can only be developed in the crucible of life (e.g., courage through fear, compassion through suffering, endurance through hardship). Father and actor Tommy Lee Jones reflects on the paradoxical parental task of providing for his children while also helping them grow up: "I don't know how to give my children everything and at the same time make sure they are self-reliant. I've never faced that before. You hope to teach children to respect money without worshipping it, and to manage it well whether they have it or not."[38] God, as our Father, generously provides for us *and* presents opportunities for us to grow up.

Furthermore, in the experience of suffering, our spontaneous response reveals our true character, our current operating beliefs and desires (e.g., 1 Cor 3:1-3). These reactions to suffering offer a window into the state of our soul, as Thomas à Kempis notes. "The beginning of all evil temptations is inconstancy of mind, and little trust in God. For as a ship without a helm is tossed to and fro with waves, so the man who is remiss, and apt to leave his purpose, is in many ways tempted. Fire trieth iron, and temptation [trieth] a just man. We know not oftentimes what we are able to do, but temptations show us *what we are*."[39]

At a practical level, how can believers make progress toward maturity and resist Satan's temptations? The focus must be at a point of awareness of our thoughts, feelings and actions. In order to sin less, believers must become aware of what needs attention (Lev 4:22-23, 27-28; Jas 4:17)—what sin patterns predominate and what temptations to sin tend to surface. Of course, ultimately sin is anything against God's nature, with or without our awareness (Lev 5:17), anything that does not please or glorify God (Rom 3:23; 1 Cor 10:31), as the Westminster Confession affirms. Yet for dealing with trials and temptations at a practical level, the Wesleyan "working" definition of sin offers help. Thus, for practical purposes, consider that what needs attention is "a *voluntary* transgression of a *known* law."[40] We can only address matters about which we are conscious, of which we are aware.

For example, in convicting us regarding a failing which needs attention, God the Spirit may use a variety of means to make us aware, such as
the teaching and study of God's Word, an experience of suffering, the
counsel or admonishment of a close and trusted friend or spouse, or the
inner witness of the Spirit. It is our job to listen and ponder the problem
without defending ourselves. We have various specific sinful patterns habituated deeply in our character that are now done with ease. To gain the
upper hand, believers must find the "place of freedom" in which to resist
Satan.

Only two years ago I realized how angry I was when drivers would cut
me off and do other stupid antics on the road. Admitting to God I was angry was a great step forward. Next I needed to monitor my heart and seek
his perspective on the matter. Two Bible passages helped me. First, I used
Jesus' words on the cross, "Father, forgive them; for they do not know
what they are doing" (Lk 23:34). I became convinced that people genuinely do not understand the full effects of their actions on others, so I began to speak these words at moments of torment on the road. Jesus' words
convicted me: "Anyone who says, 'You fool!' will be in danger of the fire
of hell" (Mt 5:22). I realized I had contempt for people who were created
in God's image (cf. Jas 3:9-10). By attending to my heart, listening to the
Spirit and using these practices over a twelve month period, great
progress was evident. I was excited the day I noticed a driver cutting in
front of me and I experienced no anger at all!

The race in character formation is not a sprint but a marathon—it requires endurance over time. Furthermore, when one is a victim of someone's habitual sin or sinful acts—depending on the depth of evil
suffered—much time may need to pass for a full sense of release of bitterness over the evil. Yet for God's peace to flood our soul, forgiving the per-
petrators of evil is a necessity (Col 3:13). In Rebecca's case—the story
shared at the beginning of the chapter—several months passed before
there was a readiness for her to forgive her ex-husband. She gave up her
desires for revenge and left that in God's hands. God is the avenger of all
evil. We must leave room for God to take vengeance (Rom 12:17-21;
1 Thess 4:6; 2 Thess 1:5-10; Rev 6:9-10).

What is our part? To begin the healing process, we must take these ones who mistreat us to our Father in prayer. "Love your enemies, do good to those who hate you, bless those who curse you, pray for those who mistreat you" (Lk 6:27-28). Of course, this requires God's love and forgiveness to permeate us and heal our souls in the process. We can monitor the kind of prayer we offer to God as an indicator of the healing that is taking place. In being honest with God, in living in a sphere of forgiveness and being a blessing to others, we defeat Satan, and he will flee (Jas 4:7). May the beloved apostle John's commendation be ours: "I write to you, young people, because you are strong and the word of God abides in you, and you have overcome the evil one" (1 Jn 2:14 NRSV).[41]

Hostage negotiator Terry Waite was himself taken hostage in Beirut, enduring four years of solitary confinement. Among his reflections of that difficult time, he noted, "I have learned to embrace solitude as a friend and I no longer experience that aching loneliness that made me such a compulsive individual."[42] Times of suffering and trial will shape and strengthen our character, and in our responses to trials, we can discern where unbelief still reigns in our heart and where there is room to grow.

Forming Christian Community in Love and Unity

Finally, trials can encourage greater unity and love among believers. Crises bond people together into deeper relationships. Through suffering, God provides a means to build community among us by drawing us together when we would naturally tend to remain isolated by ourselves, especially those of us accustomed to a radically individualistic culture. We do not realize how much we need each other until trials invade our life. Believers are given the opportunity to grow in love for each other by giving of themselves and reaching out to others through praying, through meeting needs, and by just being present (Acts 4:32-35; 1 Cor 12:16-27; 1 Pet 5:9). Jesus himself said, "It is more blessed to give than to receive" (Acts 20:35). Swinburne notes that it is "a good thing to be of use, to help, to serve. . . . Helping is an immense good for the helper."[43] Moreover, in our experience of suffering, we are able to identify with the suffering of saints in other parts of the world, growing deeper within our solidarity as fellow members of God's family scattered around the globe (Heb 13:3; 1 Pet 5:9).

Reflecting on the lengthy grief experienced regarding his wife's illness,

Feinberg notes, "Another major factor in helping me to cope, though I did not realize it at the time, was seeing that God and others really do care. . . . In the midst of those feelings [of abandonment and helplessness], God used various people to show me that He and others knew what I was going through and cared."[44]

Paul urges believers to "mourn with those who mourn" (Rom 12:15). Christians need to create safe places within the church family for greater honesty and for raw emotions to flow freely for those in affliction. Certainly God invites openness in sharing our heart of turmoil with him (Ps 38:6-9). Furthermore, believers may need to learn how to comfort those in sorrow. For example, the expression "I know exactly how you feel" must be banned from our lips. Likewise, handing out intellectual explanations of why suffering comes, like some quick-fix-for-the-soul band aids, displays arrogance and is itself hurtful.

Rather, the sorrowful need comfort, a coming alongside, a listening ear, help with basic material needs—these are welcome. Here, caring actions speak louder than words. Feinberg offers this advice for family and friends: "We must show those who are hurting that we really do care. We must show it by our deeds. And by all means, we must show it by not avoiding those who suffer. We must be there, even if only to listen."[45] And when the trial is far past, when there is a readiness to ponder past times of trouble, then there may be open dialogue to glean insights about this sorrowful journey of the past.

Trials only offer an occasion to realize the good that could come. Five broad themes of benefits have been identified, but they are potential, never automatic. Within the affliction, we intentionally must trust God, receive supernatural empowerment and move away from the evil toward the good (e.g., 1 Cor 10:13). The following account beautifully portrays how a person can colabor with God to bless rather than curse a perpetrator of a hideous evil (Rom 12:14).

A Missed Christmas
Five days before Christmas, a lanky ten-year-old got off the school bus in a Miami suburb.[46] A well-dressed middle-aged man approached Hugh. "Hi, I'm a friend of your father's. We're throwing a party for your dad, but I have some questions about what gifts to get him. Could you help me

pick them out? We'll come right back." Wanting to please his dad, Hugh followed the stranger to his motor home, parked two blocks away. In entering that vehicle, Hugh was ushered into a twilight zone of terror that still sends chills up his spine today. It turns out the stranger, David McAllister, was seeking revenge for being fired by Hugh's father. Far out of town on a secluded road, McAllister let Hugh out, shot him in the head and left him to die. Six days later Hugh suddenly awoke from an unconscious state, staggered to the road and was picked up by a passing motorist. The bullet had passed through his left temple, severing the optic nerve and rendering him permanently blind in that eye. Furthermore, no evidence could ever link McAllister to the attempted murder, and so he was never convicted.

Hugh was traumatized. For the first three years he slept on the floor near his parents' bed with a growing sense of insecurity. Additionally, he felt overly self-conscious of his drooping half-shut injured eye. Hugh was fearful and full of resentment. At age thirteen, Hugh sought solace at the neighborhood church and found Jesus, beginning a process of healing and forgiveness and launching him to share his story and his newfound faith. After college and seminary, Hugh was married and a became youth pastor at his local church, fully engaging in life with zest and purpose.

Then in 1996 a phone call brought all the hidden memories of twenty-two years ago to the forefront again. Officer Scherer, who had worked on the original case, had located McAllister in a nursing home nearby and asked if Hugh wanted to confront the man who tried to kill him. The next day, as Hugh walked toward McAllister's room, his stomach began to tighten. McAllister, a withered seventy-seven-year-old, weighing only seventy pounds, initially denied any knowledge of the episode in his usual cocky manner. But then something gave way and he began to cry, taking Hugh's hand in his own frail hand. "I'm sorry. I'm so sorry." With tenderness, Hugh responded, "I just want you to know that I have been blessed. What you did was not the end of meaning in my life. It was a beginning." This opening began a three-week period of almost daily visits. McAllister used to believe that God was something only "suckers believed in," but now he prayed.

The day McAllister died, Hugh told him, "I'm planning on going to heaven, and I want you there too. I want our friendship to continue." The apostle Peter urges us, "Do not repay evil with evil or insult with insult, but with blessing, because to this you were called so that you may inherit a blessing" (1 Pet 3:9). Christopher "Hugh" Carrier won a difficult victory over Satan in working along with God's grace. First Hugh forgave a man who, without a conscience, left him blinded in one eye and lying unconscious for almost a week. Then Hugh became a blessing to that same man, so that McAllister could be released from slavery to Satan and also receive the divine forgiveness freely offered by God. In the battlefield of life, believers must be wary of the real enemy and find the places of freedom to resist their adversary and to bless the victims of Satan, who has "taken them captive to do his will" (2 Tim 2:26).

Wasting Time with God: Lament

Experiencing evil may seem a radical feature of God's plan for us, yet our response of surrender is crucial if we wish to embrace trials so that God's good purposes can be served. Which responses can be constructive to the process and fit with an underlying posture of submission to God? Actually, Scripture records a wide array of reactions that should foster a refreshing honesty to God about our experience. One of the distinctive benefits of experiencing evil, as suggested in this chapter, is that our responses to evil can indicate the present state of our heart. In fact, such trials may be the only clear means we have to discern the depths of our operating beliefs and desires. This hidden blessing offers one important reason for us to begin to welcome trials in our life as God's custom tutoring. It is this unique benefit we need to explore further here.

God desires that we bare our soul to him. We can fully open our hearts and acknowledge our thoughts and feelings before God; he invites us to be honest. How honest? The holy Scriptures record the complaints of disappointed saints. Although we usually turn to the book of Psalms for songs of praises to God, we can also find solace here when suffering invades our soul. Does King David's plea express the cry of your heart sometimes?

> My God, my God, why have you forsaken me?
>   Why are you so far from saving me,
>   so far from the words of my groaning?
> O my God, I cry out by day, but you do not answer,
>   by night, and am not silent. (Ps 22:1-2)

Among the 150 psalms, the largest category consists of laments. Daniel Harrington suggests that believers should read and meditate on these lament psalms to "help sufferers develop a vocabulary about their condition, raise the theological issues at stake in their suffering, and recognize that as human beings and religious people we belong to a community of fellow sufferers" [Heb 13:3; 1 Pet 5:9].[47]

Bingham Hunter asks, "What can you tell God, if he knows everything? . . . The point is that since God already knows *everything* about you and still loves you, then there is nothing you can tell him that will change his feelings for you. . . . Nothing you ever tell God will cause him to turn his back on you."[48] What comfort God offers us. What an invitation to bare our soul to one who loves and accepts us unconditionally, as affirmed by David, "Surely you desire truth in the inner parts" (Ps 51:6).

Furthermore, Deryck Sheriffs claims that in the Old Testament, confrontation with God is shown to be an important component of our relationship with God. Consider the classic example of Job, who experienced tragedy upon tragedy. First roving bands of raiders stole his wealth; then natural disasters took away his sons and daughters. Finally, he experienced such physical agony in his sickness that he despaired of life. Where was God for Job? "Why do you hide your face and consider me your enemy?" (Job 13:24). "I cry out to you, O God, but you do not answer; I stand up, but you merely look at me" (Job 30:20). Sheriffs notes, "Job and Jeremiah are outstanding models of an Old Testament spirituality that has room for confrontation with God. The strength of their relationship with God allows for the use of the strongest language, language that both questions God, demands his response, argues and expresses anger."[49] Sheriffs explains that "confrontation is a part of intimacy, albeit a hazardous one. . . . Intimacy and confrontation with God are very evidently part of Old Testament spirituality. . . . Jeremiah and Job go beyond lament to confront God with the full force of their feelings."[50] Is this kind of relational openness common in our circles? Perhaps writing a contemporary psalm of lament—even confrontation with God—is one avenue of redress.

Disappointment with God's apparent absence is a common feeling, whether in biblical times or our times. Have we ever wondered that we were in some kind of limbo, just spinning our wheels and getting nowhere? Others were out playing in the game of life, but there we sat on the bench, watching life go by. That may have been how Joseph felt from ages seventeen to thirty. Sold into slavery by his brothers at age seventeen, Joseph was then falsely accused and languished in prison during what he may have thought were his prime years of his life; yet God blessed the work of his hand (Gen 39:21). Such in-between times may seem hard to endure.

But after some of the tears and sorrow have subsided, there will be time for further reflection: "What are you teaching me, Lord?" Such an inquiry captures the instructive spirit of welcoming trials. And we can share our concerns and anxious thoughts with God (Phil 4:6; 1 Pet 5:7). Consider these reflections from philosopher Nicholas Wolterstorff after the untimely loss of his adult son. In the preface to *Lament for a Son* he writes, "I wrote the following to honor our son and brother Eric, who died in a mountain-climbing accident in Austria in his twenty-fifth year, and to voice my grief. Though it is intensely personal, I have decided now to publish it, in the hope that it will be of help to some of those who find themselves with us in the company of the mourners." [51] Although warned against rehearsing his regrets of neglecting to do more with Eric, Wolterstorff opines, "I shall allow the memories to prod me into doing better with those still living. And I shall allow them to sharpen the vision and intensify the hope for that Great Day coming when we can all throw ourselves into each other's arms and say, 'I'm sorry.'"[52] What is God prodding in our life through past trials?

In suffering we are in God's classroom. No matter what purposes God may be achieving for others, God wishes for us to grow in our relationship with him, to form our character, to grow in community within his family and to defeat Satan. God the Spirit will prompt our growing awareness of what is still lacking in our lives.[53]

Wasting Time with God: Advocacy

Besides openly displaying our grief, another important response to suffering is to do good and so overcome evil (Rom 12:20-21), to be an advocate for God's righteousness and justice in a world where Satan is active and much suffering abounds (Prov 31:8-9). "And what does the Lord require of you? To act justly and to love mercy and to walk humbly with your God" (Mic 6:8). Much of the Old Testament prophetic ministry dealt with matters of injustice, oppression and suffering resulting from the selfish actions of kings, priests and the rich within Israelite society. As a result, God expressed a particular concern for the orphan, the widow and the alien (Deut 10:18-19; 24:17; Ps 94:6; Is 1:17; Jer 7:5-7; Zech 7:8-10). Walter Brueggemann explains, "Thus 'widow, orphan, alien' are ciphers for those most vulnerable and powerless and marginated in a patriarchal society, who are without legal recourse or economic leverage."[54] The New Testament reaffirms this commitment: "Religion that God our Father accepts as pure and faultless is this: to look after orphans and widows in their distress" (Jas 1:27) and to "remember those in prison as if you were their fellow prisoners, and those who are mistreated as if you yourselves were suffering" (Heb 13:3; cf. 1 Pet 5:9).[55]

Advocacy will involve being God's representative in our daily encounters, looking for those who cannot defend themselves and those in need. Robert Pazmiño notes, "As Christians we have an advocate, the Lord Jesus Christ, who represents us (1 Jn 2:1). We as Christians must stand up for those who may not have an advocate."[56] As believers, we should become alert to matters of fairness and injustice.[57] Within our spheres of influence, we need to ask, Who needs justice, who needs a helping hand to get basic needs met at home, at work, at school, at church, in the neighborhood? We can ask the Lord to bring to mind one who needs help this day.[58]

Let me share one of the opportunities I've had. During a tour of duty with the U.S. military, Jerry and Jill Smith[59] sensed God's leading to the mission field. Following seminary graduation—each with their own earned degree—they joined a well-respected evangelical missionary organization to serve God in a needy part of the world. While they were still engaged in deputation, speaking in churches to develop prayer and financial sponsors, I received a plaintive telephone call from them. Without any warning and without a clear rationale, the missionary leadership had pulled the plug on them. Jill and Jerry were out of the mission—they had been fired for no substantial reason! Rumors shot up like weeds surrounding them. Formerly sought after by churches as missionary candidates, they were now outcasts, tarred and feathered by false accusations.

Since I saw no basis for the dismissal, I became an advocate for Jerry and Jill to the mission agency. I wrote detailed letters and met with a few personnel and presented the actual lifestyle of our friends to counter misinformation. For example, one rumor labeled them as being on the spendy side of the ledger, substantiated by evidence of owning a Mercedes and dressing expensively. The Smiths actually drove a used Volvo and cautiously lived on a shoestring budget during seminary—we helped them buy groceries now and then. Jill had a knack for finding bargain clothes so that with a small wardrobe and great creativity, the family dressed well. After much grief and effort, a day-long meeting was scheduled and led by a representative of the Christian Mediation Service. I never did get a clear reason for the dismissal, but the mission organization finally provided an undisclosed statement and monetary compensation for significant lost financial support so the Smiths could continue deputation with another sending agency. If I had not gotten involved, I am not certain the matter would have received any further attention by the mission agency.

What matters could use your advocacy? What injustices might prevail without your efforts to make a difference?

Conclusion

Puzzling as it is, God has permitted evil in the world to bring about good for his kingdom program *and* for us. Can we trust God, yield to him and welcome trials of our life? We must admit that we do not always know the rest of the story—we may never know why some evils come our way. The varied goals of God's kingdom project are probably as complex as God is. God's purposes for specific instances of suffering may become obvious much later, or they may elude us our whole life. Regardless, we must leave room for God's greater wisdom. God has not revealed his full plans in the Bible (Deut 29:29). But in all that God does, his goodness is assured (Rom 8:28).

The crises that come our way offer an opportunity to listen to God, to welcome his work in our heart, no matter which individual perpetrated this evil. Are we open to what God wants to teach us? Such suffering may offer an opportunity to know God better, to learn the destructive consequences of evil, to do battle with God against Satan and all evil, to grow in our own character, and to grow in friendship and community with other believers.

Will God seriously consider our prayers for protection from suffering, for healing in the midst of illness? What other kind of requests can we make to God? In the final chapter, we ponder Jesus' promise to answer prayer (Jn 15:7) as an invitation for believers to make requests to God. Yet how does this fit within God's rule of world affairs? Furthermore, why pray if God already knows the requests and he already has a master plan for the future? Does prayer just change me? Or does prayer actually change things? To these important issues we now turn.

8

PARTNERSHIP

ASKING THE GOD WHO ANSWERS

"If you remain in me and my words remain in you,
ask whatever you wish, and it will be given you."

JOHN 15:7

"You do not have, because you do not ask God."

JAMES 4:2

JESUS' EXAMPLE

Peter remembered and said to Jesus, "Rabbi, look! The fig tree you cursed has withered!"
"Have faith in God," Jesus answered. "I tell you the truth, if anyone says to this mountain, 'Go, throw yourself into the sea,' and does not doubt in his heart but believes that what he says will happen, it will be done for him. Therefore I tell you, whatever you ask for in prayer, believe that you have received it, and it will be yours."

MARK 11:21-25

To my shame I could have been described as a functional atheist for much of my Christian life in the matter of prayer. Why bother making any specific requests if God had already scripted every detail of my life—and everyone else's—without genuinely considering our prayers? Of course, I regularly talked with God, but I did not persist in prayer. Since it seemed to me that God was going to do what he wanted to do anyway, I believed my particular prayer was inconsequential to the final outcome.

But my perspective was jolted because of an accident through which God visited me in a special way by answered prayer. As I described in chapter seven, in the midst of a friendly game of roller hockey, my left eye was blinded by a hockey ball. A week later at the office visit on Friday, my ophthalmologist confirmed suspicions that more bleeding had occurred. Although hesitant to take this step earlier, he now advised me I must undergo surgery on Wednesday. He would flush the blood from the eye to aid the cleansing process. Beth and I were discouraged by the prognosis, but encouraged that some relief might come. Later that day, while listening to a cassette tape on the subject of prayer from Luke 18, I was challenged to persist in prayer and to pray specifically.

Had I really prayed persistently and specifically about my eye? Oh, I did talk to God about my injury and ask him to heal me—but I felt something was lacking. So I took up the challenge with the invasive eye surgery only two days away. "Would you heal my eye, or tell me why the surgery is necessary?" Monday night I went to sleep with anticipation. Tuesday morning came with no change, but I kept praying. On surgery morning, I slowly opened my left eye. Still no change. But I kept praying. Surgery was scheduled for 11:00 a.m. Beth drove me to the hospital, and my nurse, Betty, helped me get ready for the operating room with reassurance and humor.

Having just finished his previous operation, the ophthalmologist examined my eye one more time before going into surgery. And then the sweetest words flowed from his lips, "Your eye is making such progress that we don't need to do the surgery." I was stunned. I sensed even the doctor was taken aback at this development. He asked us if we had done anything differently, to which Beth quickly replied, "We prayed about it." That day became a watershed event for me in my relationship with God. I gained more confidence that God answers my specific prayers.[1] That day, God showed me he cared about the details of my life.

Accounts of answered prayer can lift our hearts as they send chills down our spine. Unfortunately, such stories can also discourage and overwhelm us with embarrassment. When discussing certain aspects of Christian living, some react by falling headlong into a slough of despondency, with self-flagellating strokes of remorse and resolutions to do better tomorrow. Take courage. This chapter does *not* attempt to play the strings of guilt to make readers feel unworthy and shameful about any lack of prayer. Rather, prayer is a grand opportunity God makes available to each believer for a variety of divine purposes.

The word *prayer* can encompass various aspects in our communion with God: worship and adoration, mourning and confession, praise and thanksgiving, as well as intercession for others and petitions for ourselves. Although all of these elements are crucial in a dynamic relationship with God, the focus of the chapter will be on prayer as request. My own frustration with prayer has primarily been in the arena of intercession and petition.

Prayer as Request

Does it appear too self-serving to devote an entire chapter to prayer as request? Not according to Jesus. The exemplary prayer given to his disciples and to us in the Sermon on the Mount includes a request in each line of the prayer (Mt 6:9-13; Lk 11:2-4), as John MacQuarrie notes:

> Christian prayer has always been basically a prayer of asking. When the disciples asked Jesus to teach them to pray, he did not respond by advising them to meditate on the good nor did he teach them sophisticated techniques of contemplation. He told them to ask, to seek, to knock; and the model prayer that he taught them is one that consists of a series of petitions. It is quite unmistakably a prayer of asking. In the teaching of Jesus Christ, therefore, the primary meaning of prayer is asking. In the modern situation, we may find that embarrassing, but I do not think we can get away from it. Indeed, prayers of petition, supplication, and intercession have from the beginning had a prominent place both in the public liturgy of the church and in private devotions of individual Christians. We cannot even repeat the Lord's Prayer without affirming, through our very act of repeating it, our commitment to that kind of prayer.[2]

Our core beliefs about God and how he runs his world will impact our prayer life. As Wayne Grudem explains, "If we were really convinced that prayer changes the way God acts, and that God does bring about remarkable changes in the world in response to prayer, as Scripture repeatedly teaches that he does, then we would pray much more than we do. If we pray little, it is probably because we do not really believe that prayer accomplishes much at all."[3] Consider the blunt honesty of Jean-Jacques Rousseau (d. 1778): "I bless God for his gifts, but I do not pray to him.

Why should I ask him to change for me the course of things, to work miracles on my behalf? I who ought to love above all the order established by his wisdom and maintained by his providence."[4]

But Scripture teaches that God answers prayer. "Then the Father will give you whatever you ask in my name" (Jn 15:16). From his unlimited bounty, God the Father[5] provides generously for our daily needs. John R. Rice (d. 1980) underscores this claim: "The outside, unbelieving world expects to get things [solely] by work or by planning or by scheming or by accident; *but God's children are taught that they are to get things by asking and that the reason we do not have is because we do not ask.*"[6]

I have found that greater effectiveness in petitionary prayer has propelled my participation in other aspects of communion with God. This chapter presents the results of a personal quest to learn more about God's viewpoint. In the process, my prayer life is being rejuvenated, and I am seeing more answers to prayer. Just as laborers grow closer as they work together, so we can grow deeper in our friendship with God as we labor with God in prayer to accomplish his kingdom goals.

Prayer and Friendship with God
Our friendship with God opens up the possibility of prayer, as Simon Chan explains: "Petition makes perfectly good sense when it is understood in the context of friendship, not in the context of physical cause and effect. . . . Real asking, giving and receiving are deep interchanges between friends."[7] In the Greco-Roman world, one of the marks of a true friend, as opposed to a flatterer, was candor or "frankness of speech" (Gk., *parresia*)—a freedom to speak one's mind (cf. 1 Thess 2:2, 5).[8] Interestingly, this term appears in the New Testament in the context of praying to God, usually translated as "confidence" (see Eph 3:12, also translated as "freedom" or "boldness" NASB).

> Let us then approach the throne of grace with *confidence* so that we may receive mercy and find grace to help us in our time of need. (Heb 4:16, emphasis added)

> Dear friends, if our hearts do not condemn us, we have *confidence* before [toward] God and receive from him anything we ask, because we obey his

commands and do what pleases him. (1 Jn 3:21-22, emphasis added; cf.
1 Jn 5:14-15)

In his commentary on the epistles of John, Stephen Smalley explains:

> The Christian's courage, in the presence of God . . . arises from a right
> relationship to him. . . . The words . . . "toward God," express the idea of
> (a friendly) relationship (between God and his own), as well as the *direction* of the Christian's confidence. . . . The child of God, who walks in the
> light and obeys the love command (cf. 1:7, 2:6, 10), has the privilege of
> "bold speech" in the presence of God.[9]

For example, note the boldness of Martin Luther (d. 1546) in a letter to
Frederick Myconius (d. 1546). On receiving his friend's farewell correspondence informing Luther of impending death due to a serious illness,
Luther immediately replied, "I command thee in the name of God to live
because I still have need of thee in the work of reforming the church. . . .
The Lord will never let me hear that thou art dead, but will permit thee to
survive me [Myconius survived Luther by two months]. For this I am praying, this is my will, and may my will be done, because I seek only to glorify the name of God."[10] As one becomes more comfortable in God's
presence, frankness of speech increases.

Petitionary prayer is but one component of an ongoing communion
with God, in which friends share deep thoughts and feelings of the heart
and make requests of each other. Through wrestling in prayer we come to
know who God really is. As Dallas Willard indicates, "Prayer, it is rightly
said, is the method of genuine theological research, the method of understanding what and who God is."[11]

Images of Prayer

As we waste time with God in focusing our attention and God's attention
through prayer, we grow deeper in our friendship with God. Contrast two
analogies of prayer. In the first analogy, prayer is like being a customer in
a restaurant. After perusing the options on the menu, we place our order
and wait for the complete meal to be served. Outside of placing the order,
our posture is rather passive.

In the second analogy, prayer is more like the actual preparation of the
meal—what takes place in the kitchen of the restaurant. Here, God is the

chief chef and the one who provides the power and resources: stove, oven, refrigerator, pots and pans, food. Our role is to labor with God in bringing the ingredients together and, relying on his power and guidance, to develop the meal for the customer. Salads are easier to prepare than entrées. Some foods must simmer longer. Most recipes require a certain sequence in preparation. As we learn how to colabor with God and sweat the details with him, the chief chef trains us to become trustworthy chefs whom he can eventually set free in his kitchen to serve others.

And so it is as we partner with God in prayer—it is a process in which we play a very active role. Along the way, God mentors us to enhance all aspects of our prayer life. We improve our proposals and requests by studying the kind of answers God provides, as well as by pondering the missing elements when answers do not come. Ultimately, after we have been fully trained, God will let us reign with him in his kingdom forever and ever (Ps 8:6; Rev 22:5).

In this final chapter we explore our partnership with God in prayer. I am surprised that I can now offer some suggestions about how to improve a person's prayer life. This has not always been the case. As theologians Gordon Lewis and Bruce Demarest note, *"Any view of God's predestination or providence that keeps people from praying indicates something out of line with the Bible's teaching."*[12] Since I had little urgency for petitioning God, I knew something was wrong about my view of God and prayer. Furthermore, published explanations of prayer and divine sovereignty left little motivation for making requests to God. Yet I have become convinced that God has so designed his eternal plan that he can genuinely respond to our requests. *Prayer can change things.* God does respond to our prayers simply because we ask. The basis for such "impetratory" prayer[13] comes from James 4:2: "You do not have because you do not ask."

In the following pages we first consider the scriptural teaching that God genuinely responds to our prayers with Old Testament examples and Jesus' promise in the New Testament. We then look at why God might be so responsive. Finally, we explore how to pray, with some guidelines regarding the practical and logistical matters of prayer.

Room Within God's Plan for Answered Prayer

By using the phrases "God changes his mind" or "God relents" (employing the Hebrew word *nicham*),[14] Scripture communicates the important principle that God considers the actions of people in his decision regarding how he will act, implying a measure of responsiveness in how God runs the universe. The general principle is recorded by Jeremiah.

> If at any time I announce that a nation or kingdom is to be uprooted, torn down and destroyed, and if that nation I warned repents of its evil, then I will relent and not inflict on it the disaster I had planned. And if at another time I announce that a nation or kingdom is to be built up and planted, and if it does evil in my sight and does not obey me, then I will reconsider the good I had intended to do for it. (Jer 18:7-10)

Relenting is one of God's attributes, as noted in two passages: "Return to the LORD your God, for he is gracious and compassionate, slow to anger and abounding in love, and he relents from sending calamity. Who knows? He may turn and have pity and leave behind a blessing" (Joel 2:13-14). Jonah uses a similar list of attributes in his reply to God (Jon 4:2). Furthermore, God had been so gracious to the rebellious nation of Judah that he grew weary of their backsliding: "I am tired of relenting!" (Jer 15:6 NASB).

This particular Hebrew word for relent is employed in four instances where God "changed his mind" in response to a request. Moses prayed that God would not destroy the Israelite nation after the golden calf episode: "Then the Lord relented and did not bring on his people the disaster he had threatened" (Ex 32:14). Later, elders of Judah, anticipating their own potential calamity during the days of Jeremiah, reminded themselves of the time when God responded to King Hezekiah's prayer regarding Assyria's assault on Judah (2 Kings 18:14—19:37). "Did not Hezekiah fear the Lord and seek his favor? And did not the Lord relent, so that he did not bring the disaster he pronounced against them?" (Jer 26:19). During the time of Amos, as God was revealing his impending judgment on Israel, the prophet asked God twice to change his mind. "Then I cried out, 'Sovereign Lord, I beg you, stop! How can Jacob survive? He is so small!' So the Lord relented" (Amos 7:5-6). And in the book of Jonah we read that the king of Nineveh declared a fast in response to Jonah's preaching, "Who knows? God may yet relent" (Jon 3:9), and God did.

What about passages that record God does not change his mind? In examining the immediate contexts, one learns that these are specific pronouncements—involving the same Hebrew word for relent—to signify the finality of God's resolve in carrying out particular actions: to bless his people and not curse them (Num 23:19-20), to declare Messiah as a priest forever (Ps 110:4) and to pronounce certain judgment on King Saul (1 Sam 15:29) and Judah (Jer 4:28; cf. Ezek 24:14). But outside of these four specific instances Scripture emphasizes the characteristic posture of a God who relents: "You are a gracious and compassionate God, slow to anger and abounding in love, a God who relents from sending calamity" (Jon 4:2).[15]

The earnest prayers of famous biblical persons demonstrate that they believed God would actually respond to their prayer. For example, in the heat of battle Joshua prayed: " 'O sun, stand still over Gibeon, / O moon, over the Valley of Aijalon.' / So the sun stood still, / and the moon stopped, / till the nation avenged itself on its enemies" (Josh 10:12-13). The editorial commendation highlights God's responsiveness: "There has never been a day like it before or since, a day when the Lord listened to a man" (Josh 10:14).[16]

King David, too, believed God would respond to his prayer. Following his sin with Bathsheba and his admission of sin, the prophet Nathan declared God's judgment: "The Lord has taken away your sin. You are not going to die. But . . . the son born to you will die" (2 Sam 12:13-14). Before the child passed away, David fasted and pleaded with God, despite a divine pronouncement of death. Why? "While the child was still alive, I fasted and wept. I thought, 'Who knows? The LORD may be gracious to me and let the child live.' " (2 Sam 12:22).

After reigning for fifteen years over Judah, King Hezekiah became deathly ill around the age of thirty-nine. The prophet Isaiah announced to the king, "This is what the LORD says: Put your house in order, because you are going to die; you will not recover" (2 Kings 20:1). Yet Hezekiah believed God might change his mind, and he prayed and "wept bitterly" (2 Kings 20:3). The divine response was "I will add fifteen years to your life" (2 Kings 20:6). All of these scriptural cases present a pattern that God is responsive to the initiatives of his people.

Always One Best Way?

Is God moved in prayer because believers have a better idea or plan? Of course not; no one can instruct God (Is 40:13-14). Then what room is there for prayer if, as one theologian summarizes, "God's wisdom means that God always chooses the best goals and the best means to those goals"?[17] But is that assumption correct that there is always only one best means to reach every goal? Is it not the case that, for many of life's situations, several equally good means could be selected? Reflect on your own experience about this point. For example, does it matter how a person keeps track of a daily schedule (e.g., a desk notebook, a pocket scheduler, a computer notepad)? Is there room for creativity and individual preferences in accomplishing many of life's tasks? Why not in prayer?

If it is the case that sometimes several equally good means can accomplish the same basic goal, then there is flexibility within God's overall plan to permit his children to have their preferences be actualized.[18] Consider the following examples in which God defers to the preferences of others in selecting means to accomplish a certain task.

To offer an acted parable, God required the prophet Ezekiel to eat barley cake cooked over human dung (Ezek 4:12). Ezekiel protested, "Not so, Sovereign LORD! I have never defiled myself." (4:14). "Very well," [the LORD] said, "I will let you bake your bread over cow manure instead of human excrement" (4:15). God lets Ezekiel's preference for cow dung stand over his own for human dung.[19] The particular means used seems inconsequential to God's overall intentions. In a similar vein, consider God's response to Moses. Although God wanted Moses to be his spokesman to Pharaoh and was angry with Moses' request that he use another, God still answered Moses' request by letting Aaron be the spokesman for Moses (Ex 4:13-14).

Or consider an example from 1 Kings 22, where we witness a scene in the court of heaven. During the days of the kings, God asked, "Who will entice Ahab into attacking Ramoth Gilead and going to his death there?" (1 Kings 22:20). Among those assembled of the heavenly host, various strategies were suggested until one proposed to become "a lying spirit in the mouths of all of his prophets" (1 Kings 22:22). God affirmed the success of this tactic and commanded the evil spirit to perform the task.[20] The objective was set by God, but God did not unilaterally decide the means, since various means were considered.

In a similar way, when King David had sinned by conducting a census of the people of Israel, God offered David three possible measures of punishment from which to choose. "Shall there come upon you three years of famine in your land? Or three months of fleeing from your enemies while they pursue you? Or three days of plague in your land?" (2 Sam 24:13). If there is always only one best means, why did God offer David three possible punishments?

The biblical data suggest two general categories of divine actions. In some cases, God *alone* determines the means, and Scripture records a divine *unconditional* statement for which God never changes his mind (e.g., not to curse Israel, Num 23:19; the death of King David's infant, 2 Sam 12:14). In other cases, God's pronouncement is *conditional*—permitting some measure of flexibility and responsiveness in God's plans—for which God might change his mind (e.g., added years for King Hezekiah, 2 Kings 20:1, 6; deliverance of the Ninevites, Jon 3:4, 10). As Robert Chisholm explains:

> Sometimes God's promises and warnings are not clearly marked as unconditional or conditional. This explains why the recipient of a divine warning sometimes does what is appropriate and then says, "Who knows? He may turn and have pity" (lit., "change his mind," Joel 2:14; see also Jon. 3:9). One must wait and see how God responds in order to know if the divine announcement is conditional or unconditional.[21]

If there is no one best way, and there are various good options from which to select, does it matter that God permits humans to influence the choice?[22] God sometimes answers prayer that is initiated by his people.[23] Willard comments:

> And God's "response" to our prayers is not a charade. He does not pretend that he is answering our prayer when he is only doing what he was going to do anyway. Our requests really do make a difference in what God does or does not do. The idea that everything would happen exactly as it does regardless of whether we pray or not is a specter that haunts the minds of many who sincerely profess belief in God. It makes prayer psychologically impossible, replacing it with dead ritual at best.[24]

Prayer *does* change things.

Divine Purposes in Responding to Prayer

But why might an omniscient God permit finite persons to have any say in how he runs his universe? Because getting what we ask for is *not* the main point. God actually has a number of purposes for instigating this process of asking and receiving. For example, as we waste time with God in petitionary prayer, our conversation with him enriches our relationship. Moreover, whenever stories of his provision through prayer are made known, believers are reminded to look to God—the God who exists and who supernaturally intervenes in our lives. John R. Rice proposes that answered prayer is the main way to alleviate our doubts about God and to help our young people grow in their faith in God.

> And until God's people can have definite, remarkable, provable answers to prayer, then we had just as well expect that our young people will grow up doubting that there is a miracle-working, prayer-hearing and prayer-answering God. The remedy for unbelief is that God's people shall pray and have their prayers answered. . . . How doubts would flee away if we should begin to pray boldly and definitely and expect God to give concrete and specific answers to our prayers day by day![25]

But more important, a major purpose for prayer—to be developed further in the following section—is that God is grooming us to reign with him in his kingdom. Why does God permit our preferences to be actualized in instances where one means is as good as another? Because God can develop our decision-making and leadership abilities by transforming for the better how we petition God and partner with him to do kingdom work

An Invitation to Participate in Leadership

God created humanity in his image with the privilege of ruling the earth (Gen 1:27-28; Ps 8:6). Since Christ's first coming, believers have been invited to reign with the Son in the age to come: "To him who overcomes, I will give the right to sit with me on my throne" (Rev 3:21); "his servants will serve him. . . . And they will reign for ever and ever" (Rev 22:3, 5). "For your Father has been pleased to give you the kingdom" (Lk 12:32; cf. Dan 7:18, 27; Jas 2:5). In the future, God's intention is to share leadership and decision making among believers regarding the affairs of his kingdom.

If he wished, God could run the world more efficiently if he did it

alone. But one of his kingdom purposes is to delegate a measure of ruler-
ship to believers. We are now in training, since wisdom in leadership
does not come fully functional at natural birth or at spiritual birth. Just as
parents supervise the growth of their children to adulthood, so God is
now growing us to learn how to rule well.

Instances in the Bible of significant human participation in God's
realm include, for example, Adam's first act of naming the animals:
"[God] brought [the animals] to the man to see what he would name
them; and whatever the man called each living creature, that was its
name" (Gen 2:19). In addition, God delegates to parents the unique privilege of bringing into existence children who never existed before ("be
fruitful and increase in number," Gen 1:28). Furthermore, God the Spirit
invited various persons throughout history to coauthor the holy Scriptures, our only authoritative standard of truth ("but men spoke from God
as they were carried along by the Holy Spirit," 2 Pet 1:21).

To illustrate God's invitation to participate in decision making and his
willingness to grant requests, consider Abraham's unusual prayer. He ne-
gotiated with God over what criterion would be used to judge Sodom and
Gomorrah. "What if there are fifty righteous people in the city? Will you
really sweep it away and not spare the place for the sake of fifty righteous
people in it? . . . Will not the Judge of all the earth do right?" (Gen 18:24-
25). Each time God granted Abraham's request: if there are 50, or 45, or
40, or 30, or 20, or even 10? (Gen 18:24-32). Yet only four righteous people were found—Lot, his wife and two daughters—so the city could not
be spared from God's judgment.

Unfortunately, ancient scribal editing of Genesis 18:22 has obscured
the importance of God's implicit invitation for Abraham's request. Our
English versions read, "The men [two angels] turned away and went toward Sodom, but Abraham remained standing before the LORD." Actually,
the original text states that the *Lord* waited, as the NIV marginal note reads:
"an ancient Hebrew scribal tradition *but the LORD remained standing before Abraham.*" Terence Fretheim explains, "The subjects were reversed
by scribes who thought it indecorous for God to stand before a human
being. 'Remained' refers more appropriately to God, who remains behind
while the two men depart. God seeks to communicate with Abraham, not
the other way around."[26] After announcing the great sin of Sodom and

Gomorrah, God said, "Shall I hide from Abraham what I am about to do?" (Gen 18:17). And the Lord "remained standing before Abraham" (Gen 18:22), waiting for Abraham to verbalize his concerns for the city in which Lot and his family resided.

Prayer plays a central role in the development of our ability to work with God in governing his kingdom. As Willard clarifies:

> Prayer as kingdom praying is an arrangement explicitly instituted by God in order that we as individuals may count, and count for much, as we learn step by step how to govern, to reign with him in his kingdom. . . . It is God's intention that we should grow into the kind of person he could empower to do what we want to do. Then we are ready to "reign for ever and ever" (Rev. 22:5). . . . In the life of prayer we are training for, we reign in harmonious union with the infinite power of God.[27]

While engaging in petitionary prayer, we partner with God to do kingdom work. As we improve our ability to make requests for our loved ones, for the church, for the nations and for ourselves, God mentors us in kingdom leadership competencies.

Views of God's Providence and Prayer

But how is God able to be genuinely responsive to human actions? There is the rub. This is a complex issue involving mysteries for which theologians throughout the ages have scratched their heads to propose solutions. Space limitations only permit a brief survey of major views regarding God's providence and foreknowledge and human freedom in relation to prayer (see table 8.1).[28] Each of the five views in the chart offers something attractive as a solution, but at the cost of minimizing a biblical truth that conflicts with the proposed solution. I do not think we have a complete explanation yet, but partial resolutions offer some help.

How does answered prayer fit into God's plan? Traditional Calvinism (A) fits best with what could be called "prayer as alignment." The prayer request was already aligned with what God alone had determined to do from eternity past, and so the prayer was "answered." Furthermore, according to this perspective, God ordains both the means (our prayer) and the end (the answer). Prayer is regarded as important, although God alone ordained the prayer as a means.

	Prayer as Alignment	Prayer as Alignment and Human Initiative			Prayer as Human Initiative
Certainty of Future	Future is certain. God knows all the details of any future event.				The future is open and uncertain. God may be surprised by future. God acts and adapts.
How God plans or acts	God unilaterally determines his eternal plan	God incorporates foreknown human actions into his eternal plan that he alone determines		Without MK, God sees the future and acts accordingly	
Views of Fore-knowledge	**OC:** God decrees what people do	**MK:** God foreknows what people would do		**SF:** God sees what people actually do	**PK:** God "predicts" what people might do
	Omni-Causality of God (OC) (and timeless "foreknowledge") (Traditional Calvinism)	with **Middle Knowledge** (MK)		with **Simple Foreknowledge** (SF) (Traditional Wesleyanism)	with **Present Knowledge** (PK) ("Openness of God" view)
	A	**B**	**C**	**D**	**E**
Author	P. Helm J. Feinberg	(MK Calvinism) T. Tiessen	W. Craig T. Flint	J. Cottrell	J. Sanders G. Boyd
Form of Human Freedom	**Compatibilism** Theological (soft) Determinism; "Power to do what you want to do, even though you could not do otherwise." God accomplishes his eternal decrees in every detail of human action	**Libertarianism** Theological Indeterminism; "Power to do what you want to do, but you could do otherwise."			

"Alignment"—answered prayers are those "aligned" with what God alone determined to do (e.g., death of Christ, Acts 2:23)

"Human Initiative"—answered prayers stem from human initiatives (e.g., God announced Hezekiah would die, Hezekiah prayed, and God answered by giving Hezekiah fifteen more years of life, 2 Kings 20:1-6).

Table 8.1. Views of prayer and God's providence

Three views of God's foreknowledge—middle knowledge (B and C) and simple foreknowledge (D)—are clustered under the heading "Prayer as Alignment and Human Initiative." Here, answers to prayer would either be something that God alone determined to do (those that are aligned), or they could also stem from God's genuine response to human initiatives in prayer (i.e., impetratory prayer, receiving an answer because of the request). In other words, in some cases God would not bring about that particular answer without the prayer being made (e.g., Jas 4:2). Views of foreknowledge B, C, D and E (present knowledge) could affirm the concept of impetratory prayer developed in this chapter. In my view, the least difficulties come with a view which affirms that God is never surprised since he has middle knowledge,[29] yet he willingly responds to the prayers and preferences of his people by incorporating them into his eternal plan.

Regardless of our current partial knowledge about how God works with prayer, we are certain that Scripture affirms God's responsiveness to our prayers. Furthermore, we can discern some of God's purposes regarding why he is willing to do so. Accordingly, God invites us to join him in deeper friendship through working together with him in prayer as asking—a point Jesus plainly makes in his teaching by the fig tree.

Jesus and the Fig Tree

In an unusual circumstance, Jesus offered his disciples an important lesson on prayer (Mt 21:18-22; parallel in Mk 11:12-14, 20-26). Being hungry and noticing a fig tree in leaf, Jesus approached it only to find leaves but no figs. He proclaimed, "May you never bear fruit again!" and it subsequently withered. There is much misunderstanding about Jesus' action. A fig tree in leaf normally indicates that it is bearing figs. At this early stage the figs are green, but still edible. D. A. Carson explains:

> That it was not the season for figs explains why Jesus went to this particular tree, which stood out because it was in leaf. Its leaves advertised that it was bearing, but the advertisement was false. Jesus, unable to satisfy his hunger, saw the opportunity of teaching a memorable object lesson and cursed the tree, not because it was not bearing fruit, whether in season or out, but because it made a show of life that promised fruit yet was bearing none. . . . Jesus is cursing those who make a show of bearing much fruit but are spiritually barren.[30]

Jesus uses this miracle as a demonstration of answered prayer. "I tell you the truth, if you have faith and do not doubt, not only can you do what was done to the fig tree, but also you can say to this mountain, 'Go, throw yourself into the sea,' and it will be done. *If you believe, you will receive whatever you ask for in prayer"* (Mt 21:21-22, emphasis added). The reference to mountain movement was a common metaphor for overcoming one's problems (cf. 1 Cor 13:2: "if I have a faith that can move mountains").[31] Jesus demonstrates and teaches that prayer can be effective. We can be confident in seeing God answer prayers on a regular basis.

Having developed a biblical rationale for impetratory prayer, we move to a discussion of the logistics and practical aspects of prayer in the rest of the chapter.

An Answer to Prayer Is Receiving What Was Requested

The purpose of asking is to receive. A child comes crying to mother to kiss a skinned knee. A teen wants to know if the car is free to drive to a friend's house. At a social gathering, a husband asks his wife for the name of the couple across the way. An employee talks to the supervisor for time off to attend a funeral. A CEO makes a proposal to the company board of directors to begin a new venture. Asking and receiving are basic to life. If there is no possibility of receiving anything, then there is no purpose in asking. Our experience in this world often includes making requests of others so we can get on with the business of working and living. God has instituted a similar approach in his plan for us—the distinct opportunity for believers to make divine requisitions to meet our daily needs: "Give us today our daily bread" (Mt 6:11).

How does one sustain a life of regular prayer? At lunch a few years ago I asked my mother why she shares her requests with God, for she is one who is good at it. When I was a college student, I remember arising early one morning, and I happened to observe my mother praying in the family room on her knees. While we waited for our meal at the restaurant, she explained to me that her parents' faith provided a foundation for her life. Yet when she and my dad, in their second year of marriage, left the comforts of their homeland and crossed the ocean to this new land of opportunity, she sensed a deep need to look to God herself. In the process, she discovered the secret to prayer—answered prayer.

Obedience to God by doing our duty to pray is commendable, but it cannot sustain a genuine experience of prayer over a lifetime. This kind of duty may degenerate into a mouthing of pious words, stemming from a heart of disbelief (cf. Mt 15:8). As I grow to know God better, my motivation for praying is changing, from praying because I have to, to praying because I want to—a transition from the prayer of duty to the prayer of desire. "Trust in the LORD and do good. . . . / Delight yourself in the LORD / and he will give you the desires of your heart. / Commit your way to the LORD; / trust in him and he will do this" (Ps 37:3-5).

The Craft of Prayer

Gregory Jones employs the concept of craft for another important aspect of Christian living: forgiveness. Jones suggests that believers grow to become forgiving as in any craft, such as art, woodworking and music. "Learning to embody forgiveness involves our commitment to the cultivation of specific habits and practices of the Church. . . . Indeed, just as Aristotle emphasized the importance of learning a 'craft' for learning how to live, so there is a craft of forgiveness that Christians are called to learn."[32] Similarly, what if we accepted the notion of a craft of prayer? As in much of life, we can grow in our ability to become better at a particular skill or hobby. What about prayer?

Richard Foster shares his own discovery that "real prayer is something we learn."

> Occasional joggers do not suddenly enter an Olympic marathon. They prepare and train themselves over a period of time, and so should we. When such progression is followed, we can expect to pray a year from now with greater authority and spiritual success than at present. . . . It was liberating to me to understand that prayer involved a learning process. I was set free to question, to experiment, even to fail, for I knew I was learning. For years I had prayed for many things and with great intensity, but with only marginal success. But then I saw that I might possibly be doing some things wrong and could learn differently. . . . To understand that the work of prayer involves a learning process saves us from arrogantly dismissing it as false or unreal. . . . We can determine if we are praying correctly if the requests come to pass. If not, we look for the "block." . . . We listen, make the necessary adjustments, and try again.[33]

Prayer is not simply a matter of saying a few choice words at a given point in time. We can learn to trust more in a God "who is able to do immeasurably more than all we ask or imagine" (Eph 3:20). We can become wiser in our prayer proposals, because "we do not [always] know what we ought to pray for" (Rom 8:26). *Believers can become better at praying.*

In the past few years I have seen answers to a variety of requests related to ministry (e.g., effects of lecture series and classes), related to physical health, as well as domestic issues (e.g., financial matters, a great vacation place last Christmas, locating the right tail light for a Volvo station wagon in a junkyard). In this chapter I specifically include answers to prayer about mundane matters of life to remind us that God delights in responding to these requests as well.

In learning to become a better pray-er it is critical to examine answers to prayer, whether our own or others. By studying specifically how God acts within the particulars of the answer, believers can discern what principles God tends to follow in doing good for others. With God's help we can learn to improve our prayer proposals and, over time, see more answers to prayer. For example, during a road trip, I discovered that answers to prayer usually include the involvement of others.

The Engine Died

After an overnight at a friend's home, we were en route to Thanksgiving dinner, but along Interstate 5, in the vicinity of Chico, California, the car engine suddenly died. A call to the Automobile Association brought a young man who towed our beloved car to the parking lot of the closest but closed auto shop of a small town. Immediately I tried to fix the situation by calling a car rental company, but none were open. Then our friends who lived about an hour away kindly offered to bring up a car for our use. Finally, I began talking to God about the situation and wondering what it was all about.

Desiring to take more risks in prayer, I decided to raise the hood and ask God to fix the engine outright—the first time I had ever done that. But no answer—my first disappointment. As we waited for our friends, we noticed a family purchasing a Christmas tree in the lot next door. The salesman then walked over and asked if he could help—he worked at the auto shop. God was beginning to offer his help—he likes to involve people. After five minutes of detective work, the friendly mechanic announced that our distributor cap was chipped, whirling around but doing no work—the second instance of help, identifying the problem. Our kind stranger looked in the shop, but could not find our part—my second disappointment. Being resourceful, the mechanic then cannibalized a similar part from a used car on the lot, and our engine worked—the third instance of help, a replacement part. We called our friends, waved goodbye to this good Samaritan and got back on the road.

What did I learn? I must pray more specifically, such as "Lord, help me rest in you and not try to fix every situation, to trust that you are aware of our need and will meet it." "Lord, please help us find out what's wrong with the engine." "Lord, if it is a broken part, could it be in stock and could that person fix our car today?" "Lord, how do you wish me to minister to the person you bring my way?" That day marked another milestone in my journey with God. I try to view trials as opportunities to learn more about God and more about myself, and to learn how to pray wisely in colaboring with God. But some habits die hard.

Natural Reactions

Do we hinder our progress in the school of prayer by regularly forgetting to leave room for God to provide for our needs? For example, we have a tendency of pulling out that credit card or making an appointment with the doctor without giving God room to answer in another way.[34] There is nothing essentially wrong with credit cards or medical science. The point is that "[we] do not have because [we] do not ask God" (Jas 4:2). So we forestall God's involvement in our life. We unconsciously sustain a lifestyle of ignoring God as our major benefactor, the one who loves to provide for our needs in his own way and time.

Supernaturally assisted living can become a routine with us, as epitomized in young David's pronouncement to Goliath, "This day the LORD will hand you over to me" (1 Sam 17:46). David had the faith to face the seasoned warrior Goliath because he had learned to trust God as a shepherd who protected his sheep from lions and bears (1 Sam 17:33-37). Little faith in God can increase to greater faith. The Bible presents many examples of unusual provision by God for daily needs, such as the ever-flowing oil jar to pay off debts (2 Kings 4:1-7) and Jesus' feeding of the five thousand (Mt 14:19-20) to expand our ideas about how life can be lived. Furthermore, God brought victory for Israel in unusual ways, creating sounds of marching troops to scare off an army (2 Sam 5:24; 2 Kings 7:6-7), precipitating confusion and panic (1 Sam 7:10; 14:15), even using forests as a weapon to defeat the enemy (2 Sam 18:8; cf. Josh 24:12).

Yet some of the Israelite kings, as is our habit today, leaned solely on human resources, buying military protection from neighboring nations rather than relying on God. When King Asa made a treaty with the Arameans, the prophet confronted the king:

> Because you relied on the king of Aram and not on the LORD your God, the army of the king of Aram has escaped from your hand. Were not the Cushites and Libyans a mighty army with great numbers of chariots and horsemen? Yet when you relied on the LORD, he delivered them into your hand. For the eyes of the LORD range throughout the earth to strengthen those whose hearts are fully committed to him. You have done a foolish thing, and from now on you will be at war. (2 Chron 16:7-9)

What particular forms of supernaturally assisted living could God bring at work, at school, at church, at home if we petitioned him about the matter? What divinely assisted strategies are needed to wage war with Satan in daily experience? Prayer is a ready resource to sustain such a lifestyle. We always pray at our current level of trust in God, but we need not remain there.

But then, when we receive an answer, does our mind automatically suggest a natural explanation as the cause, rather than a supernatural one? On a recent day of prayer at Biola University, a loud honking noise started to blare from a car alarm system, disrupting the spirit of the moment. As I was moving along the prayer walk, I asked God to stop the noise. At that very moment, it stopped. But then I wondered if it happened by other means—maybe it ran its course or maybe the owner returned. In *The Screwtape Letters*, C. S. Lewis suggests that this mind game can destroy a life of prayer, as articulated in this piece of devilish advice offered to the younger demon-in-training.

> But you worry him with the haunting suspicion that the practice [of prayer] is absurd and can have no objective result. Don't forget to use the "Heads I

win, tails you lose" argument. If the thing he prays for doesn't happen, then that is one more proof that petitionary prayers don't work; if it does happen, he will, of course, be able to see some of the physical causes which led up to it, and "therefore it would have happened anyway," and thus granted prayer becomes just as good a proof as a denied one that prayers are ineffective.[35]

To make progress in this school of prayer, I am giving God the benefit of the doubt that, apart from any explicit evidence to the contrary, God stopped that horn in answer to my prayer. And if I am wrong, God will help me refine my understanding through future answers.

Persisting in Prayer

God may not answer a request the first time around in order to help us continue in prayer about the matter. In the parable of the woman and the judge (Lk 18:1-8), Jesus teaches us to pray persistently. Both Paul and Jesus prayed three times before receiving specific answers to their requests (Paul in 2 Cor 12:8-9; Jesus in Mt 26:44; cf. Heb. 5:7). Persistence paid off for the Canaanite woman who kept on asking Jesus to heal her daughter (Mt 15:21-28). Have we ever really agonized in prayer (e.g., Col 4:12)? How burdened are we about our requests? Do we tend to make a request known once to God and then figure it is on his to-do list and not ours anymore?

In this particular aspect, we fail to understand prayer as a means of growing in our relationship with God. Rather than the once-for-all-time prayer request, similar to dropping a bomb and flying away, it may be more helpful to view prayer as if we were cooking a prayer request over a slow burner.[36] Consider that almost all prayer requests require some cooking time—some more, some less. We cook the request repeatedly and persistently throughout the day by bringing it to our attention *and* God's attention. As we continue in prayer, we may ponder how our prayer can become more focused, what other factors need to be included as well and what God's view is on the matter. Other means can help our concentration and demonstrate to God our resolve: extended times for prayer (e.g., several hours, Acts 12:5, 12; all night prayer, Lk 6:12) and prayer with fasting (e.g., Moses fasted and prayed for forty days regarding Israel's sin with the golden calf, Deut 9:11-20; cf. Acts 13:2).

For What Can We Pray?

We can pray for anything that is good for others and for ourselves—anything that concerns us or that our heart desires (Ps 37:4; cf. Ps 34:10; 84:11). "Do not be anxious about anything, but *in everything* by prayer and petition, with thanksgiving, present your requests to God" (Phil 4:6, emphasis added).[37] We can pray for our daily needs. We can pray for the people we love and care about. We can pray for our church's ministry. We can pray for the work we do at our job during the week. We can take anything and everything to God in prayer. For example, I have received answers to prayer regarding our refrigerator working, buying a used car, proposals being approved at work, ideas and organization in writing this book, and the safety of a friend in harm's way.

Furthermore, based on the kinds of prayers we offer, could we tell whether or not a prayer was answered? Consider the kinds of prayers spoken in any gathering of Christians, at a class or in a home Bible study. I noticed that my own requests to God tended to be general, laced with customary prayer speech, rather than appealing to God for specific matters. As John R. Rice warns, "The modern idea and the modern practice about prayer is so indefinite that it is silly. . . . I say that where there is no definiteness in prayer, it is because there is no burden, no urgency, no heart desire."[38] How definite are our prayers?

For example, when moving to another state to serve with a campus ministry, a friend of mine prayed specifically about the house he wanted to rent. He wanted it to have a touch of home to minister to the college students who would enter its doors. His prayer list included these particulars: that the house would be within two miles of the college, that rent would be under a certain monthly amount and that the house would have a white picket fence as a symbol of warmth for students away from home. Through some coincidental circumstances, God answered that prayer. Because of these particular details, my friend was assured that God answered his prayer—too many details were involved that could not be explained by chance alone.

A few years ago Beth and I thought it best to move closer to Biola University, where I teach, where she now works, and where both our son and daughter are students. After listing our house on the market at the end of January, many people walked through the house, but no offers came. After three months we wondered over the delay since our price was reasonable and other homes coming on the market after ours were selling in our neighborhood. So in April, Beth and I began regularly beseeching the Lord with these specific requests: that we would be out of the house by Memorial Day, May 31, that the buyers would want a particular large and heavy piece of furniture (which we did not want to move), and that the house would meet the needs of the buyers as it had met ours. On May 4 we accepted an offer, requesting a less-than-thirty-day escrow. And the buyers wanted that piece of furniture (which was just one of the many attractive features for them). Through such answers to prayer, Beth and I are gaining more confidence to pray to God with greater belief that he genuinely cares for our daily needs.

God also responds to requests for healing; I have experienced a few myself. Physician Larry Dossey has collected documented experimental effects of healing prayer.

> Approximately 150 experiments in laboratories, clinics, and hospitals have put distant healing influence to the test. More than half of these studies have produced statistically significant results, meaning that they cannot be explained by chance. . . . After scrutinizing this body of data for almost two decades, I have come to regard it as one of the best-kept secrets in medical science. I am convinced that the distant nonlocal effects are real and that healing happens.[39]

We can pray about anything and everything. As the old hymn "What a Friend We Have in Jesus" (Joseph Scriven, 1857) reminds us:

> What a friend we have in Jesus, all our sins and griefs to bear!
> What a privilege to carry, everything to God in prayer!
> O what peace we often forfeit, O what needless pain we bear,
> All because we do not carry everything to God in prayer!

In other words, if we deem something appropriate to do or to purchase, why not make it a matter of prayer? As Rice notes, "If you want it, pray for it! If it is not right to pray for it, then it is not right to want it. . . . But anything we have a right to want, anything we have a right to work for, anything we have a right to try to buy or plan about, that we have a right to pray for, too!"[40] God invites us to make our requests to him for anything that is good.[41]

In the following section we consider what kinds of answers may come and why God may delay an answer to our prayer, for Jesus' promise is that our prayers can be answered (Jn 15:7).

Expectations and God's Answers

Sometimes God's answer comes, but we are not able to recognize it. Foster explains, "Another reality to keep in mind is the simple fact that many times our prayers are indeed answered, but we lack the eyes to see it. . . . A part of our petition must always be for an increasing discernment so that we can see things as God sees them."[42] God's answer may arrive in a different manner and at a different time than we expect. Table 8.2 may help expand our way of seeing answered prayer, employing just two factors: manner, the *what* of the prayer, and time, *when* the prayer is answered. We look for category #1 answers, yet God might respond as in categories #2-4.

Evangelical philosopher Gary Habermas maintains a lengthy prayer list of names of students and others for whom he seeks divine sustenance. When his eighty-seven-year-old grandmother became deathly ill, he earnestly prayed for her. And God graciously prolonged her life. Then sickness hit much closer to home, for Debbie, his beloved wife of twenty-three years, was diagnosed with terminal stomach cancer. And Gary prayed and prayed. He prayed that God's will might be done in her life. But he also prayed that she might be restored to full health. She died four months later.[43] In spite of Gary's grief, God thrilled his soul with an answer to prayer. One day while undergoing treatment in the hospital, Debbie experienced God's presence as never before. "God spoke to me. Three words: I love you." Gary's joy in God's answer stems from the fact that Debbie "had doubted God's love all her life, yet now she was as sure of his love as she was of mine. I trust him to have a good answer to my prayers. That's not the same as [always] knowing what that answer is."[44]

When Answers to Prayer Are Delayed

Sometimes we may have to wait awhile to see the answers to our prayers. For example, God may be withholding an answer to get our attention on matters of higher priority to God. It might be that we are not quite ready to receive the answer. For example, a parent will give a

	What? Manner	When? Timing	Illustration from the Bible
#1	same	now	King Hezekiah prayed that he would not die, and God extended his life fifteen more years. (2 Kings 20:1-7)
#2	same	later	Abraham prayed for an heir, and twenty-five years later Isaac was finally born (Gen 15:1-6)
#3	different/better	now	Jonah prayed that God would take his life; instead God attempted to teach Jonah about God's views. (Jon 4:2)
#4	different/better	later	David desired to build a temple, a "house" for God, yet God only let him gather the resources so Solomon could build it. Rather God promised David an "enduring house," establishing an eternal Davidic dynasty (although God informed him of the answer at that time). (2 Sam 7:1-17)

Table 8.2. Alternative affirmative answers from God

child a two-wheel bicycle when he or she is old enough to ride it. In the same way, God may need to grow us more before an answer comes. Sometimes, as Foster admits, "we simply are not prepared for what we have asked."[45]

For example, after faithfully serving in various capacities as a police officer and then as assistant chief, Randy Gaston applied for the opening to become the new police chief of the city of Anaheim. Although Randy prayed about the matter, an outsider was selected. God used this difficult turn of events in Randy's life to deepen his faith in God. Several years later, with further development as a believer, Randy applied again for the opening. Even though a national search was conducted, Randy was tapped as Anaheim's new police chief. Waiting can be challenging, but God's timing is always good.

In some cases God may delay an answer until we invite others to join us in prayer about the matter, to counter our radical individualism and solo efforts in prayer. One important purpose in the plan of God is our unity—as Jesus prayed—"that they may be one as we are one" (Jn 17:22). As developed in the last chapter, God permits crises to come our way so that believers can bond together, especially through the human activity of praying in unity (Acts 12:5). Besides our practice of worship, nothing unites the body of Christ more than praying with one mind about a matter. Praying together testifies to our love for God *and* our love for each other.

Keith Ward notes, "It is no use disobeying God in most things, not caring about him or bothering to establish a firm relationship with him, and then complaining that our prayers do not seem to 'work.' The difference is between asking a stranger to do something and asking a dearly loved friend to do something."[46] Have we been totally honest with God about our dealings with others? God blocked Israel's victory in the battle against Ai because one person disobeyed God's ban on keeping anything from the victory over Jericho (Josh 7:6-12). Also, God values maintaining good relationships with other believers (e.g., Mt 5:23-24; 6:12; husbands may have their prayers hindered if treating their wives inappropriately, 1 Pet 3:7).

As Bill Craig notes, "It is clear from Jesus' promise that unanswered prayer ought to be the exception, not the norm, of our prayer life. For the Christian abiding in Christ, answers to his prayers ought to be his regular experience."[47] Jesus promises that the norm and ideal in our relationship with God is that more of our prayers can be answered than currently is the case (Jn 15:7). As Rice encourages, "If you do not get just what you pray for, then you should set out today to find what is wrong with your prayers. Do not claim to have the answer until you get what you pray for."[48]

Are we clueless about what the barrier might be if an answer is delayed? No matter, as Rice suggests, God will bring it to mind. "At the very place where you come to talk to God, to make your gift to God, to ask God's blessing, there God is most likely to reveal the things that grieve Him. Nowhere in the world is the conscience so alive as in the place of prayer!"[49]

God's Silence

What if God foresees that were he to fulfill our request, it would not bring about good, but misery or disaster for us or our loved ones in the long run? Thomas Flint explains, "Perhaps the prayers he doesn't answer are cases where what we have prayed for *wouldn't* have been good, for ourselves, or for others."[50] Just as a parent might deny a child something that would be harmful, so God protects us from our own misguided notions. That God does not answer every prayer of ours can become a comfort to us; he has something much better in mind. P. T. Forsyth (d. 1921) affirms, "We shall come one day to a heaven where we shall gratefully know that God's great refusals were sometimes the true answers to our truest prayer."[51]

Furthermore, God may impose his own seasons of silence in which he does not answer our prayer. All believers will experience periodic dark nights of the soul in which we experience limited or no answers to prayer at all. As discussed in chapter five, God withdraws his usual presence to move us away from our dependence on other things and to move closer to him.

Pressing On in Our Prayer Life with God

Ultimately, a life of prayer grows out of a love relationship with God. While Peter, James and John were witnessing the overwhelming glory of Jesus in his transfiguration on the mountaintop, the other nine disciples below worked at casting out a demon, but nothing happened. After the embarrassing episode, the disciples asked Jesus why—although they had been successful in previous cases (Mk 6:7-13)—they were unable to cast the demon out. The problem was not with the mechanics or technique of prayer. The problem was, as Jesus said, "You have so little faith" (Mt 17:20). D. A. Carson explains:

> At a superficial level the disciples did have faith: they expected to be able to exorcise the demon. They had long been successful in this work, and now they are surprised by their failure. But their faith is poor and shoddy. . . . In Mark [9:29], Jesus tells them that this case requires prayer—not a form or an approved rite, but an entire life bathed in prayer and its concomitant faith. In Matthew, Jesus tells his disciples that what they need is not giant faith (tiny faith will do) but true faith—faith that, out of a deep personal trust, expects God to work.[52]

And so with prayer, there is room to grow in our faith.

How do we know if we are making progress in our friendship with God? Consider a classic formulation offered by Bernard of Clairvaux (d. 1153), a monk who became the abbot of the Clairvaux monastery around age twenty-five and remained there until his death. With the clever transposition of a few key phrases, Bernard outlined four general stages or degrees in loving God.[53] In the final or fourth stage, we experience such oneness with God that our prayer requests routinely reflect the heart of God.

First degree: We love ourselves for our own sake. The starting point in learning to love God is to recognize our own natural self-love, alluded to in the command to "Love your neighbor as yourself" (Lev 19:18; Mt 22:39; cf. Eph 5:29). Furthermore, we can love our neighbor since our neighbor has the same nature and rights as we do—to care for themselves just as we care for ourselves—also being created in God's image. Then as we move beyond meeting our own needs and begin to meet the needs of others first, we are on the path of learning how to love.

Second degree: We love God for our own sake. In caring for the needs of our neighbor first, we temporarily put aside our own needs. We then ask, Who will meet our needs? It is God who will generously supply our lack. "Seek first his kingdom and his righteousness [for example, by loving your neighbor], and all these things will be given to you as well" (Mt 6:33). Moreover, we can only love our neighbor when we love our neighbor in God, that is, if we love God first. To help us turn toward God, Bernard explains, "The same creator wills that man be disciplined by tribulations so that when man fails and God comes to his help, man, saved by God, will render God the honor due him."[54] The beginnings of our love for God stem from his goodness: we love God because God is good to us. Thus, we seek God to meet our needs. In this second degree, the urgency of our needs defines our relationship with God. Another turning point occurs to gain freedom from this necessity.

Third degree: We love God for God's sake. Through our experience of suffering and trials, God begins to soften our hard hearts, to sensitize them to the grace of God. We begin to love God not merely for our own sake, but to love God for himself. The psalmist's plea becomes our own: "Taste and see that the LORD is good" (Ps 34:8). We love God not just because he is good to us, but because God is good. A more pure love for

God blossoms, without strings attached. Believers are weaned away from a sense of duty or obligation as the primary motive for submission. Bernard notes, "He loves God truthfully and so loves what is God's. He loves purely and he does not find it hard to obey a pure commandment, purifying his heart, as it is written, in the obedience of love."[55] Furthermore, it is easier to love others as well. We love God for God's sake, not just our own sake.

Fourth degree: We love ourselves for God's sake. In this final stage, believers become one in mind and heart with God: "Your will be done on earth as it is in heaven" (Mt 6:10). Believers become "inebriated with divine love . . . hastening towards God and clinging to him, becoming one with him in spirit," as Bernard phrases it.[56] It is rare to experience this here, since the physical "body keeps one busy to the point of distraction."[57] Yet Bernard identifies martyrs as partial exemplars of this supreme kind of love. The rest of us will experience such fullness of love for God in the future, when at the resurrection—with our new bodies not being as needy—we can begin to attend to God completely.

It is this fourth degree form of love which God wishes to cultivate in us through our prayer life so that in the future—as we experience oneness with God—we can direct God's power on any matter whenever we wish. That is the ideal underlying Jesus' promise from the fig tree episode: "Therefore I tell you, whatever you ask for in prayer, believe that you have received it, and it will be yours" (Mk 11:24).

From Scripture perhaps we can identify a few who experienced moments of such fourth-degree love. These heroes of faith in God entered into a form of supernatural living and received great answers to their prayers (cf. Heb 11:32-35), such as Abraham, who was "called God's friend" (Jas 2:23); Moses, who spoke with God "face to face, as a man speaks with his friend" (Ex 33:11); David, whom God called "a man after my own heart" (Acts 13:22; 1 Sam 13:14); and Daniel, who was "highly esteemed" by God (Dan 10:11; cf. Ezek 14:14, 20). A life of prayer is a natural outcome of a growing and deepening friendship with God. As Foster notes, "Real prayer comes not from gritting our teeth but from falling in love."[58]

In Harm's Way

My friend was in danger, and I prayed like I had never prayed before. A few days after the terrorist bombings of the American embassies in Nairobi, Kenya, and Dar es Salaam, Tanzania, on August 7, 1998, a close friend of mine, Dr. Brian Kidwell, an American psychologist with the United Nations Department of Peacekeeping Operations in New York, arrived for a peacekeeping mission in Dushanbe, Tajikistan. But then on August 20 the United States military, in response to the embassy bombings, dropped destruction on a suspected terrorist base of Osama bin Laden in Afghanistan, near the border of Tajikistan, and on a pharmaceutical factory in North Khartoum, Sudan, suspected to be a chemical weapons facility. As an American, Kidwell was in the wrong place at the wrong time. That evening he packed his bags but could not leave because of fighting in the vicinity and because, having arrived on UN-chartered aircraft, no scheduled airlines were departing that evening or the next couple days.

To make matters worse, a Dushanbe UN-mission staff member had been murdered in a complicated arrangement made to appear like a suicide. The motive was not clear, but it was obvious local forces wanted to retaliate for supposed wrongs committed by the local government. In the streets it was common to hear gunfire and occasional hand grenade blasts. Consequently, fear permeated the atmosphere at this UN compound. With tensions rising, UN authorities approved a partial evacuation of foreign staff and contingency plans were prepared over the next five days. Later we learned that a complicated diversion had to be created to permit the convoy safe passage to the airport during a window of opportunity when two UN-chartered planes landed to rescue the staff.

As soon as we heard of this life-threatening situation, my wife, Beth, and I prayed. These circumstances stretched my comfort zone of prayer, and God offered me an opportunity to partner with him about a dear friend in harm's way. Furthermore, I invited many to pray with us about this matter close to our heart. Daily we called Anne, his wife, for any updates, but news was scarce due to the possibility of communication lines being compromised.

Finally Dr. Kidwell arrived safely at a military base in Western Europe, but I did not hear the great news till the next day, because I arrived home late that night with Beth already asleep. Early the next morning as I was getting up, Beth shared the good news she had heard the night before:

Brian had arrived safely. I began tearing up, so I went out to the living room and there wept uncontrollably. Amidst the tears flowing freely, I wondered, *Why am I crying so much?* Of course, I love my dear friend and am ecstatic he was safe. But I asked the Lord, *Is there something more involved?* I sensed that through my tears God was telling me, "Your prayers mattered. Brian is safe and sound because you prayed." In working on this particular project with God, I grew in my confidence that God the Father desires to consider my requests.

Wasting Time with God: Faith-Stretching Prayer

Petitionary prayer is best learned by experience: initiating requests, persisting in prayer, noting answers and then reflecting back on the whole encounter to glean insights for future proposals. God wishes to colabor with us to meet our needs and accomplish his kingdom goals. Jesus' parable of the talents (Mt 25:14-30) can launch believers into opportunities for supernaturally assisted, faith-stretching prayer. The basic storyline of the parable involves three servants being entrusted with certain amounts of his wealth, one, two and five talents respectively. During the landowner's absence, two servants invested these funds in certain business ventures and doubled the money. The third servant buried it in a hole.[59] When the landowner returned, the two servants were praised for their great accomplishment, and the third was scolded for his laziness.

As this parable illustrates, Jesus encourages his followers actually to take appropriate risks with God's resources. King David announced, "With your help I can advance against a troop; with my God I can scale a wall" (Ps 18:29; cf. v. 32-36). In what arenas does God wish to stretch our faith with prayer requests beyond our comfort zone? A recurring phrase in the owner's praise for his faithful servants was, "You have been faithful with a few things; I will put you in charge of many things. Come and share your master's happiness" (Mt 25:21, 23). For additional help in improving our praying we can follow Foster's example. "As I was learning [to pray] I sought out persons who seemed to experience greater power and effectiveness in prayer than I and asked them to teach me everything they knew."[60]

Henry Blackaby shares an account in which the finance committee members came to him as pastor and asked how they might walk by faith regarding the church budget. The church prayed and decided God would want them to trust him for more funds than had been budgeted. "The budget of our church normally would have been $74,000. The budget we set was $164,000. We pledged to pray daily that God would meet our needs. . . . At the end of the year we had received $174,000. God taught our church a lesson in faith that radically changed us all."[61]

There are many ways we can stretch our faith through prayer. For example, my parents, in their late sixties, trusted God for his provision when they joined their church's mission trip to Brazil to spend two weeks in the jungle helping construct a church building for local believers. After years of searching for the right place in response to God's direction, Judy and Gene TenElshof, with the help of many financial partners, recently purchased a fifty-eight-acre property near Crestline, California, containing a six-thousand-square-foot house, which they will develop into a retreat center specifically for the personal renewal of pastors. Frank and Gina Pastore are being stretched beyond their comfort zones as they walk with God in a new business venture.

As we contemplate the needs of family, friends, others and ourselves, we can develop a list of three, six or ten items toward which we are willing to expend a lot of time directing our attention and God's. Do we have specific requests that strain our comfort zone of faith? The qualifying factor is not God's ability, but *our belief in God's ability*. As Willard notes, "The cautious faith that *never* saws off the limb on which it is sitting never learns that unattached limbs may find strange, unaccountable ways of not failing."[62] Then, regularly throughout the day and at special times devoted to prayer, we cook these requests over and over before and with God. Do we sense God's view on the matter or his suggestions to revise the proposal? When answers come, we contemplate the particulars to grow in our ability to direct God's resources to matters about which we are concerned.

James states that "the prayer of a righteous man is powerful and effective" (Jas 5:16). Furthermore, prayer becomes a great opportunity to labor with God in doing kingdom work and, through the answers God provides, to encourage the faith of believers and to testify to all that "he exists and that he rewards those who earnestly seek him" (Heb 11:6).

Wasting Time with God: Practicing the Presence of God

As our journey in this book comes to an end, it may be helpful to be reminded of the various ways of wasting time with God suggested in each chapter. I draw together the spiritual disciplines previously described into a summary list to stimulate a practice of living more and more in God's presence (see table 8.3). The long-term goal is to sense God's presence more regularly in the hustle and bustle of life. Henri Nouwen explains, "Although the discipline of solitude [treated in chapter five] asks us to set aside time and space, what finally matters is that our hearts become like quiet cells where God can dwell, *wherever we go and whatever we do.* The more we train ourselves to spend time with God and him alone, the more we will discover that God is with us at *all times and in all places.*"[63] A close friendship with God is not just a lofty ideal but a distinct reality for those who wish to seek it.

We can personalize God's presence by connecting with God throughout our day—especially during times we tend to be "alone" with our thoughts.

1. *Press the "pause button."* Throughout your day take thirty-second breaks to have a word with God. Recite a special verse, a favorite chorus or prayer. And get "physical"—speak aloud, kneel or lift up your arms (Rom 6:13; see pp. 141-43, 162).

2. *Look around.* See God's invisible attributes in his handiwork (Rom 1:20). God, the Artist-Engineer-Creator, makes things beautiful as an added touch (see pp. 102-4).

3. *Become aware of good "coincidences."* Notice unplanned meetings with acquaintances, the lost item that is suddenly found, protection from danger. God is more active in our lives than we know (see pp. 115-17).

4. *Meditate on Scriptures.* Ponder one passage all day long (Ps 1:2). Ask questions about it, read what commentators have said, and ask God for insight into its meaning and significance for your own life (see pp. 32-33, 166-67).

5. *Monitor your heart.* Share your anxious thoughts and concerns with God. He promises to overwhelm us with his peace (Phil 4:6-7; see pp. 148-49, 175).

6. *Fast from food.* Skip a meal now and then (but keep drinking fluids); let the rumblings of your stomach remind you to reconnect with God (e.g., Acts 9:9; 13:2; see pp. 117-18).

7. *"Fast" from a good activity.* Skip a normal activity of life—TV, a favorite hobby, credit cards—to remind yourself that God is your first priority. Take a short retreat from all activities to waste time with God (e.g., 1 Cor 7:5; see pp. 117-18).

8. *Journal.* Jot down thoughts, feelings and actions throughout your day. Did anything move you closer to or away from God? Write your own psalm (see, e.g., Ps 55; 84.)

9. *Find a spiritual friend.* Challenge one another to connect with God more and more throughout your days (2 Tim 2:22; see pp. 64-65).

10. *Find a spiritual mentor.* Meet regularly with someone who walks closely with God to help you discern God's movements in your life (e.g., 2 Tim 1:16; see pp. 180-81).

Table 8.3.   Ten Spiritual Practices for the Road

Summary

Seeking God is not a one-time affair, but a lifelong and eternity-long adventure. But our hearts tend to be crowded, so we must clear the clutter to make room for God. Knowledge gained through personal relationships is of a different texture than what can be learned about someone through a resume or even a story. As we become more intimate with and more trusting of our close friends, we increase our capacity for greater intimacy with God. For our God of love is an eternally existing Trinity—a fellowship of persons who love each other deeply and who extend an invitation for us to experience this love more fully in friendship with God

In many ways God will be a unique spiritual friend. To honor his holiness, we bow down in our hearts, humbling ourselves before him, honestly facing the pockets of pride that implicitly pronounce "I don't need God." Furthermore, we look to see the unseen as we increasingly walk by faith, not sight, seeing more and more of the invisible God and his kingdom of light all about us. With all of our heart, mind, soul and strength, we become more intentional about wasting time with God.

God is personal. As we grow in our awareness and ability to walk with God the Spirit who indwells us, the Spirit himself—the agent of the Trinity—mediates God's presence to us. As we engage in two-way communication with the Spirit in a process of informed and willing consent, the fullness of divine guidance can become routine.

In yielding to God in our suffering, we let God be God and plead for endurance while we freely share our grief with him. We recognize that larger kingdom purposes may have brought on our suffering; nonetheless, we can desire the good that can come our way in the end. Furthermore, these same kingdom purposes include divine responsiveness to our pleas and initiatives in human prayer. In partnership with God in prayer, we deepen our friendship as he trains us to reign with him forever.

As a final action of the book—related to the personal retreat idea within the "Pause" category of table 8.3—may I suggest looking at your present schedule to identify a few particular times to wait on God?

□ A weekly time (e.g., an hour or two you can regularly schedule with God)

☐ A seasonal and an annual time (e.g., an evening, full day, overnight or weekend for a personal retreat)

Is a calendar or daily planner handy? Consider penciling in a time in the next few days to waste time with God. In addition, mark down an extended time of solitude in the near future to engage in the habit of investing premium time for a personal retreat with God. The promise is sure:

Come near to God and he will come near to you. (Jas 4:8)

Notes

Chapter One: The Quest

[1]Dallas Willard proposed this word picture in a lecture on Biola's campus, October 19, 1998.

[2]The analogy is adapted from one suggested by Garry DeWeese in a conversation about this subject.

[3]There are some verses in Scripture about seeking God that do apply to believers, for example, Jeremiah 29:11-14; Lamentations 3:25; Zephaniah 2:3; Acts 17:26-27; Hebrews 11:6.

[4]Wayne Grudem, *Systematic Theology* (Grand Rapids, Mich.: Zondervan, 1994), p. 151.

[5]In the future eternal state, whatever thoughts we have about God will be true, for "we shall see face to face" (1 Cor 13:12) and "we shall see him as he is" (1 Jn 3:2), but they still will not be complete. This kind of accurate knowledge is what Paul has in mind in 1 Corinthians 13:12, as Grudem explains, "The phrase 'know fully' is simply an attempt to translate *epiginosko*, which suggests deeper or more accurate knowledge (or perhaps, in contrast with present partial knowledge, knowledge free from error or falsehood). Paul never says anything like, 'Then I shall know all things,' which would have been very easy to say in Greek (*tote epignosomai ta panta*) if he had wished to do so" (*Systematic Theology*, p. 151 n. 2).

[6]The true story of their love is told by Sheldon Vanauken, *A Severe Mercy* (New York: Harper & Row, 1977).

[7]A. W. Tozer, *The Knowledge of The Holy* (New York: Harper & Row, 1961), p. 9.

[8]Tozer, *Knowledge of the Holy*, p. 8.

[9]Dallas Willard, *Hearing God: Developing a Conversational Relationship with God* (Downers Grove, Ill.: InterVarsity Press, 1999), p. 194.

[10]"NASA Scientists Blush Red As Mars," *The Orange County Register*, October 1, 1999. Also see Charles Petit, "NASA's Costly Deviation," *U.S. News & World Report*, October 11, 1999, p. 63; and "NASA Officially Quits on Missing Mars Polar Lander," *The Oregonian*, January 18, 2000.

[11]"By using the case at hand, [Jesus] simply upset the prevailing general assumption about God and riches" (Dallas Willard, *The Divine Conspiracy* [San Francisco: HarperSanFrancisco, 1998], p. 108).

[12]J. B. Phillips, *Your God Is Too Small* (New York: Macmillan, 1954), p. v (emphasis added).

[13]Gordon Fee, *Paul, the Spirit, and the People of God* (Peabody, Mass.: Hendricksen, 1996), p. 37.

[14]John Feinberg, *The Many Faces of Evil* (Grand Rapids, Mich.: Zondervan, 1994), p. 336 (emphasis added). The details of their family ordeal is recounted in John Feinberg, *Deceived By God? A Journey Through Suffering* (Wheaton, Ill.: Crossway, 1997).

[15]Philip Yancey, *What's So Amazing About Grace?* (Grand Rapids, Mich.: Zondervan, 1997), p. 70.

[16]Gerald Hawthorne notes that "this expression, 'the peace of God,' is found nowhere else in the NT." He goes on to explain what the phrase means: "Paul seems here to be referring to the tranquility of God's own eternal being (Caird), the peace of God which God himself has (Barth), the calm serenity that characterizes his very nature . . . and which grateful, trusting Christians are welcome to share" *(Philippians,* vol. 43 of Word Biblical Commentary [Waco, Tex.: Word, 1983], p. 184).

[17]D. A. Carson, "When Is Spirituality Spiritual? Reflections on Some Problems of Definition," *Journal of the Evangelical Society* 37, no. 3 (1994): 391-92.

[18]J. I. Packer, *Knowing God* (Downers Grove, Ill.: InterVarsity Press, 1973), p. 35.

[19]Neil T. Anderson and Robert Saucy, *The Common Made Holy: Being Conformed to the Image of God* (Eugene, Ore.: Harvest House, 1997), p. 377.

[20]Chuck and Nancy Missler, *Faith in the Night Seasons* (Coeur d'Alene, Idaho: Koinonia House, 1999), p. 249.

[21]In theology a distinction is sometimes made between positional truth, what is an objective fact regardless of our experience of it, and experiential truth, what is in fact experienced. For example, all believers are positionally righteous before God, based on Christ's righteousness. But in our Christian living we are at various stages of becoming righteous persons. Likewise, knowing God requires engagement of both aspects.

[22]Noel D. O'Donoghue, *The Holy Mountain* (Dublin: Dominican Publications, 1983), p. 17, quoted in Gary Badcock, *Light of Truth and Fire of Love: A Theology of the Holy Spirit* (Grand Rapids, Mich.: Eerdmans, 1997), p. 144.

[23]Henry T. Blackaby and Claude V. King, *Experiencing God* (Nashville: Broadman & Holman, 1994), pp. 147, 151, 153.

[24]D. A. Carson, "When is Spirituality Spiritual?" p. 381.

[25]In the ecumenical series on spirituality edited by Bernard McGinn, the full title of the series is *World Spirituality: An Encyclopedic History of the Religious Quest* (New York: Crossway), which includes discussions of religiosity of non-Christian forms from around the world. Of the twenty-one volumes describing particular spiritualities, three volumes specifically address Christian spirituality.

[26]"Introduction," in *Christian Spirituality: Origins to the Twelfth Century,* World Spirituality, ed. Bernard McGinn, John Meyendorff and Jean Leclercq (New York: Crossroad, 1997), 16:xv.

[27]McGinn et al., "Introduction," *Christian Spirituality,* pp. xv-xvi. It seems McGinn et al. incorporated elements from Louis Bouyer's definition, which differentiated spirituality from dogmatic and moral theology: "Spirituality concentrates on those [human acts] in which the reference to God is not only explicit but immediate. It concentrates, that is, above all on prayer and on everything connected with prayer in the ascetical and mystical life—in other words, on religious exercises as well as religious experiences" *(The Spirituality of the New Testament and the Fathers,* A History of Christian Spirituality [New York: Seabury, 1982], 1:ix).

For a list of various definitions see Lawrence S. Cunningham and Keith J. Egan, *Christian Spirituality: Themes from the Traditions* (New York: Paulist, 1996), pp. 22-28.

[28]Murray J. Harris notes, "Paul grounds his pastoral appeal for unity of spirit and for the rejection of discord (vv. 11, 12) in the theological doctrine of the Trinity. . . . This embryonic Trinitarian formulation is noteworthy for the unusual 'economic' order of Son, Father, Spirit. It is through the grace shown by Christ (8:9) in living and dying for men that God demonstrates his love (Rom 5:8) and the Spirit creates the fellowship (Eph 4:3). This order also reflects Christian experience" ("2 Corinthians," in *Expositor's Bible Commentary*, ed. Frank E. Gaebelein [Grand Rapids, Mich.: Zondervan, 1976], 10:405).

[29]"The New Testament term *spiritual (pneumatikos)* occurs twenty-six times and primarily refers to the Holy Spirit." Gordon Fee explains that "the word functions primarily as an adjective for the Spirit, referring to *that which belongs to, or pertains to, the Spirit" (God's Empowering Presence* [Peabody, Mass.: Hendrickson, 1994], p. 29).

Consider the following definitions of *spirituality:* From Lewis Sperry Chafer (d. 1952), "What, then, is true spirituality? It is the unhindered manifestations of the indwelling Spirit" (*He That Is Spiritual* [1918; reprint, Grand Rapids, Mich.: Zondervan, 1967], p. 133). From Bradley Holt, "Christian spirituality is a style of walking in the Holy Spirit" (*Thirsty for God: A Brief History of Christian Spirituality* [Minneapolis, Minn.: Augsburg, 1993], p. 123). From Jürgen Moltmann, "Literally, spirituality means life in God's Spirit, and a living relationship with God's spirit. . . . In a strictly Christian sense, the word has to mean what Paul calls the new life *en pneumati* [in the spirit]" (*The Spirit of Life: A Universal Affirmation* [Minneapolis: Fortress, 1992], p. 83). Moltmann does not remain with the literal definition as he continues his discussion in the rest of the chapter.

[30]In this category, I would also include empirical investigations in the natural sciences and social sciences. Data do not, in themselves, prove anything. One must use a research design and make interpretations and conclusions from the findings. Thus, reason is primary in such investigations.

[31]Gordon Lewis and Bruce Demarest, *Integrative Theology* (Grand Rapids, Mich.: Zondervan, 1987), p. 8.

In another framework articulated by John Wesley (d. 1791), tradition or previous theological statements and interpretations of Scripture is added as a fourth component. This four-factor interpretive framework has been called the Wesleyan quadrilateral. Historian Roger Olson explains that this framework consists of "four essential sources and tools of theology—Scripture, reason, [theological] tradition, and experience. . . . [Wesley] believed that all these inevitably play roles in Christian thought and that rather than rejecting them, Christians ought to acknowledge their proper place as tools of scriptural interpretation and value the contributions they can make to formulating biblical doctrines that are truly catholic (faithful to the spirit of the church fathers and Reformers), reasonable (coherent, intelligible) and practical (relevant to experience). . . . [Wesley] never tired of emphasizing the supreme authority of Scripture and never allowed tradition, reason or experience to overshadow or control it" (*The Story of Christian Theology* [Downers Grove, Ill.: InterVarsity Press, 1999], p. 513). For example, if an assessment of a claim is measured by the Westminster Confession (1646), it would be a case illustrating Wesley's category of tradition, not Scripture.

For further reading, see Donald A. Thorsen, *The Wesleyan Quadrilateral: Scripture, Tradition, Reason and Experience as a Model of Evangelical Theology* (Grand Rapids,

Mich.: Zondervan, 1990).

[32]John Feinberg, *The Many Faces of Evil*, p. 72.

[33]Studying an example from Jesus in each chapter of the book offers a further extension of our three tests in that we will be looking at Scripture, thinking about the claims Jesus made in his teaching and pondering Jesus' own experience as recorded in Scripture.

[34]Richard Osmer, *A Teachable Spirit* (Louisville, Ky.: Westminster John Knox, 1990), p. 175.

[35]Unfortunately, within the traditional categories of theology, the subject of a relationship with God is unintentionally deemphasized, although it should be preeminent above any other aspect of Christian living. Consequently, it is time for Christian spirituality—discussion of growing a relationship with God—to become a recognized theological component, meriting its own chapter in systematic theology. As it stands now, within the theological encyclopedia, principles about a relationship with God are usually treated in discussions of prayer or as an aspect of the work of the Spirit, placed within treatment of the doctrine of sanctification. Yet sanctification primarily refers to the process in which Christians become more righteous and Christlike. Of course, the doctrines of spirituality and sanctification are related, but Scripture always makes our relationship with God the ultimate focus and goal of Christian living (e.g., Jn 17:3). In addition, the process of sanctification is traditionally understood to be finished at the onset of glorification, yet our spirituality——our relationship with God—continues on into eternity.

Furthermore, confusion is apparent in the literature. For example, on the same page one theologian offers two differing definitions of Christian spirituality. One emphasizes the relational element (A: "Christian spirituality is a reflection on the whole Christian enterprise of achieving and sustaining a relationship with God, which includes both public worship and private devotion, and the results of these in actual Christian life"), while the other focuses more on the process of sanctification (B: "Christian spirituality concerns the quest for a fulfilled and authentic Christian existence, involving the bringing together of the fundamental ideas of Christianity and the whole experience of living on the basis of and within the scope of the Christian faith"; Alister McGrath, *Christian Spirituality: An Introduction* [Oxford: Blackwell, 1999], p. 2). A similar confusion is evident in definitions offered by theologian Bruce Demarest (*Satisfy Your Soul: Restoring the Heart of Christian Spirituality* [Colorado Springs: NavPress, 1999], p. 74). Aside from these definitional matters, both books are excellent resources.

By marking off a distinct subject of Christian spirituality for study and reflection along the lines of the first definition above, we bring greater clarity to the discussion, and at the same time heighten the importance of pursuing our relationship with God above the matters of sanctification, although they are related in Christian living. The issue is which should be given prominence, both in theory (e.g., theological texts) and in practice (e.g., what best motivates character formation). For me, pursuing a closer relationship with God has yielded various positive outcomes in my character formation as well.

[36]D. A. Carson, "The Difficult Doctrine of the Love of God," parts 1 and 4, *Bibliotheca Sacra* 156 (January-March 1999): 7-9; (October-December 1999): 397-98.

[37]G. K. Beale notes that Revelation 3:20 is specifically written for believers: "This is an

invitation not for the readers to be converted but to renew themselves in a relationship with Christ that has already begun, as is apparent from v. 19. . . . The focus of v. 20 is on the immediate present and conditional coming of Christ rather than his definite final coming. . . . This is highlighted by Christ's initial statement that he presently 'stands at the door' and presently is 'knocking'" *(The Book of Revelation,* The New International Greek Testament Commentary [Grand Rapids, Mich.: Eerdmans, 1999], p. 308).

[38]Augustine [d. 430], *The Confessions of St. Augustine,* trans. John K. Ryan (Garden City, N.J.: Image, 1960), p. 44.

[39]This book does not attempt to treat all the issues within Christian spirituality. The unique contribution is that it primarily addresses the *puzzling* aspects of our relationship with God that have not been satisfactorily addressed in the general Christian literature—at least to my satisfaction. There are good treatments of other important topics regarding one's relationship with God (e.g., worship, the ordinances), thus eliminating the need to address these themes in this book.

[40]On the first page of each chapter, the second Scripture verse printed below the chapter title refers to Jesus' example regarding the subject matter of the chapter.

[41]My particular strength is taking material from diverse and difficult sources and offering an integrative synthesis that is faithful to Scripture and relevant for life. I would ask my colleagues who are more technically minded to read my proposals within a context of being colaborers in the Lord's vineyard, rather than as adversaries. The following extended excerpt from James Dunn's preface to his *Christology in the Making* [(Grand Rapids, Mich.: Eerdmans, 1989), p. ix.] may help convey the tone of my offering to the body of Christ in this book—although I make no claim to be Professor Dunn's equal in scholarship.

> The opportunity [to add a fresh foreword] is welcome for several reasons. Not least because it enables me to underline a feature of my writing which perhaps should have been given a clearer expression before this. That is, that I regard any writing (and lecturing) which I do as part of an ongoing dialogue. While striving to put my thoughts and insights in as finished a form as possible I have never presumed I was giving the final word on a subject. Writing helps me to clarify my own thinking; but my hope is also to help clarify the particular issues and considerations most relevant to these issues for others. Naturally I seek to find answers to my questions and offer up my own conclusions. But not in any attempt to bully readers into agreement: more with the objective of provoking them to respond, to join in the dialogue, in the hope that out of the continuing and larger dialogue a clearer and fuller picture will emerge—for myself as well as for others engaged in the dialogue.

[42]Marjorie J. Thompson, *Soul Feast: An Invitation to the Christian Spiritual Life* (Louisville, Ky.: Westminster John Knox, 1995), p. 11.

[43]Henri Nouwen, *Making All Things New: An Invitation to the Spiritual Life* (San Francisco: Harper & Row, 1981), p. 68. Greek philosopher Aristotle offers this insight: "So it is a matter of no little importance what sort of habits we form from the earliest age—it makes a vast difference, or rather all the difference in the world" (*Nichomachean Ethics,* trans. J. A. K. Thomson, rev. Hugh Tredennick [London: Penguin, 1976], pp. 91-92).

[44]In a few cases, I have suggested a discipline that is supported by Scripture but not particularly identified in the literature. The disciplines are presented for individuals, yet ultimately they work best when practiced in community (e.g., 2 Tim 2:22).

The best general treatment of the subject of spiritual disciplines is Dallas Willard, *The Spirit of the Disciplines* (San Francisco: HarperSanFrancisco, 1988). The most extensive treatment of particular classic disciplines is Richard Foster, *Celebration of Discipline: The Path to Spiritual Growth* (San Francisco: HarperSanFrancisco, 1998). Additional books describing specific disciplines include Donald S. Whitney, *Spiritual Disciplines for the Christian Life* (Colorado Springs: NavPress, 1991); Marjorie J. Thompson, *Soul Feast: An Invitation to the Christian Life* (Louisville, Ky.: Westminster John Knox, 1995); Dorothy Bass, ed., *Practicing Our Faith: A Way of Life for a Searching People* (San Francisco: Jossey-Bass, 1997); Simon Chan, *Spiritual Theology: A Systematic Study of the Christian Life* (Downers Grove, Ill.: InterVarsity Press, 1998); and Joseph Driskill, *Protestant Spiritual Exercises* (Harrisburg, Penn.: Morehouse, 1988).

For those hesitant about engaging in spiritual disciplines, I include the following report from an international graduate student, after completing a class assignment in which students were to practice a discipline of their choice.

> I am surprised that I have accomplished this project and have meaningful results. There are several insights that I gained from this project. Before the project, I thought discipline was a rigid way to reach a goal. Now, I realize that disciplines or strategies can be flexible and adjustable. We need to adjust our strategies according to the changes in our lives so that we may reach the goal more effectively. Before this project, I viewed discipline as hard work. Now, I am convinced that an effective discipline is one of the ways to make life easier. In addition, the lesson that I learned from this project is not only "a small thing makes a big difference if I practice it on a daily basis," but also "the Lord is always there and ready to give me rest" (April 29, 1999).

[45]The distinction between *meaning* and *significance* was proposed by E. D. Hirsch:

> *Meaning* is that which is represented by a text; it is what the author meant by his use of a particular sign sequence; it is what the signs represent. *Significance*, on the other hand, names a relationship between that meaning and a person, or a conception, or a situation, or indeed anything imaginable. . . . Failure to consider this simple and essential distinction has been the source of enormous confusion in hermeneutic theory. (*Validity in Interpretation* [New Haven, Conn.: Yale University, 1967], p. 8.)

For general guides on biblical hermeneutics, see Walt Russell, *Playing with Fire: How the Bible Ignites Change in Your Soul* (Colorado Springs: NavPress, 2000), and Gordon D. Fee, *New Testament Exegesis: A Handbook for Students and Pastors*, rev. ed. (Louisville, Ky.: Westminster John Knox, 1993). For a comprehensive treatment of the matters of hermeneutics, see William Klein, Craig Blomberg and Robert Hubbard, *Introduction to Biblical Interpretation* (Waco, Tex.: Word, 1993), and Grant R. Osborne, *The Hermeneutical Spiral: A Comprehensive Introduction to Biblical Interpretation* (Downers Grove, Ill.: InterVarsity Press, 1991).

[46]Klein, Blomberg and Hubbard, *Introduction to Biblical Interpretation*, p. 406. Later on they clarify further, "Rather than speak of single intent or single meaning with multiple applications or significances, however, it seems to us better to speak of fixed meaning with varying significances" (p. 406 n. 13).

[47]Peter Toon, *The Art of Meditating on Scripture* (Grand Rapids, Mich.: Zondervan, 1993), p. 74.

[48]Ibid., p. 74

[49]J. P. Moreland, *Love Your God with All Your Mind* (Colorado Springs: NavPress,

1997), p. 164.

⁵⁰The traditional spiritual discipline of *Lectio Divina* (divine or sacred or spiritual reading), a practice of reading Scripture aloud and slowly, is described by Walt Russell, *Playing with Fire*, pp. 92-94, and by Gabriel O'Donnell , "Reading for Holiness: *Lectio Divina*," in *Spiritual Traditions for the Contemporary Church*, ed. Robin Maas and Gabriel O'Donnell (Nashville: Abingdon, 1990), pp. 45-50. For a more extensive resource, see Susan Muto, *A Practical Guide to Spiritual Reading* (Denville, N.J.: Dimension, 1976). A somewhat humorous and honest example is shared by James B. Smith, "The Jogging Monk and the Exegesis of Heart," *Christianity Today*, July 22, 1991, pp. 29-31.

⁵¹See Roy Zuck, *Teaching as Jesus Taught* (Grand Rapids, Mich.: Baker, 1995) for a complete list of Jesus' questions and questions asked of Jesus.

⁵²An outstanding educational resource on asking questions, although out of print, is J. T. Dillon, *Questioning and Teaching: A Manual of Practice* (New York: Teachers College, 1988).

Chapter 2: Friendship

¹One main piece of evidence that relationships with God and believers continue on after death comes from Jesus' postresurrection appearances: Jesus was recognizable to his followers (e.g., disciples, Jn 20:19-31; Mary Magdalene, Jn 20:16; two followers on the road to Emmaus, Lk 24:31; although in both of the latter encounters, Jesus was not recognized right away). After his resurrection Jesus asked Peter three times if Peter loved him, in light of the three times Peter had denied the Lord before his crucifixion (Jn 21:15-20). The designation of John as "the disciple whom Jesus loved" (Jn 20:2; 21:7, 20) was applied to John both before and after Jesus' death and resurrection (e.g., Jn 13:23; 19:26), indicating a seamless designation without break in continuity due to Jesus' death. Also, the tone of the encounters with Jesus and the eleven disciples recorded in John 20 implies a continuity with no break in the disciples' relationship with Jesus from before Jesus' death.

The major problem raised by some believers concerns what kind of memories we will have in heaven of our past life—with all its suffering and knowing that some family members are not in heaven—since the Bible promises no more tears in heaven (Rev 21:4). It may be that we will view our past sufferings and past relationships of those not in heaven with new eyes—with the same godly perspective that God has now. (Note that believers often make statements like, "I'll ask Noah or Daniel or Lazarus about [something from their life experience] when I get to heaven." The underlying assumption is that these people will have continuing memories of their life experience on earth to be able to answer such questions.)

²Friendship with God is a theme among a few biblical scholars of the past. For example, Paul Wadell directs our attention to medieval theologian Thomas Aquinas (d. 1274), who "believes we can, are called to be, and must be friends of God. That is what our life is, a life of ever-deepening friendship with God" (*Friendship and the Moral Life* [Notre Dame, Ind.: University of Notre Dame, 1989], p. 120).

³Two primary core beliefs hinder us from intensifying our relationships: a radical individualism imbibed from Western culture and an overly task-oriented life that permits no time to nurture relationships.

⁴The Lord's prayer also highlights this linkage: "Forgive us our debts, as we also have

forgiven our debtors" (Mt 6:12). Jesus explains, "But if you do not forgive men their sins, your Father will not forgive your sins" (Mt 6:15).

[5]J. I. Packer, *Concise Theology* (Wheaton, Ill.: Tyndale House, 1993), p. 42. Packer's brief summary of the doctrine is worth stating in full.

> The basic assertion of this doctrine is that the unity of the one God is complex. The three personal "subsistences" (as they are called) are coequal and coeternal centers of self-aware-ness, each being "I" in relation to two who are "you" and each partaking of the full divine essence (the "stuff" of deity, if we may dare to call it that) along with the other two. They are not three roles played by one person (that is *modalism*), nor are they three gods in a cluster (that is *tritheism*); the one God ("he") is also, and equally, "they," and "they" are always together and always cooperating, with the Father initiating, the Son complying, and the Spirit executing the will of both, which is his will also.

[6]Wayne Grudem, *Systematic Theology* (Grand Rapids, Mich.: Zondervan, 1994), p. 226.

[7]Millard Erickson, *Christian Theology* (Grand Rapids, Mich.: Baker, 1986), p. 338.

[8]Immanuel Kant, *Der Streit der Fakultaeten*, PhB 252, 333; quoted in Jürgen Molt-mann, *The Trinity and the Kingdom* (1980; reprint, Minneapolis, Minn.: Fortress, 1993), p. 6.

[9]Here I lean on Millard Erickson's discussion, *Christian Theology*, pp. 337-38.

[10]Erickson, *Christian Theology*, p. 337.

[11]Ibid.

[12]Gordon Lewis and Bruce Demarest, *Integrative Theology* (Grand Rapids, Mich.: Zondervan, 1987), 1:271.

[13]Current discussions regarding the doctrine include to what extent social aspects exist within the Godhead and to what extent each person of the Trinity is a distinct center of consciousness or not. The New Testament records each of the persons speaking: the Father to the Son (Mt 3:17; 17:5; Jn 12:28); the Son to the Father (Jn 12:28; 17:1-26); and the Spirit to Philip (Acts 8:29) and to Peter (Acts 10:19-20). The biblical evidence indicates that each person of the Trinity is a center of consciousness and communication, thus constituting three centers of consciousness within the Godhead.

Two developments in the doctrine guard against the possibility of tritheism— *perichoresis* (coinherence, mutual interpenetration) and appropriation. Theologian Alister McGrath explains, "The concept of *perichoresis* allows the individuality of the persons to be maintained, while insisting that each person shares in the life of the other two. . . . Each person, while maintaining its distinctive identity, penetrates the others and is penetrated by them. . . . The doctrine of appropriation insists that the works of the Trinity are a unity; every person of the Trinity is involved in every outward action of the Godhead. . . . [Yet] despite the fact that all three persons of the Trinity are implicated in creation, it is properly seen as the distinctive action of the Father. . . . Taken together, the doctrines of *perichoresis* and appropriation allow us to think of the Godhead as a 'community of being,' in which all is shared, united, and mutually exchanged" (*Christian Spirituality* [Oxford: Blackwell, 1999], pp. 50-51).

[14]For a helpful pictorial treatment of the Trinity, see Fred Sanders, *Dr. Doctrine's Christian Comix on the Trinity* (Downers Grove, Ill.: InterVarsity Press, 1999).

[15]Roger Olson, *The Story of Christian Theology* (Downers Grove, Ill.: InterVarsity Press, 1999), p. 512.

[16]Ibid., emphasis added.

[17]C. S. Lewis, *The Four Loves* (New York: Harcourt Brace & Co, 1960), p. 1.

[18]Grudem, *Systematic Theology,* p. 247.

[19]Daniel Fuller, *The Unity of the Bible: Unfolding God's Plan for Humanity* (Grand Rapids, Mich.: Zondervan, 1992), pp. 132, 139.

[20]According to Gary Badcock:

> There are only two significant trinitarian traditions in Western medieval theology: the Augustinian, which is mediated by Anselm and Peter Lombard and which culminates in Thomas Aquinas, and that initiated by Richard of St. Victor [d. 1173], which continues in the Franciscan tradition in Alexander of Hales and Bonaventure (pp. 246-47). . . . In the practical sense, his trinitarian theology of love provides a basis for the Christian community, and the community of human beings generally (p. 248). . . . Richard's trinitarian theology offers a coherent alternative within Western theology to the predominant Augustinian position. . . . The trinitarian relations Richard has in view similarly depend upon whether or not the trinitarian persons as persons are capable, in themselves, of genuinely interpersonal relations of love. In the other main trinitarian tradition of the West, the persons are not strictly conceived as such; but for Richard they are, and in this respect his position is representative of the social doctrine of the Trinity. (*Light of Truth and Fire of Love: A Theology of the Holy Spirit* [Grand Rapids, Mich.: Eerdmans, 1997], p. 251)

[21]A discussion of the person and ministry of the Holy Spirit, the third person of the Trinity, is offered in chapter six.

[22]An expression adapted from colleague Walt Russell.

[23]Gerald Bray, *The Doctrine of God* (Downers Grove, Ill.: InterVarsity Press, 1993), p. 242.

[24]D. A. Carson, "God is Love," (Part 2) *Bibliotheca Sacra* 156 (April-June 1999): 137, 140.

[25]Paul's discussion of the believer with weaker faith in Romans 14 is relevant to this point.

[26]Richard Swenson, *Margin: Restoring Emotional, Physical, Financial, and Time Reserves to Overloaded Lives* (Colorado Springs: NavPress, 1992), pp. 54-55.

[27]Larry Crabb continues to call the church to deeper relationships in *Connecting* (Waco, Tex.: Word, 1997) and *The Safest Place on Earth* (Waco, Tex.: Word, 1999).

[28]Another avenue for clarifying the scope of the subject is to examine the particular Greek terms for *love,* as done by Leon Morris, *Testaments of Love: A Study of Love in the Bible* (Grand Rapids, Mich.: Eerdmans, 1981), and Lewis, *Four Loves.*

[29]The three groups I identify happen to parallel a similar clustering proposed by an early sociologist, Charles H. Cooley, who coined the term *primary group* to refer to the three sets of relationships that impact child development: family, playmates [friends], and neighbors (*Social Organization* [New York: Scribner, 1909]). The term *primary group* is still used in sociological circles but is no longer tied just to these three groups.

[30]Here I develop a theological clustering of concepts that in some cases can be loosely associated with certain Greek terms. But these particular Greek terms do not expressly make such distinctions within the biblical text: "love of strangers" (*philoxenia,* e.g., Rom 13:12; Heb 13:2); "brotherly love" (*philadelphia,* e.g., Rom 12:10; 2 Pet 1:7); and "friend" (*philia,* e.g., Lk 16:9; Jn 15:14).

[31]Derek Kidner, *Proverbs,* Tyndale Old Testament Commentary (Downers Grove, Ill.: In-

terVarsity Press, 1964), p. 44.

[32]D. A. Carson notes, "Many have tried to assign the love of God, and derivatively Christian love, to one particular word-group. . . . . What is now clear to almost everyone who works in the field of linguistics and semantics is that for several reasons such an understanding of love cannot be tied in any univocal way to the *agapao* word-group" ("God is Love," p. 131-32).

[33]Aelred of Rievaulx, *Spiritual Friendship*, trans. Mary Eugenia Laker (Kalamazoo, Mich.: Cistercian, 1977), p. 74.

[34]Gilbert Meilander, *Friendship: A Study in Theological Ethics* (Notre Dame, Ind.: University of Notre Dame Press, 1981), p. 66. Aelred of Rievaulx suggests that "friendship is, so to say, a stage toward the love and knowledge of God" *(Spiritual Friendship,* p. 74).

[35]Deborah Tannen, " . . . So talk between women and men is cross-cultural communication," in *You Just Don't Understand: Women and Men in Conversation* (New York: Ballantine, 1990), p. 18.

[36]Note the variation in order of names: "Paul and Barnabas" (Acts 13:42; 15:2, 22); "Barnabas and Paul" (Acts 14:12, 14; 15:12, 25).

[37]In employing the concept of mentoring, I do not wish to affirm any kind of permanent dependent status, for I regard it as a permeable status, for we are all brothers and sisters in Christ. I do suggest that giving and receiving are normal aspects of living. Because of their experience and wisdom, some will have a greater giving role in our lives, and we may have very little of a giving role for these persons. Likewise, we may have a similar giving role in the lives of others. Sometimes being on the receiving end is difficult, especially the older we get. Here, humility is the requisite posture.

[38]Jerome, a comment on Micah 3:8, *Patrologiae cursus completus, series Latina* [PL], ed. J. P. Migne (Paris, 1878-1890), quoted in Aelred of Rievaulx, *Spiritual Friendship*, p. 115 n. 82 [PL 25:1218f.].

[39]Aelred of Rievaulx, *Spiritual Friendship*, p. 90. Cf. 2 Cor 8:9.

[40]Aquinas *Summa Theologica* 2-2, 23, 3, ad 1; quoted in Francis de Sales, *An Introduction to the Devout Life*, trans. John K. Ryan (Garden City, N.J.: Image, 1972), p. 177. Francis de Sales notes, "Here I do not refer to the simple love of charity we must have for all men but of that spiritual friendship by which two, three, or more souls share with one another their devotion and spiritual affections and establish a single spirit among themselves" (p. 175).

[41]Personal communication, April 14, 1997.

[42]The term *friend* occurs mostly in the Gospels, usually as a part of Jesus' parabolic teaching. James also employs the phrase "God's friend" with Abraham (Jas 2:23) and calls "adulterous people" those who are friends with the world and not God (Jas 4:4).

[43]John T. Fitzgerald explains, "In his correspondence with the church at Philippi, Paul uses a number of terms that belong to the ancient *topos* on friendship [*topos* = stock treatments of moral subjects]" ("Philippians in Light of Some Ancient Discussions of Friendship," in *Friendship, Flattery, and Frankness of Speech: Studies on Friendship in the New Testament World*, ed. John T. Fitzgerald [London: E. J. Brill, 1996], p. 141). The following discussion is informed by Fitzgerald's research.

[44]Aristotle, *Nichomachean Ethics,* trans. J. A. K. Thomson, rev. Hugh Tredennick (London: Penguin, 1976), p. 301.

[45]A similar phrase is used in the ancient Pentateuch, predating Aristotle: Deut 13:6,

"your friend who is as your own soul" (NASB).

[46]Marcus Tullius Cicero *De amicitia/Laelius* 20, quoted in Aelred of Rievaulx, *Spiritual Friendship*, p. 53.

[47]The Greek phrase can be located in the Greek version, Sir Alexander Grant, *The Ethics of Aristotle* (New York: Arno, 1973), p. 298.

[48]The point here is not the issue of asking for forgiveness when we have wronged someone, but of making public confession within a small community of believers. "James, then, is speaking of confession in the community meetings (although he certainly does not exclude more detailed and private confession to another person), to one another" (Peter H. Davids, *The Epistle of James*, NIGTC [Grand Rapids, Mich.: Eerdmans, 1982], p. 196).

[49]The famous love chapter, penned by the apostle Paul in 1 Corinthians 13, would be another helpful checklist.

[50]Michael Wilkins, *Following the Master: Discipleship in the Steps of Jesus* (Grand Rapids, Mich.: Zondervan, 1992), p. 247.

[51]Robert Stein, *Jesus the Messiah: A Survey of the Life of Christ* (Downers Grove, Ill.: InterVarsity Press, 1996), p. 218.

[52]For example, in relation to marriage Stanley Hauerwas notes, "The character necessary to sustain the life of marriage . . . is not formed by the family but by the church. . . . Indeed that is why marriage is only possible if it is sustained by a community more significant than the marriage itself" ("The Family as a School for Character," *Religious Education* 80 [spring 1985]: 280, 282).

[53]Luke 5:10 states that James and John were partners (Gk., *koinonoi*) with Simon.

[54]Simon Chan, *Spiritual Theology* (Downers Grove, Ill.: InterVarsity Press, 1998), p. 179. The essential nature of genuine Christian community, both at the congregation level as well as the pastoral staff level, has been severely underemphasized in much of the existing church ministry literature.

[55]One metaphor for the church is the family, involving a spiritual kinship bond in that Timothy is encouraged to relate to older men as "fathers," older women as "mothers," and younger women as "sisters" (1 Tim 5:1-2).

[56]Michael Wilkins, *In His Image: Reflecting Christ in Every Day Life* (Colorado Springs: NavPress, 1997), p. 100.

[57]Paul J. Wadell, *Friendship and the Moral Life* (Notre Dame, Ind.: University of Notre Dame Press, 1989), p. xiii.

[58]Jack Deere, *Surprised by the Voice of God* (Grand Rapids, Mich.: Zondervan, 1996), p. 289.

[59]Henri Nouwen, *Reaching Out* (Garden City, N.J.: Image, 1975), p. 83.

[60]Steve Duck, *Understanding Relationships* (New York: Guilford, 1991), p. 4.

[61]Mihalyi Csikszentmihalyi, *Flow* (New York: Harper & Row, 1990), pp. 189-90.

[62]James Houston, *The Transforming Friendship: A Guide to Prayer* (Oxford: Lion, 1989), p. 150.

[63]Em Griffin suggests four benefits of self-disclosure: it draws us closer to those who listen, it can relieve the tension and emotional energy required to hide, we become known to others, and we come to know more about ourselves. There are also drawbacks such as confidential matters shared with gossips may be leaked to others (*Getting Together* [Downers Grove, Ill.: InterVarsity Press, 1982], pp. 116-18).

[64]Susan Besze Wallace, "The Club: 15 friends and 40 years," *The Orange County Regis-*

ter, June 14, 1999, Metro, p. 1. One of the original members recently passed away due to ovarian cancer, leaving fourteen members.

[65]Houston, *The Transforming Friendship,* p. 11.

Chapter 3: Humility

[1]Jim Cymbala with Dean Merrill, *Fresh Wind, Fresh Fire: What Happens When God's Spirit Invades the Hearts of His People* (Grand Rapids, Mich.: Zondervan, 1997), pp. 141-43. The remaining quotations comes from this source.

[2]Cymbala, *Fresh Wind,* p. 143. David was later married and was hired by the church to work on the maintenance crew.

[3]Justin Kruger and David Dunning, "Unskilled and unaware of it: How difficulties in recognizing one's own incompetence lead to inflated self-assessments," *Journal of Personality and Social Psychology* 77, no. 6 (1999): 1,132.

[4]Ibid.

[5]Ronald Allen, "Numbers," in *The Expositor's Bible Commentary,* ed. Frank E. Gaebelein (Grand Rapids, Mich.: Zondervan, 1990), 2:830. Numbers 15:30 states, "But anyone who sins defiantly, whether native-born or alien, blasphemes the LORD, and that person must be cut off from his people." Psalm 19:13 states, "Keep your servant also from willful sins."

[6]Kenneth E. Bailey, *Poet and Peasant: A Literary Cultural Approach to the Parables in Luke* (Grand Rapids, Mich.: Eerdmans, 1976).

[7]Bailey, *Poet and Peasant,* p. 195.

[8]Henri Nouwen, *The Return of the Prodigal Son* (Garden City, N.J.: Image, 1992), p. 71.

[9]Bailey, *Poet and Peasant,* p. 197 (emphasis added).

[10]Rembrandt's painting *The Return of the Prodigal Son* combines these two parables of Jesus by including the character of the humble tax collector seated in the background. See Nouwen's *The Return of the Prodigal Son* for an interesting elaboration of Rembrandt's painting and life in relation to Jesus' parable.

[11]Helmut Thielicke, *A Little Exercise for Young Theologians,* trans. by Charles Taylor (Grand Rapids, Mich.: Eerdmans, 1962), p. 31.

[12]Some evangelical scholars consider these verses to have a dual or indirect reference, one to the king of Babylon and then to the ultimate opposing king, Satan himself (e.g., Geoffrey W. Grogan, "Isaiah," in *The Expositor's Bible Commentary,* ed. Frank E. Gaebelein [Grand Rapids, Mich.: Zondervan, 1986], 6:105).

[13]Dallas Willard, *Hearing God: Developing a Conversational Relationship with God* (Downers Grove, Ill.: InterVarsity Press, 1999), p. 38 (emphasis added).

[14]Jack Deere, *Surprised by the Voice of God* (Grand Rapids, Mich.: Zondervan, 1996), p. 39.

[15]The Jewish scribes could not fathom such humility on the part of God, so they reversed the references. The NIV text reads "but Abraham remained standing before the LORD," but the marginal reading is "but the LORD remained standing before Abraham." Terence E. Fretheim explains, "The subjects were reversed by scribes who thought it indecorous for God to stand before a human being. 'Remained' refers more appropriately to God, who remains behind while the two men depart. God seeks to communicate with Abraham, not the other way around" ("Genesis," in *The New Interpreter's Bible,* ed. Leander Keck [Nashville: Abingdon, 1994], 1:468).

[16]Deere, *Surprised by the Voice of God,* p. 39.

[17]David's installation as king took place in two phases: first over Judah (2 Sam 1:4), and finally over the whole nation of Israel (2 Sam 5:1-5), almost seven years later.

[18]Gene Edwards, *A Tale of Three Kings: A Study in Brokenness* (Wheaton, Ill.: Tyndale House, 1980), pp. 47, 49.

[19]Ibid., pp. 97-98.

[20]Whenever Moses was challenged about his authority (e.g., by his own sister and brother, Num 12:1-15, and by Korah, Num 16:1-40), Moses preferred that God arbitrate the matter, rather than defend himself. The prophet Daniel did not seek extraordinary means to defend himself to King Darius against the spurious charges. He awaited God's deliverance in the lion's den (Dan 6:1-28). Furthermore, having great wisdom does not guarantee a continuing humble heart, as evident in the life of King Solomon (1 Kings 11:4).

[21]Chapter seven on suffering and submission will develop this theme further.

[22]St Jerome, "To Eustochium," letter CVIII in "Letters and Select Works," in Philip S. and Henry Wace, eds., *The Nicene and Post-Nicene Fathers,* 2nd series, (1890, print, Peabody, Mass.: Hendrickson, 1994), 6:195-211, quoted in John R. Tyson, ea *Invitation to Christian Spirituality: An Ecumenical Anthology* (New York: Oxford University Press, 1999), p. 101 [with omissions and minor linguistic emendations].

[23]Becoming more aware of the various defense mechanisms identified by Sigmund Freud (d. 1939) could help us better monitor the times when pride is reigning our hearts (e.g., denial, repression, hiding, compensation, procrastination). For further study see Gerald May, *Addictions and Grace* (San Francisco: HarperSanFrancisco, 1988).

[24]David Harned, *Patience: How We Wait upon the World* (Cambridge, Mass.: Cowley, 1997), p. 54.

[25]Additional means of becoming aware of pride influencing our actions: (1) notice the consequences of our actions on others and their reactions, (2) seek out and listen to the counsel of trusted friends who know us (invite them to offer feedback when they deem best; the need for close friends in our spiritual journey was developed in chapter two), and (3) listen to the inner promptings of God the Holy Spirit (this aspect is developed further in chapter six).

[26]Dallas Willard, *The Spirit of the Disciplines* (San Francisco: HarperSanFrancisco, 1988), p 187-88.

[27]Joseph Luft, *Of Human Interaction* (Palo Alto, Calif.: Mayfield, 1969), p. 13. This model of behavior in groups was developed by Joe Luft and Harry Ingram, hence the name *Johari,* during a summer session in 1955 and subsequently published later that year in the *Proceedings of the Western Training Laboratory in Group Development* by the UCLA Extension Office.

[28]Richard Foster, *Celebration of Discipline: The Path to Spiritual Growth* (San Francisco: HarperSanFrancisco, 1998), p. 130.

[29]Ibid., p. 112.

[30]Ibid., pp. 129-30.

Chapter 4: Faith

[1]From "Someone to Guide Him," in Kelsy Tyler, *Heaven Hears Each Whisper* (New York: Berkeley, 1996), pp. 27-34.

[2]The Bible uses terms like *host* (an army or very large number) and *myriad* (ten thousand or an immense number) as a way to indicate their numbers: "a multitude of the heavenly host" (Lk 2:13 NRSV) and "of many angels; . . . they numbered myriads of myriads" (Rev 5:11 NRSV).

[3]Dallas Willard, *The Divine Conspiracy* (San Francisco: HarperSanFrancisco, 1998), p. 61.

[4]Many Protestants and Catholics hold that Jesus did not need faith. "Aquinas and the subsequent Catholic theological tradition held that in his human mind Jesus enjoyed the beatific vision and hence lived by sight, not by faith. Aquinas expressed classically this thesis: 'When the divine reality is not hidden from sight, there is no point in faith. From the first moment of his conception Christ had the full vision of God in his essence. . . . Therefore he could not have had faith (*Summa theologiae*, 3a. 7. 3 *resp.*)" (Gerald O'Collins, *Christology: A Biblical, Historical and Systematic Study of Jesus* [Oxford: Oxford University Press, 1995], pp. 254-55). A growing number of New Testament scholars dispute this view, as I indicate in my subsequent comments.

[5]In Hebrews 12:2, both the NIV and NSRV insert the word *our* prior to faith, which is not in the Greek text. The NASB excludes this insertion.

[6]William L. Lane, *Hebrews 9-13*, Word Biblical Commentary (Waco, Tex.: Word, 1991), p. 412.

[7]An interpretative matter arises in understanding the relationship between the word *faith* and the word *Christ* or *Son of God*. Of course, there is general agreement that believers must place their faith *in* Jesus, as taught in various New Testament passages (e.g., Jn 3:16; Acts 20:21; Col 1:4). But the issue here regards whether the genitive noun (Jesus, or Son of God) is either objective or subjective in seven verses of Paul (Rom 3:22, 26; Gal 2:16 [twice], 20; 3:22; Eph 3:12; Phil 3:9), as well as Acts 3:16 and Revelation 14:12. The translation as "faith *of* Christ" or "faith *of* the Son of God"—as I have rendered Galatians 2:20—interprets the genitive as subjective (i.e., Christ's own faith or faithfulness), indicating that Jesus himself experienced faith in God during his incarnation. In agreement with Hebrews 12:2, Jesus was the pioneer of faith as previously discussed. On the other hand, the traditional translation of these particular verses as placing our "faith *in* Christ" or "faith *in* the Son of God" treats the genitive as objective. If Jesus did not need to experience faith himself, as Aquinas taught, then the proper rendering is as an objective genitive.

Daniel Wallace summarizes these grammatical options in *An Exegetical Syntax of the New Testament* (Grand Rapids, Mich.: Zondervan, 1996), pp. 115-16, and concludes that "although the issue is not to be solved via grammar, on balance grammatical considerations seem to be in favor of the subjective gen. view [i.e., the faith or faithfulness of Christ]." For further treatment of this important issue see Morna D. Hooker, "Pistis Christou," *New Testament Studies* 35 (1989): 321-42; Gerald O'Collins and Daniel Kendall, "The Faith of Jesus," *Theological Studies* 53 (1992); 403-23.

[8]Since I am referring explicitly to Jesus' earthly pilgrimage, I will use past tense, although Jesus continues to live now as the God-man.

[9]Gerald O'Collins, *Christology*, p. 261.

[10]Philip Yancey, *Reaching for the Invisible God* (Grand Rapids, Mich.: Zondervan, 2000), p. 105.

[11]Ibid., p. 106.

[12]For a philosophical critique of scientific naturalism, see J. P. Moreland, "Theistic Sci-

ence and Methodological Naturalism," in *The Creation Hypothesis: Scientific Evidence for an Intelligent Designer,* ed. J. P. Moreland (Downers Grove, Ill.: InterVarsity Press, 1994).

[13]George Marsden, *The Soul of the American University* (New York: Oxford University Press, 1994), p. 430.

[14]Phillip Johnson, "Foreword," in Moreland, *The Creation Hypothesis,* p. 7.

[15]The field of philosophy may be a notable exception where prominent philosophers are willing to affirm publicly their belief in God, as indicated by one book which presents personal views of various philosophers: Kelly James Clark,ed., *Philosophers Who Believe* (Downers Grove, Ill.: InterVarsity Press, 1994).

[16]Peter Rose Range, "God & the News," *TV Guide,* August 6, 1994, p. 19. The report was based on evening news shows from ABC, NBC, CBS, CNN and PBS. Out of more than 18,000 news stories aired during 1993, only 212 dealt with specifically religious themes.

[17]Ibid., p. 22.

[18]Richard Swinburne, *The Existence of God* (Oxford: Oxford University Press, 1996), p. 139.

[19]Dallas Willard used this phrase in a lecture on Biola's campus on October 20, 1999.

[20]The brain is a uniquely complex physical organ. A brain is necessary for humans to interact appropriately in a physical world. If it were possible to perform a brain transplant, I see no moral problem, assuming that a person's immaterial nature or soul is associated with the whole and not just one particular organ. Of course, the brain may be like a worn piece of clothing, having become custom-fitted to a person. (It may be easier to transplant the upper brain in contrast to the brain stem—but this is all speculation at this time.)

[21]The mind-body problem is an enduring philosophical topic of debate. For further discussion, see J. P. Moreland and Scott B. Rae, *Body and Soul: Human Nature and the Crisis in Ethics* (Downers Grove, Ill.: InterVarsity Press, 2000).

[22]Melvin Morse with Paul Perry, *Closer to the Light: Learning from the Near-Death Experiences of Children* (New York.: Random House/Villard, 1990), pp. 3-9, quoted in Gary R. Habermas and J. P. Moreland, *Beyond Death: Exploring the Evidence for Immortality* (Wheaton, Ill.: Crossway, 1998), p. 163.

[23]Elizabeth Kubler-Ross, *On Children and Death* (New York: Macmillan/Collier, 1983), p. 208, quoted in Habermas and Moreland, *Beyond Death,* p. 163.

[24]John Gibbs, "Three Perspectives on Tragedy and Suffering: The Relevance of Near-Death Experience Research," *Journal of Psychology and Theology* 16 (1988): 26-27.

[25]Furthermore, if believers are solely constituted by physical parts without an immaterial soul, how do they exist in between death and the second coming of Christ? Only at that future event will all believers, dead or alive, receive a resurrected body, similar to the body our Lord possessed upon his resurrection (Rom 8:23; 1 Cor 15:50-54). During this period of time (called "paradise" or the "intermediate state") believers will, temporally, exist without a body, in between (thus "intermediate") having an earthly body and receiving a resurrection body.

[26]Willard, *Divine Conspiracy,* pp. 75, 77-78.

[27]Ibid., pp. 72-73.

[28]Our resurrection bodies will be constituted of some kind of materiality, of "flesh and bones," similar to Jesus' resurrection body that the disciples saw (Lk 24:36-43). To be

human is to be constituted of both body and soul.

[29]"The central theme of the teaching of Jesus is the coming of the kingdom of God" (Robert Stein, *The Method and Message of Jesus' Teaching* [Louisville, Ky.: Westminster John Knox, 1994], p. 60).

[30]In the episode with the rich young ruler, Matthew includes all three terms as being near equivalents: "to get eternal life" (Mt 19:16), "to enter the kingdom of God" (Mt 19:24), "being saved" (Mt 19:25).

> In this regard the concept of the kingdom of God, is parallel with the Johannine concept of eternal life and the Pauline concept of salvation. Precisely as those who put their faith in the atoning work of Christ are said to possess eternal life, to be in Christ or to be saved, in spite of the fact that eternal life or salvation are essentially eschatological concepts, so also believers may be said to have entered into the kingdom of God despite the fact that the kingdom of God, like eternal life and salvation, can be properly experienced only at the end of time. (C. C. Carougis, *Dictionary of Jesus and the Gospels*, ed. Joel Green et al. [Downers Grove, Ill.: InterVarsity Press, 1992], p. 425)

[31]Willard, *Divine Conspiracy*, pp. 21, 25.

[32]Richard N. Longenecker, "The Acts of the Apostles" in *The Expositor's Bible Commentary*, ed. Frank E. Gaebelein (Grand Rapids, Mich.: Zondervan, 1981), 9:254.

[33]Chuck and Nancy Missler, *Faith in the Night Seasons* (Coeur d'Alene, Idaho: Koinonia House, 1999), p. 102.

[34]Personal e-mail, May 30, 2000.

[35]"Amazing Grace: The Lives of Children and the Conscience of the Nation," *The Orange County Register*, December 2, 1995, p. 16. "[Immanuel] Kant points out . . . that the sight of justice unfulfilled on earth fills the average mind with a longing for something to even it all out. (He calls this 'the postulate of immortality')" (Michael Gelvin, *Spirit and Existence: A Philosophical Inquiry* [Notre Dame, Ind.: University of Notre Dame, 1990], pp. 86-87).

[36]Peter T. O'Brien, *Colossians, Philemon*, Word Biblical Commentary (Waco, Tex.: Word, 1982), p. 171.

[37]Bible scholars have suggested differing end-time scenarios prior to the destruction of this earth and following the tribulation period and the second coming of our Lord to this earth, described in Revelation. The disagreement revolves around whether or not there will be a one-thousand-year period (i.e., millennium) in which our Lord, as Messiah and King, will reign on this same earth; for further study see Darrell Bock, ed., *Three Views on the Millennium and Beyond* (Grand Rapids, Mich.: Zondervan, 1999).

[38]*Bright Side,* May 1999, p. 4. *Bright Side* is a publication for the staff family of Campus Crusade for Christ.

[39]That we will learn in eternity is suggested by Ephesians 2:7, "so that in the ages to come He might show the surpassing riches of His grace in kindness toward us in Christ Jesus" (NASB). For a brief discussion of this topic, see Habermas and Moreland, *Beyond Death,* p. 271.

[40]*The Journals of Jim Elliot*, ed. Elisabeth Elliot (Old Tappan, N.J.: Revell, 1983), p. 174 [Oct. 28, 1949].

[41]J. P. Moreland, *Love Your God with All Your Mind* (Colorado Springs: NavPress, 1997), p. 73.

[42]Willard, *Divine Conspiracy*, p. 307, emphasis added.

[43]Richard Swinburne, *The Evolution of the Soul* (Oxford: Clarendon, 1986), p. 127.

[44]Richard Swinburne, *Providence and the Problem of Evil* (Oxford: Clarendon, 1998), p. 55.

[45]Jeff Astley, *The Philosophy of Christian Religious Education* (Birmingham, Ala.: REP, 1994), p. 218.

[46]The genius of this system of the passive acquisition of beliefs that God designed is that young children are able to learn core beliefs without the need for mature cognitive reflection to supervise the process.

[47]"A person's character is her system of desires and beliefs" (Swinburne, *Providence,* p. 91).

[48]*Parade Magazine,* December 29, 1996, p. 7.

[49]David Merkh, "Antidotes for Spiritual Amnesia," *Kindred Spirit* (summer 1997): 12.

[50]Of course, the issue of evil coming our way is a more complex matter, since Satan is ultimately behind all evil in our world. We take up this subject in chapter seven.

[51]Jesus most likely engaged in fasts on a regular basis during his hidden years in order to have the ability to conduct a forty-day fast following his baptism (Mt 4:2).

[52]Most of these categories are developed by Kent Berghuis, "Teaching Biblical Fasting," presentation at the Evangelical Theological Society annual meeting, 1998. Berghuis cites four New Testament passages in which the word *fasting* has been added to the text: Mt 17:21; Mk 9:29; Acts 10:30; 1 Cor 7:5. Berghuis includes this quotation from Marion Fink: "These textual variations indicate the growing interest in the church in the practice of fasting, especially after the second century; and they have some significance for a consideration of fasting after the New Testament period" (Marion Michael Fink, Jr., "The Responses in the New Testament to the Practice of Fasting" [Ph.D. diss., The Southern Baptist Theological Seminary, 1974], 143).

[53]For further information, see Richard Foster, *Celebration of Discipline: The Path to Spiritual Growth* (San Francisco: Harper & Row, 1998), chap. 4.

[54]M. Shawn Copeland, "Saying Yes and Saying No," in *Practicing Our Faith: A Way of Life for a Searching People,* ed. Dorothy Bass (San Francisco: Jossey-Bass, 1997), p. 67.

[55]John of the Cross, *Living Flame of Love,* paraphrased in *You Set My Spirit Free: A 40-Day Journey in the Company of John of the Cross,* ed. David Hazard (Minneapolis: Bethany House, 1994), pp. 45-46.

[56]C. S. Lewis, *Christian Behavior* (New York: Macmillan, 1945), p. 55.

Chapter 5: Commitment

[1]See also Elijah's encounter with God in 1 Kings 19:11-12.

[2]This aspect of God's hiddenness is illustrated in Brennan Manning's parable *The Boy Who Cried Abba* (San Francisco: HarperSanFrancisco, 1997). Willie Juan, the boy, asks the Medicine Man, the Christ figure, "But why didn't you come to the cave with trumpets and angels and a great big show?" The Medicine Man replies, "I didn't want to frighten you, my friend. If I came displaying all the glory of El Shaddai, you would find it utterly unbearable and, more importantly, you'd be afraid to come close to me" (pp. 61-62).

[3]Blaise Pascal claims, "God therefore being hidden, any religion which does not say that God is hidden is not true. And any religion which does not give the reasons why does not enlighten. Ours does all this" (*Pensees and Other Writings,* trans. H. Levi

[Oxford: Oxford University Press, 1995], p. 81). Pascal closes this fragment by quoting Isaiah 45:15: "Truly you are a God who hides himself." The Latin term, *Deus absconditus* ("hidden God") comes from Jerome's translation of this particular verse. For a popular introduction to the subject, see Thomas Morris, *Making Sense of It All: Pascal and the Meaning of Life* (Grand Rapids, Mich.: Eerdmans, 1993). A detailed study of the Old Testament passages can be found in Samuel Ballantine, *The Hiddenness of God: The Hiding of the Face of God in the Old Testament* (New York: Oxford University Press, 1983). For further study on the hiddenness of God, see Paul Moser, "Cognitive Idolatry and Divine Hiding," in *Divine Hiddenness*, ed. Daniel Howard-Snyder and Paul Moser (New York: Cambridge University Press, forthcoming), and *Why Isn't God More Obvious?* (Atlanta: Ravi Zacharias International Ministries, 2000). A technical philosophical study (and suggesting that God's hiddenness argues against God's existence) is by J. L. Schellenberg, *Divine Hiddenness and Human Reason* (Ithaca, N.Y.: Cornell University Press, 1993).

[4]I am adapting the concept of relational space from John Hick's concept of epistemic distance, although I fundamentally disagree with his philosophy of religion. *Evil and the God of Love*, rev. ed. (San Francisco: HarperSanFrancisco, 1977), p. 281.

[5]I. Howard Marshall, *Commentary on Luke*, New International Greek Testament Commentary (Exeter, U.K.: Paternoster, 1978), p. 897.

[6]Kenneth Bailey, *Poet and Peasant: A Literary Cultural Approach to the Parables in Luke* (Grand Rapids, Mich.: Eerdmans, 1976), pp. 161-62.

[7]Ibid., p. 164.

[8]A story told by Howard Hendricks, from a seminary class session too many years ago.

[9]Scott Horrell, personal communication, September 10, 1999.

[10]Busyness in ministry or devotional exercises is no guarantee of spirituality, as noted by Jonathan Edwards: "That persons are disposed to abound and to be zealously engaged in the external exercises of religion, and to spend much time in them, is no sure evidence of religion, and to spend much time in them, is no sure evidence of grace; because such a disposition is found in many that have no grace" (*The Religious Affections* [1746; reprint, Edinburgh: Banner of Truth Trust, 1961], p. 92).

[11]Simon Chan, *Spiritual Theology* (Downers Grove, Ill.: InterVarsity Press, 1998), pp. 114-15.

[12]I have been working with this model for over a decade. The first published appearance involved further tinkering with my friend, as the 4 C's: communion, community, commission and character; see Ronald Habermas and Klaus Issler, *Teaching for Reconciliation: Foundations and Practice of Christian Educational Ministry* (Grand Rapids, Mich.: Baker, 1992), p. 47-57. Another adaptation turned up in Klaus Issler and Ronald Habermas, *How We Learn: A Christian Teacher's Guide to Educational Psychology* (Grand Rapids, Mich.: Baker, 1994), as a circle diagram, figure 10.1, p. 172. No framework can be perfectly comprehensive. Yet I suggest that these four themes encompass the bulk of what is important for Christian living with God.

[13]John H. Sailhamer, "Genesis," in *The Expositor's Bible Commentary*, ed. Frank E. Gaebelein (Grand Rapids, Mich.: Zondervan, 1990), 2:38.

[14]William L. Lane, *Hebrews 1-8*, Word Biblical Commentary (Waco, Tex.: Word, 1991), p. 104.

[15]Terence E. Fretheim, "The Book of Genesis," in *The New Interpreter's Bible* (Nashville: Abingdon, 1994), 1:347.

[16]Richard Swenson, *Margin: Restoring Emotional, Physical, Financial, and Time Reserves to Overloaded Lives* (Colorado Springs: NavPress, 1992), pp. 227-28.

[17]Ibid., p. 228.

[18]Dallas Willard develops this point in *An Anchor for Our Soul,* taped presentation (North Hills, Calif.: The Sowers Yield, n.d.).

[19]For this chapter and the next, due to the nature of the material treated, I place the discussion of one spiritual discipline at a point within the chapter and the other at the end of the chapter.

[20]A more structured approach for daily communing with God could involve the monastic eight "offices" or hours of the day, when prayer, praise, singing and meditative chants were offered to God: lauds (3 a.m. or dawn), prime (6 a.m.), terce ("third," 9 a.m.), sext ("sixth," noon), none ("ninth," 3 p.m.), vespers (6 p.m. or dusk), compline (9 p.m. or before bed), vigils (midnight). The seven times of the day were based on the verse "Seven times a day I praise you for your righteous laws" (Ps 119:164). The one occasion during the night comes from "At midnight I rise to give you thanks for your righteous laws" (Ps 119:62).

[21]John Wijngaards, *Experiencing Jesus* (Notre Dame, Ind.: Ave Maria, 1981), p. 149.

[22]Ibid., p. 151.

[23]Henri Nouwen, *Making All Things New: An Invitation to the Spiritual Life* (San Francisco: Harper & Row, 1981), pp. 69, 71.

[24]Dallas Willard, *The Spirit of the Disciplines* (San Francisco: HarperSanFrancisco, 1988), p. 160.

[25]Nouwen, *Making All Things New,* pp. 72-73.

[26]Three of the elements of the ACTS framework for communication with God are identified by King David in his assignments to the Levites (1 Chron 16:4). The element of confession can be seen in Nehemiah 1:4-11 and 9:16-38, for example.

[27]For more information about music in this regard, see Don E. Saliers, "Singing Our Lives," in *Practicing Our Faith: A Way of Life for a Searching People,* ed. Dorothy Bass (San Francisco: Jossey-Bass, 1997), pp. 179-93.

[28]Louis Bouyer, *The Spirituality of the New Testament Fathers* (New York: Seabury, 1960), 1:314.

[29]John Coe, "Stages of Life in the Spirit," (lecture given at Institute of Spiritual Formation, Biola University, Oct. 18, 1999).

[30]Richard Foster, *Prayer: Finding the Heart's True Home* (San Francisco: HarperSanFrancisco, 1992), p. 20.

[31]Ibid., p. 21.

[32]The phrase "dark night of the soul" comes from the book of that title by the Spanish mystic John of the Cross. It was the continuation of a previous work, entitled *Ascent of Mount Carmel.* In these two works he discusses the "active night" and the "passive night" (Dark Night) in moving through purgation, illumination on to union with God. For an introduction to his thought, see E. W. Trueman Dicken, "Teresa of Jesus and John of the Cross," in *The Study of Spirituality,* ed. Cheslyn Jones, Geoffrey Wainwright and Edward Yarnold (New York: Oxford University Press, 1986), p. 371.

[33]For my discussion, I am following Foster's brief summary in *Prayer,* pp. 21-23

[34]Foster, *Prayer,* p. 22.

[35]Ibid., pp. 22-23.

[36]While on the cross being judged for the sins of the world, Jesus himself appears to

have also experienced God's silence. It was near the end of this three-hour period of literal darkness over the land when Jesus cried, "My God, my God, why have you forsaken me?" (Mt 27:46).

[37]Chuck and Nancy Missler, *Faith in the Night Seasons* (Coeur d' Alene, Idaho: Koinonia House, 1999), pp. 28-29, 159.

[38]Mme. Jeane Guyon, *Final Steps in Christian Maturity* (formerly entitled *The Spiritual Adventure*, excerpts of a larger, three-volume work entitled *Justifications*), (1915; reprint, Gardiner, Maine: Christian Books, 1985), p. 35.

[39]Missler, *Night Seasons*, pp. 324-25.

[40]Millie de Beers, "Waiting in Solitude," *Bright Side*, September 1997, p. 3.

[41]James Houston outlined the development of the double knowledge in a lecture on Biola's campus: "The Recovery of the Double Knowledge: Self-knowledge in the Light of the Knowledge of God," (lecture given at the Institute for Spiritual Formation Lecture, Biola University, Oct 11, 1999).

[42]John Calvin, *Institutes of Christian Religion*, vol. 1, trans. Ford Lewis Battles (Philadelphia: Westminster, 1960), pp. 35, 37. In the footnote section, the editor cites others who use the notion of the double knowledge (see pp. 36-37).

[43]Augustine, "Soliloquies," 2.1.1, in *Nicene and Post-Nicene Fathers*, ed. Philip Schaff (1888; reprint, Peabody, Mass.: Hendricksen, 1995), 7:547.

[44]Blaise Pascal, *Pensees and Other Writings*, trans. H. Levi (Oxford: Oxford University Press, 1995), fragment 225, p. 64.

[45]Morton T. Kelsey, *Adventure Inward* (Minneapolis: Augsburg, 1980), p. 11. Kelsey offers this caution: "Because a journal can provide the moisture to crack the husk, it should be used carefully, particularly by young people and people in crisis" (p. 81).

[46]For a popular study of Jesus' emotions by a Christian psychologist, see Dick and Jane Mohline, *Emotional Wholeness: Connecting with the Emotions of Jesus* (Shippensburg, Penn.: Treasure House, 1997).

[47]Deryck Sheriffs, *The Friendship of the Lord: An Old Testament Spirituality* (London: Paternoster, 1996), p. 211.

[48]The following framework is adapted from friend, Ray Hergert, who uses these questions daily to monitor his experience of God's peace as a means to stay connected with God.

[49]John of the Cross, *Living Flame of Love*, in *You Set My Spirit Free: A 40-Day Journey in the Company of John of the Cross*, ed. David Hazard (Minneapolis: Bethany House, 1994), pp. 49-50.

Chapter 6: Communication

[1]Charles H. Spurgeon, *The Autobiography of Charles Spurgeon* (London: Curts & Jennings, 1899), 2:226.

[2]Ibid. Spurgeon continues:

> I could tell as many as a dozen similar cases in which I pointed at somebody in the hall without having the slightest knowledge of the person, or any idea that what I said was right, except that I believed I was moved by the Spirit to say it; and so strikingly has been my description, that the persons have gone away, and said to their friends, "Come, see a man that told me all things that ever I did; beyond a doubt, he must have been sent of God to my soul, or else he could not have described me so exactly." (p. 227)

[3]"In the Garden," by C. Austin Miles, 1912.

[4]Dallas Willard, *Hearing God: Developing a Conversational Relationship with God* (Downers Grove, Ill.: InterVarsity Press, 1999), p. 22.

[5]Klaus Bockmuehl (d. 1989) comments, "He is *doctor internus*, the 'teacher within,' as the ancient Church called him. . . . His is an ongoing ministry of teaching, and, although the passages mentioned do not speak of listening, his teaching extends to us a continuous invitation to listen to him" (*Listening to the God Who Speaks* [Colorado Springs: Herder & Herder, 1990], p. 63).

[6]Gary Badcock, *Light of Truth and Fire of Love: A Theology of the Holy Spirit* (Grand Rapids, Mich.: Eerdmans, 1997), p. 233. Badcock points to excesses within each of these movements and is not making a categorical statement about these movements.

[7]The miraculous gifts of the Spirit and speaking in tongues are secondary issues and peripheral to the present discussion. Neither of these have I personally experienced. In this regard, I write as a noncharismatic about the importance of the ministry of the Holy Spirit for the church and each believer.

[8]Daniel R. Wallace, "Who's Afraid of the Holy Spirit? The Uneasy Conscience of a Noncharismatic evangelical," *Christianity Today*, September 12, 1994, p. 35.

[9]Theologian Jim Sawyer has used this phrase.

[10]Wallace, "Who's afraid?" p. 37.

[11]Willard, *Hearing,* p. 35.

[12]An episode along these lines occurred in Numbers 11:26-29 when Joshua urged Moses to hinder some "unauthorized" prophesying (cf. also Mk 9:38-40). Moses' response is instructive to us today: "Are you jealous for my sake? I wish that all the LORD's people were prophets and that the LORD would put his Spirit on them!" (v. 29).

[13]A century ago Albrecht Ritschl complained that up to that time, "neglect of the subject [of the Holy Spirit] has had this unfortunate practical consequence, that theologians either abstain from using the idea altogether, or understand by it a kind of resistless natural force which runs athwart the regular course of knowledge and the normal exercise of the will" (*The Christian Doctrine of Justification and Reconciliation*, ed. H. R. Mackintosh and A. B. Macaulay [Edinburgh: T & T Clark, 1900], p. 533). More recently, Gary Badcock notes, "There is to this extent a pronounced pneumatological deficit in Christian theology over against, for example, its enormous elaboration of the doctrine of Christ" (*Light of Truth and Fire of Love*, p. 1).

[14]Wayne Grudem, *Systematic Theology* (Grand Rapids, Mich.: Zondervan, 1994), p. 634.

[15]Also 2 Thessalonians 2:8 and Revelation 13:15.

[16]Jan Karon, *A New Song* (New York: Penguin, 1999), p. 393 (emphasis added).

[17]J. I. Packer, *Keep In Step With the Spirit* (Old Tappan, N.J.: Revell, 1984), p. 235. John McIntyre makes the case another way, "My fear is rather for those of both sides who carelessly speak of grace as if it were a *substance* (even though 'supernatural'), a power which, though it may originate from God or the Spirit, is appropriated by the believers, thus *physically* supplementing or sanctifying their natural powers. . . . In short, to say that the believers have received the gift of grace would rightly be taken as an alternative way of saying that the Spirit indwells them" (*The Shape of Pneumatology: Studies in the Doctrine of the Holy Spirit* [Edinburgh: T & T Clark, 1997], p. 248 [emphasis added]).

[18]Debbie Schuster, Christian Spirituality class, Talbot School of Theology, Biola Univer

sity, fall 1999.

[19]Packer, *Keep In Step*, p. 261.

[20]Peter Toon, *The Art of Meditating on Scripture* (Grand Rapids, Mich.: Zondervan, 1993), p. 54.

[21]Gordon Fee, *God's Empowering Presence* (Peabody, Mass.: Hendricksen, 1994), p. 30.

[22]Terry Fulham, *On Eagle's Wings,* (Fullerton, Calif.: Emmanuel Tape Ministry, n.d.), audio-cassette.

[23]For a more personal analogy in which two living beings are paired for life, consider a blind person (like the believer) and a seeing-eye dog (like the Holy Spirit). As the relationship grows over time, these two eventually function as one unit. The blind person has a distinct limitation that the seeing-eye dog can overcome, if the blind person is willing to entrust himself or herself to the resources of the dog.

[24]J. I. Packer contrasts the concepts of monergism and synergism in the Christian life:

> Regeneration was a momentary monergistic act of quickening the spiritually dead. As such, it was God's work alone. Sanctification [and spirituality], however, is in one sense synergistic—it is an ongoing cooperative process in which regenerate persons, alive to God and freed from sin's dominion (Rom. 6:11, 14-18), are required to exert themselves in sustained obedience. God's method of sanctification is neither activism (self-reliant activity) nor apathy (God-reliant passivity), but God-dependent effort (2 Cor. 7:1; Phil. 3:10-14; Heb. 12:14). (*Concise Theology* [Wheaton, Ill.: Tyndale, 1993], pp. 170-71)

[25]For New Testament believers since Pentecost, the Holy Spirit, at the moment of regeneration, indwells each believer (Jn 14:16; 1 Cor 6:19), baptizes us (1 Cor 12:13), seals us (Eph 4:30) and inaugurates regular prayer for each believer (Rom 8:26). As we walk with the Spirit (Gal 5:16, 25), the Spirit fills (Eph 5:18), teaches (Jn 16:12-15), guides (Rom 8:14) and assures us (Rom 8:16).

[26]Frank Laubach, *Learning the Vocabulary of God: A Spiritual Diary* (Nashville: Upper Room, 1956), p. 84.

[27]Ibid., p. 76.

[28]Ibid., p. 84.

[29]Peter Toon, *Meditating on Scripture*, p. 31.

[30]The following points are adapted from friend and colleague J. P. Moreland, "Prayer as a Spiritual Discipline," audiotape of lecture given on Oct. 4, 1999. The audiotape is available from the Biola Library Media Center for a nominal fee: (562) 903-6000.

[31]Consider to whom we pray. Many of us usually address the Father in our praying. We may wish to begin acknowledging the other members of the Trinity when we converse with God. A contemporary chorus directs our attention to all three persons: "Father, I adore you." Then, in succeeding verses, one replaces "Father" with "Jesus" and finally "Spirit" (by Terry Coelho, 1992 Maranatha! Minstries).

Regarding the Jesus Prayer, rather than a vain repetition or a meaningless mantra, this is a meditation on Scripture; it is a telegram request to our Lord and Savior Jesus Christ. For discussions of the origins of the Jesus Prayer, see Kalistos Ware, "The Origins of the Jesus Prayer: Diadochus, Gaza, Sinai," in *The Study of Spirituality*, ed. Cheslyn Jones, Geoffrey Wainwright and Edward Yarnold (New York: Oxford, 1986), pp. 175-84, 272.

[32]For a discussion of the significance of the Holy Spirit in Jesus' life see Gerald Haw-

thorne, *The Presence and the Power: The Significance of the Holy Spirit in the Life and Ministry of Jesus* (Waco, Tex.: Word, 1991), and Klaus Issler, "The Spiritual Formation of Jesus: The Significance of the Holy Spirit in the Life of Jesus," *Christian Education Journal* 4, no. 2 (2000): 5-24.

[33]Bockmuehl, *Listening to the God Who Speaks*, p. 64.

[34]John McIntyre describes this synergism:

> There are, I believe, two points at which we are able to come to terms with the paradox. The first is the recognition which comes to us when, having lived through some situation which requires of us a concentrated output of effort on our part, success begins to overtake us, that it was by the power of the indwelling Spirit of God that we did succeed. Both arms of the paradox are held together as constituting the truth. The second point of enlightenment comes when in prayer we seek the strength of God's Spirit to enable us to obey some command of God's, and at the same time recognize that the answer to that prayer is no release for us from the obligation to put the most strenuous effort into the resultant action. (*The Shape of Pneumatology* [Edinburgh: T & T Clark, 1997], p. 247)

[35]Derek Kidner, *Psalms 1-72* (Downers Grove, Ill.: InterVarsity Press, 1973), p. 135. Klaus Bockmuehl affirms this contrast, based on his study of the book of Acts: "[God] guides, not as we might guide a child by the hand or a horse by the reins, but through the instructions he speaks—instructions that we hear and then act upon" (*Listening to the God who Speaks*, p. 83).

[36]I have not discussed an audible voice from God since I have no experience with that. Francis Schaeffer had such an experience, hearing God say, "Uncle Harrison's house," in response to a need for living arrangements early in their family life (quoted in Edith Schaeffer, *The Tapestry* [Waco, Tex.: Word, 1981], pp. 384-85).

[37]Walt Russell, *Playing with Fire: How the Bible Ignites Change in Your Soul* (Colorado Springs: NavPress, 2000), pp. 63-64.

[38]Ibid., p. 77.

[39]Ibid., p. 78.

[40]Jack Deere, *Surprised by the Voice of God* (Grand Rapids, Mich.: Zondervan, 1996), p. 113.

[41]Charles Swindoll, *Flying Closer to the Flame* (Grand Rapids, Mich.: Zondervan, 1993), pp. 96-97.

[42]I do not imply a dictation theory of inspiration. God superintended the writing of the Scriptures by the human authors (2 Pet 1:20-21) so that, incorporating their individual personalities, literary styles and interests (e.g., free expression, Rom 9:1-3; research, Lk 1:1-4), these human authors composed and recorded God's authoritative message in the words of the original manuscripts.

[43]During the first five centuries of the early church, according to Morton Kelsey (*God, Dreams and Revelations: A Christian Interpretation of Dreams* [Minneapolis: Augsburg, 1991]), dreams were viewed as an important means of divine communication. For example, in his *Confessions* (bk. 3, chap. 11) Augustine reports a dream his mother, Monica, had assuring her that her son would eventually become converted. Although Jerome's life course was significantly influenced toward more biblical studies by a stunning dream, in his Latin translation of the Bible (the Vulgate, which became the standard version of the Bible for a thousand years) Jerome associated "observing dreams" as a practice of sorcery in three particular Old Testament verses (Lev 19:26; Deut 18:10; 2 Chron 33:6). The Hebrew word for sorcery or divination

(anan) is used ten times in the Old Testament: Lev 19:26; Deut 18:10, 14; Judg 9:37; 2 Kings 21:6; 2 Chron 33:6; Is 2:6; 57:3; Jer 27:9; and Mic 5:12. As Kelsey notes, "In translating Leviticus 19:26 and Deuteronomy 18:10 with one word different from other [similar] passages, a direct mistranslation, as we shall show, Jerome turned the law: 'You shall not practice augury or witchcraft [i.e., soothsaying]' into the prohibition: 'You shall not practice augury nor observe dreams.' Thus by the authority of the Vulgate, dreams were classed with soothsaying, the practice of listening to them with other superstitious idea" (*God, Dreams,* pp. 138-39). Kelsey argues that along with other factors these mistranslations in the Vulgate contributed to the Christian community's negative view of listening to dreams as a means of divine communication. Due to my limited experience I have passed over this subject, but I look forward to learning more about this avenue of divine communication. One contemporary resource by an evangelical psychiatrist and psychologist exploring this issue is Paul Meier and Robert Wise, *Windows of the Soul* (Nashville: Thomas Nelson, 1995).

[44]Augustine, *The Confessions of St. Augustine,* p. 92 [bk. 3, chap. 12].

[45]Ibid., p. 92.

[46]Laubach, *Learning the Vocabulary,* p. 5.

[47]Chuck and Nancy Missler, *Faith in the Night Seasons* (Coeur d' Alene, Idaho: Koinonia House, 1999), p. 266.

[48]Ibid.

[49]Willard, *Hearing God,* pp. 99-100.

[50]Laubach, *Learning the Vocabulary of God,* p. 87. He continues this particular entry: "As the years passed, I have found that obedience to God's voice is even more difficult than hearing Him speak. I find in my 1950 diaries scores of pages on how to make obedience absolute. I was having more trouble with a rebellious will than a deaf ear."

[51]Parallel passages: Mt 10:19-20 and Lk 12:11-12 (also Lk 21:13-15, of different context, but similar topic). The critique is rehearsing some kind of response to officials solely on our own without the aid of the Spirit. See I. Howard Marshall, *Commentary on Luke* (Grand Rapids, Mich.: Eerdmans, 1978), p. 768.

[52]Marshall, *Commentary on Luke,* p. 520.

[53]Swindoll, *Flying Closer to the Flame,* p. 98.

[54]Ibid.

[55]Anita Kessels, "Front Porch," *Focus on the Family,* June 2000, back cover.

[56]I have often had great insights given me as I was writing this book project.

[57]Swindoll, *Flying Closer to the Flame,* p. 155.

[58]Ibid., p. 72. The following quotations also come from this page.

[59]Ibid.

[60]Willard, *Hearing God,* pp. 90-91.

[61]Ibid., pp. 108-9

[62]Even when we know it is God speaking, the word may come to test us, as it did the Recabites (Jer 35:1-14).

[63]E. Stanley Jones, *A Song of Ascents* (Nashville: Abingdon, 1989), p. 190, quoted in Willard, *Hearing God,* pp. 175-76.

[64]Bockmuehl, *Listening to the God who Speaks,* p. 132.

[65]For further help on corporate divine guidance, see Richard Foster, "Guidance," in *Celebration of Discipline: The Path to Spiritual Growth* (San Francisco: HarperSan-

Francisco, 1998).

[66]E. Stanley Jones, "For Sunday of Week 41," in *Victorious Living* (Nashville: Abingdon, 1938), p. 281, quoted in Willard, *Hearing God*, p. 28.

[67]The definition is adapted from one used at the Institute for Retreat/Spiritual Direction, Archdiocesan Spirituality Center, Two Chester Place, Los Angeles, California.

[68]Kenneth Leech, *Soul Friend: An Invitation to Spiritual Direction* (San Francisco: HarperSanFrancisco, 1980), pp. 88-89.

[69]For additional help on spiritual mentoring, see Keith R. Anderson and Randy D. Reese, *Spiritual Mentoring: A Guide for Seeking and Giving Direction* (Downers Grove, Ill.: InterVarsity Press, 1999).

[70]Bockmuehl, *Listening to the God who Speaks*, p. 8.

Chapter 7: Apprenticeship

[1]Rebecca's story is told by Philip Yancey in *What's So Amazing About Grace?* (Grand Rapids, Mich.: Zondervan, 1997), pp. 104-6.

[2]Reflections of Billy Graham, *U.S. News & World Report*, May 3, 1993, p. 72.

[3]Frances Young, "Suffering," in *The Westminster Dictionary of Christian Theology*, ed. Alan Richardson and John Bowden (Philadelphia: Westminster Press, 1983), p. 556.

[4]Recent treatments of the problem of evil include Daniel Harrington, *Why Do We Suffer? A Scriptural Approach to the Human Condition* (Franklin, Wis.: Sheed & Ward, 2000); Marilyn McCord Adams, *Horrendous Evils and the Goodness of God* (Ithaca, N.Y.: Cornell University Press, 1999); Richard Swinburne, *Providence and the Problem of Evil* (Oxford: Clarendon, 1998); John Stackhouse, *Can God Be Trusted? Faith and the Challenge of Evil* (New York: Oxford University Press, 1998); Michael L. Peterson, *God and Evil: An Introduction to the Issues* (Boulder, Colo.: Westview, 1998).

[5]Traditional arguments to the problem of evil have included the "free will defense" and the "greater good defense." Paul Moser proposes a "divine purposes reply" as encompassing these other explanations, yet permitting additional factors beyond what can be known. "God hides for various purposes, not just one purpose, just as God apparently allows evil for various purposes. Still, the exact details of God's purposes are sometimes unclear to us, as should be expected given God's transcendence" ("Knowing the God Who Hides and Seeks," [paper presented at the Society of Christian Philosophers' Conference, Portland, Ore., April 1999], p. 3-4). By offering potential benefits that may come from suffering, I am not simply advocating a "greater good" argument. I think Moser's proposal is a more comprehensive approach to the problem of evil.

[6]Gordon Lewis and Bruce Demarest, *Integrative Theology* (Grand Rapids, Mich.: Zondervan, 1986), 1:275-76. Gordon Fee comments in a footnote, "It should be noted that, unless otherwise specified, the word 'God' in Paul always refers to God the Father" (*Paul, the Spirit, and the People of God* [Peabody, Mass.: Hendrickson, 1996], p. 35 n. 7).

[7]William L. Lane, *Hebrews 9-13*, Word Biblical Commentary (Waco, Tex.: Word, 1991), p. 426.

[8]Scripture affirms God's knowledge of the future: the term *foreknowledge* is employed (e.g., Acts 2:23; Rom 8:29; 1 Pet 1:2); future events foretold come true (e.g., visions of Daniel); the true prophets of God are vindicated by their predictions becoming a real-

ity (e.g., Deut 18:21-22). One's view of God's foreknowledge also has implications for prayer, which will receive some attention in the next chapter.

[9]Lewis and Demarest, *Integrative Theology*, 1:315.

[10]God experiences his own grief (e.g., Gen 6:6-7; Ps 78:40; Is 63:10; Jer 42:10; Eph 4:30).

[11]Theologians are revising their conceptions of the traditional doctrine of God's impassability—that God is without passions and cannot be affected by feelings, thus he endures no suffering (as is affirmed in the Wesminster Confession). Although in usual agreement with this confessional statement, Wayne Grudem takes exception to its affirmation of this doctrine. "But the idea that God has no passions or emotions *at all* clearly conflicts with much of the rest of Scripture, and for that reason I have not affirmed God's impassibility in this book" (*Systematic Theology* [Grand Rapids, Mich.: Zondervan, 1994], p. 166).

[12]Douglas Moo, *The Epistle to the Romans*, NICNT (Grand Rapids, Mich.: Eerdmans, 1996), p. 506.

[13]Thomas à Kempis, *The Imitation of Christ*, ed. Paul Bechtel (Chicago: Moody, 1980), p. 124 [bk. II, chap. 12].

[14]Since Job received no particular answer for his suffering but rather a vision of God, Marylyn McCord Adams proposes that the goodness of the incommensurate future relationship with God be the response to the problem of evil. "If postmortem, the individual is ushered into a relation of beatific intimacy with God and comes to recognize how past participation in horrors is thus defeated, and if his/her concrete well-being is guaranteed forever afterward so that concrete ills are balanced off, then God will have been good to that individual despite participation in horrors" (*Horrendous Evils*, p. 168).

[15]Richard Swinburne, *Providence and the Problem of Evil* (Oxford: Clarendon, 1998), p. 25. Aquinas offered a similar comment, as quoted by Swinburne: "Many goods are present in things which would not occur unless there were evils" (p. 162 n. 2 [*Summa contra Gentiles* 3.71.6]).

[16]Steven S. Smalley, *1, 2, 3 John*, Word Biblical Commentary (Waco, Tex.: Word, 1984), p. 155.

[17]A detailed discussion of human free will is beyond the scope of the book. Two major traditions have emerged among evangelicals, compatibilism (soft determinism) and libertarian (incompatibilist) free will. An overview of the features of each is provided by David Ciocchi, "Human Freedom," in *Christian Perspectives on Being Human: A Multidisciplinary Approach to Integration*, ed. J. P. Moreland and David M. Ciocchi (Grand Rapids, Mich.: Baker, 1993), pp. 87-108

[18]Richard Swinburne, *Providence and the Problem of Evil*, p. 250.

[19]Alvin C. Plantinga, *God, Freedom, and Evil* (Grand Rapids, Mich.: Eerdmans, 1974), p. 49.

[20]Thomas Aquinas, *A Summa of the Summa*, ed. Peter Kreeft (San Francisco: Ignatius Press, 1990), p. 173 [I, 22, 4].

[21]The promise of 1 Cor 10:13 may be understood in two ways. Either God promises an individualized amount of evil that we can bear at the time, or God's promise may offer a general limitation to the evil he permits in this present world for any believers.

[22]Note Jesus' statement that our present physical life is not of utmost value. "Do not be afraid of those who kill the body but cannot kill the soul. Rather, be afraid of [God]

who can destroy both soul and body in hell" (Mt 10:28).

[23]Henry T. Blackaby and Claude V. King, *Experiencing God* (Nashville: Broadman & Holman, 1994), p. 134.

[24]Abraham Kuyper, *To Be Near unto God,* trans. John Hendrick de Vries (1918; reprint, Grand Rapids, Mich.: Eerdmans, 1925), p. 307.

[25]Richard Swinburne, *Providence and the Problem of Evil,* p. 188-89.

[26]Daniel B. Wallace, "Who's Afraid of the Holy Spirit?" *Christianity Today,* September, 12, 1994, p. 36.

[27]"Pauline blows stranded trio to their rescue," *The Orange County Register,* Saturday, October 11, 1997.

[28]Philip Yancey, "A Bad Week in Hell," *Christianity Today,* October 27, 1997, p. 112.

[29]Ibid.

[30]Benjamin Musyoka, Professor, International School of Theology, Nairobi, Kenya; personal communication, July 15, 1999.

[31]C. S. Lewis, *The Problem of Pain* (New York: Macmillan, 1962), p. 93, emphasis added.

[32]Such a reminder may especially be needed for those who enter heaven without any personal adult experience of this world, such as those aborted, those who died in infancy and those who were mentally incompetent.

[33]Philosopher William James, a pacifist, reluctantly acknowledged how war uniquely benefits both character and community formation.

> The [moral] virtues that prevail, it must be noted, are virtues anyhow, superiorities that count in peaceful as well as in military competition; but the strain on them, being infinitely intenser in the latter case, makes war infinitely more searching as a trial. No ordeal is comparable to its winnowings. Its dread hammer is the welder of men into cohesive states, and nowhere but in such states can human nature adequately develop its capacity. . . . So far, war has been the only force that can discipline a whole community, and until an equivalent discipline is organized, I believe that war must have its way. (*The Moral Equivalent of War and Other Essays,* ed. John K. Roth [New York: Harper & Row, 1971], pp. 10-11)

[34]John Feinberg, *The Many Faces of Evil* (Grand Rapids, Mich.: Zondervan, 1994), p. 337.

[35]Jesus' proclamation can be understood literally, indicating a vision Jesus saw, or figuratively as referring to a Jewish tradition of the fall of Satan. Gerald Hawthorne argues for a literal vision: "Thus the very positioning of the saying about Jesus' experience of seeing the downfall of the devil—an experience not unlike that which happened some years later to one of his own Spirit-inspired prophets (Rev 12:7-12; cf. 1:10-12; 4:1-2; 17:3; 21:10)" (*The Presence and the Power: The Significance of the Holy Spirit in the Life and Ministry of Jesus* [Waco, Tex.: Word, 1991], p. 150).

[36]Regarding the petition in Matthew 6:13, "lead us not into temptation," D. A. Carson develops the idea that

> it is possible that the causative form of the Lord's Prayer is, similarly, not meant to be unmediated but has a permissive nuance: "Let us not be brought into temptation [i.e., by the devil]." This interpretation is greatly strengthened if the word "temptation" can be taken to mean "trial or temptation that results in a fall" and this appears to be required in two NT passages (Mark 14:38; Gal 6:1). . . . Thus the Lord's model prayer ends with a petition that, while implicitly recognizing our own helplessness before the Devil whom Jesus alone could vanquish (4:1-11), delights to trust the heavenly Father for deliverance from the Devil's

strength and wiles. ("Matthew," in *The Expositor's Bible Commentary,* ed. Frank Gaebelein [Grand Rapids, Mich.: Zondervan, 1984], 8:173-74)

[37]See Clinton E. Arnold, *Three Crucial Questions About Spiritual Warfare* (Grand Rapids, Mich.: Baker, 1997) for responses to the following questions: What is spiritual warfare? Can a Christian be demon possessed? Are we called to engage territorial spirits?

[38]Tommy Lee Jones, "I'm optimistic—it creates possibilities," *Parade,* June 8, 1997, p. 4 (emphasis added).

[39]Kempis, *Imitation of Christ,* p. 45 [bk. I, chap. 13] (emphasis added).

[40]John Wesley, quoted in Thomas C. Oden, *John Wesley's Scriptural Christianity* (Grand Rapids, Mich.: Zondervan, 1994), p. 324 (emphasis added).

[41]The theme of overcoming, of being victorious, is a pervasive theme in Scripture, particularly in the Johanine literature: Jn 16:33; 1 Jn 2:13, 14; 4:4; 5:4, 5; Rev 2:7, 11, 17, 26; 3:5, 12, 21; 5:5; 17:14; 21:7.

[42]Terry Waite, *Footfalls in Memory* (New York: Doubleday, 1997), pp. 181-82.

[43]Swinburne, *Providence and the Problem of Evil,* p. 101.

[44]Feinberg, *The Many Faces of Evil,* p. 327.

[45]Feinberg, *The Many Faces of Evil,* p. 329. This advice is tested by his own troubling experience regarding his wife's diagnosis of a genetic brain disease, described in John Feinberg, *Deceived by God? A Journey Through Suffering* (Wheaton, Ill.: Crossway, 1997).

[46]Christopher "Hugh" Carrier, "From Darkness to Light," *Readers' Digest,* May 2000, pp. 101-6.

[47]Daniel Harrington, *Why Do We Suffer? A Scriptural Approach to the Human Condition* (Franklin, Wis.: Sheed & Ward, 2000), p. 3. Some of the lament psalms would include these series of psalms: 5—7, 22, 25—28, 42—43, 54—57, 69—71 and 140—143. For a complete list, see Walter Russell, *Playing with Fire: How the Bible Ignites Change in Your Soul* (Colorado Springs: NavPress, 2000), p. 144-45. Regarding acrostic poems (e.g., Psalms, Lamentations), David Hubbard explains that "this carefully wrought, highly artificial style seems to have a further purpose: 'to encourage completeness in the expression of grief, the confession of sin and the instilling of hope' (N. K. Gottwald, *Studies in the Book of Lamentations,* 1954), p. 28" ("Lamentations, Book of," in *New Bible Dictionary,* ed. J. D. Douglas [Grand Rapids, Mich.: Eerdmans, 1962], p. 707).

[48]W. Bingham Hunter, *The God Who Hears* (Downers Grove, Ill.: InterVarsity Press, 1986), pp. 41-42.

[49]Deryck Sheriffs, *The Friendship of the Lord: Spirituality in the Old Testament* (London: Paternoster, 1996), pp. 248-49.

[50]Ibid., p. 210.

[51]Nicholas Wolterstorff, *Lament for a Son* (Grand Rapids, Mich.: Eerdmans, 1987), p. 7.

[52]Ibid., p. 65.

[53]Do we ever provide a safe place in our corporate worship for lamentation before God? Where is there a time to "mourn with those who mourn" (Rom 12:8)? In a presentation at Biola University, Keith Anderson suggested that holding a special lament service now and then may provide a corporate and public forum in which believers can mirror the thoughts of feelings of persons like Job and Jeremiah and bare their

soul in the midst of a loving and caring community. Such a meeting may involve readings (e.g., lament psalms, other relevant passages from Scripture, including the passion of our Lord, contemporary poetry or writing), prayers, laments and reports concerning specific suffering of believers today near and around the world), singing of hymns and choruses that help us express our sorrow (e.g., "No One Knows the Trouble I've Seen," "O Sacred Head, Now Wounded"), moments of silence and tears, all undertaken during a time of fasting (e.g., sackcloth and ashes). James's commendation is fitting: "Grieve, mourn and wail. Change your laughter to mourning and your joy to gloom. Humble yourselves before the Lord, and he will lift you up" (Jas 4:9-10).

[54]Walter Brueggemann, *Theology of the Old Testament* (Minneapolis, Minn.: Fortress, 1997), p. 645.

[55]Jesus spoke of visiting those in prison as an act of loving him (Mt 25:36-40).

[56]Robert Pazmiño, *Principles and Practices of Christian Education* (Grand Rapids, Mich.: Baker, 1992), p. 52.

[57]Of course, in our pursuit of exposing evil and seeking justice, we must leave room for God's unique role of judgment and vengeance. "And will not God bring about justice for his chosen ones, who cry out to him day and night?" (Lk 18:7; cf. Rom 12:17-19).

[58]One older resource on settling Christian disputes out of court was written by two members of the Christian Legal Society, Lynn R. Buzzard and Laurence Eck, *Tell It to the Church: Reconciling out of Court* (Elgin, Ill.: David C. Cook, 1982).

[59]Names have been changed.

Chapter 8: Partnership

[1]I had requested that my eye be fully healed or that God would communicate a reason for why the surgery was needed. God answered with a third option: healing my eye sufficiently to make cleansing surgery unnecessary.

[2]John MacQuarrie, *The Humility of God* (Philadelphia: Westminster Press, 1978), p. 43.

[3]Wayne Grudem, *Systematic Theology* (Grand Rapids, Mich.: Zondervan, 1994), p. 377.

[4]Jean-Jacques Rousseau, *Emile*, book 2 in *Oeuvres Completes* (Paris: Baudouin Freres, 1826), 4:198, quoted in Donald Bloesch, *The Struggle of Prayer* (Colorado Springs: Helmers & Howard, 1988), p. 73.

[5]As mentioned in the last chapter, Scripture indicates a division of labor within the Trinity and that answering prayer is a primary distinctive of the Father (Mt 6:9; Eph 3:14). Additionally, the other two members of the Godhead pray for us: the Son as High Priest (Heb 7:25; cf. Rom 8:34) and as Advocate-*Paracletos* (1 Jn 2:1), and the Spirit as Divine Mentor-*Paracletos* (Rom 8:26-27). The inference is that they pray to the Father, who coordinates how prayers are answered.

[6]John R. Rice, *Prayer—Asking and Receiving* (Wheaton, Ill.: Sword of the Lord, 1942), p. 28 (emphasis added). "If prayer is asking, then the answer to prayer must be receiving" (p. 54).

[7]Simon Chan, *Spiritual Theology: A Systematic Study of the Christian Life* (Downers Grove, Ill.: InterVarsity Press, 1998), p. 140.

[8]John T. Fitzgerald, ed., *Friendship, Flattery, and Frankness of Speech. Supplement to Novum Testamentum,* vol. 82 (Leiden: Brill, 1996).

[9]Stephen S. Smalley, *1, 2, 3 John,* Word Biblical Commentary (Waco, Tex.: Word,

1984), pp. 130, 204.

[10]A 1540 letter by Martin Luther, quoted in O. Hallesby, *Prayer,* trans. Clarence Carlsen (Minneapolis: Augsburg, 1931), p. 131.

[11]Dallas Willard, *The Divine Conspiracy* (San Francisco: HarperSanFrancisco, 1998), p. 194.

[12]Gordon R. Lewis and Bruce A. Demarest, *Integrative Theology* (Grand Rapids, Mich.: Zondervan, 1990), 2:112. The italics are original.

[13]The word *impetrate* means "to obtain by request or entreaty" (*Webster's New Collegiate Dictionary* (Springfield, Mass.: 1981), p. 570. (In pronouncing *impetratory,* the accent is on the second syllable as in *impetuous.*) The term is used by Peter Geach, *God and the Soul* (London: Routledge & Kegan Paul, 1969), p. 87: "Christians who rely on the word of their Master, are confident that some prayer is impetratory: that God gives us some things, not only *as* we wish, but *because* we wish." The biblical basis for this concept is developed in the following pages.

[14]The Hebrew word *nicham* is used at least seventeen times regarding situations in which God will change or did change his mind: Exodus 32:12, 14; 2 Samuel 24:16; Psalm 106:45; Jeremiah 15:6; 18:8; 26:3, 13, 19; 42:10; Joel 2:13-14; Amos 7:3, 6; Jonah 3:9-10; 4:2.

[15]When Scripture talks of God having physical characteristics (e.g., hands, face, back, Ex 33:23; even wings, Ps 17:8), we recognize the use of anthropomorphic language, ascribing human (or animal) features to God. Using this label for other descriptions of God, such as emotions (Gen 6:6; 1 Sam 15:11), is where the difficulty lies. Robert Chisholm disputes such labeling in the present case: "Passages declaring that God typically changes His mind as an expression of His love and mercy demonstrate that statements describing God as relenting should not be dismissed as anthropomorphic" ("Does God 'Change' His Mind?" *Bibliotheca Sacra* 152 [1995]: 399).

[16]The scope of the uniqueness may apply to the context of warfare as Robert Coote suggests. "This cannot mean that God has never answered a prayer; it probably means that God has never taken orders from anyone in battle" ("Joshua," in *The New Interpreter's Bible,* ed. Leander Keck [Nashville: Abingdon, 1998], 2:647).

[17]Grudem, *Systematic Theology,* p. 193.

[18]Only if a person assumed that there was always only one best means to each goal could John Calvin's claim be correct, that if God actually responded to the petition of his children, then one of three problems had occurred: either divine "ignorance, or error, or powerlessness" (*Institutes of Christian Religion,* trans. Ford Lewis Battles, ed. John T. McNeill [Philadelphia: Westminster Press, 1960], 1.17.12). Calvin's dictum is applicable to these limited cases in which there is only one best means (e.g., Jesus' death for our atonement, Acts 2:23). But as will be demonstrated, Scripture offers significant accounts in which God defers to the preferences of others.

[19]But might God be testing Ezekiel's sensibilities? An example of such testing is illustrated by the Recabites in Jeremiah 35. God proposed a certain course of action for this clan, knowing they would refuse, for he wanted to use their example as an illustration. But the contextual cues in Ezekiel 4 do not confirm any testing motif for Ezekiel. The focus is on preparing this elaborate acted parable for the Israelites.

[20]John Calvin identifies the evil spirit as Satan. "Therefore, whatever men or Satan himself may instigate, God nevertheless holds the key, so that he turns their efforts to carry out his judgments. God wills that the false King Ahab be deceived; the devil offers his

services to this end" (*Institutes of the Christian Religion* 1.18.1).

[21]Robert Chisholm, "Does God Change His Mind?" *Kindred Spirit* 22, no. 2 (1998): 5.

[22]Thomas Constable suggests that God could permit human prayer to "affect the timing of some of God's foreordained acts" (*Talking to God: What the Bible Teaches About Prayer* [Grand Rapids, Mich.: Baker, 1995], p. 151). It seems the biblical examples indicate that prayer involves more than just an adjustment of timing.

[23]We must also be sensitive to join in where we sense God is already working, as suggested by Henry Blackaby and Claude King: "When you see the Father at work around you, that is your invitation to adjust your life to Him and join Him in that work" (*Experiencing God* [Nashville: Broadman & Holman, 1994], p. 76). In addition, I believe God also encourages us to take initiatives in areas that we do not yet happen to see the Father working around us, but for which God may be open to begin his work with us.

[24]Willard, *Divine Conspiracy*, p. 244.

[25]Rice, *Prayer*, p. 36.

[26]Terrence E. Fretheim, "Genesis," in *The New Interpreter's Bible*, ed. Leander Keck (Nashville: Abingdon, 1994), 1:468.

[27]Willard, *Divine Conspiracy*, p. 250.

[28]For table 8.1, the following authors are cited: Paul Helm, *The Providence of God* (Downers Grove, Ill.: InterVarsity Press, 1994); John Feinberg, "God Ordains All Things," in *Predestination and Free Will: Four Views of Divine Sovereignty and Human Freedom*, ed. David Basinger and Randall Basinger (Downers Grove, Ill.: InterVarsity Press, 1986); Terrance Tiessen, *Providence and Prayer: How Does God Work in the World?* (Downers Grove, Ill.: InterVarsity Press, 2000); William Craig, *The Only Wise God: The Compatibility of Divine Foreknowledge and Human Freedom* (Grand Rapids, Mich.: Baker, 1987); Thomas Flint, *Divine Providence: The Molinist Account* (Ithaca, New York: Cornell University Press, 1998); Jack Cottrell, *What the Bible Says About God the Ruler* (Joplin, Mo.: College Press, 1984); John Sanders, *The God Who Risks: A Theology of Providence* (Downers Grove, Ill.: InterVarsity Press, 1998); Greg Boyd, *God of the Possible* (Grand Rapids, Mich.: Baker, 2000).

In *Providence and Prayer*, Tiessen surveys seven models of providence evangelicals have held: openness, church dominion, redemptive intervention, Molinist, Thomist, Barthian, Calvinist, and middle knowledge Calvinist (Tiessen's own view). Another survey is forthcoming: *Divine Foreknowledge: Four Views* (Downers Grove, Ill.: InterVarsity Press), including Paul Helm on timelessness, William Craig on middle knowledge, David Hunt on simple foreknowledge, and Gregory Boyd on openness.

[29]William Craig (view C) admits that "while having some biblical support, [the doctrine of middle knowledge] ought to be accepted mainly because of its great theological advantages. It provides a basis for God's foreknowledge of the future free acts of individuals" (*The Only Wise God*, p. 151). Terrence Tiessen (view B) suggests that for both traditional Calvinism (view A) and traditional Wesleyanism (view D), their models of divine providence cannot work if God has no "middle knowledge" (*Providence*, pp. 140, 345). Something along these lines may also taint the timeless view (part of view A).

Middle foreknowledge might be illustrated in God's answer to King David, hiding in the city of Keilah to avoid capture by King Saul. David asked God, " 'Will the citizens of Keilah surrender me and my men to Saul?' And the LORD said, 'They will' " (1 Sam

23:12). So David left Keilah. A brief overview of middle knowledge: Luis de Molina (d. 1600) identified three logical moments in God's knowledge, in relation to the decision to create a world (in a manner of speaking, these moments involve narrowing scopes of content):

(1) God's *natural* knowledge, essential to God (prior to the decision to create [prevolitional], of necessary truths [e.g., $7 + 5 = 12$], including all possible creatures he could create and their actions and reactions in all possible worlds);

(2) God's *"middle* knowledge"—in between his natural and free knowledge (knowledge of counterfactuals of creaturely freedom, knowing how any particular creatures he might create would freely act if placed in any circumstance [nondetermining]; thus God knew what possible worlds he could actually create, since free creatures will act differently, assuming God does not coerce creatures to go against their will [e.g., in some possible worlds I would exist and impact others, yet in other possible worlds I would not be born and would not impact others, sadly]. And "after" deciding to create one possible world based on his middle knowledge) comes

(3) God's *free* knowledge (postvolitional knowledge of contingent truths of everything that will happen, how every creature he is going to create will freely act in the one actual world he will create).

Making "middle knowledge" a category distinct from God's natural or free knowledge was Molina's unique contribution. Note that God's natural knowledge is always the same and is essential to God; yet God's middle knowledge could be different, for it is knowledge of what free creatures might do and they can choose a variety of actions. God's free knowledge could also be different if he happened to have created and actualized another world than this one.

For further discussion of these matters, see Klaus Issler, "Divine Providence and Impetratory Prayer: A Review of Issues from Tiessen's *Providence and Prayer,"* *Philosophia Christi* (forthcoming). I wonder if further help on this issue might come from exploring the intratrinitarian division of labor among the persons of the Trinity? For example, is there some point of entry from the fact that God the Son and God the Spirit pray to the God the Father on our behalf (Rom 8:26, 34)?

[30]D. A. Carson, "Matthew," in *The Expositor's Bible Commentary,* ed. Frank E. Gaebelein (Grand Rapids, Mich.: Zondervan), 8:444-45.

[31]Ibid., p. 391. In Mark's account, it is clear that "moving a mountain" is the result of a request and accomplished by God's power ("it will be done for him," Mk 11:23).

[32]L. Gregory Jones, *Embodying Forgiveness: A Theological Analysis* (Grand Rapids, Mich.: Eerdmans, 1995), p. xii.

[33]Richard Foster, *Celebration of Discipline: The Path to Spiritual Growth* (San Francisco: HarperSanFrancisco, 1998), pp. 35-36, 38.

[34]For example, King Asa of Judah was condemned by God for his lifestyle of neglecting God, as exemplified in the king's primary consultation of physicians rather than God for his disease (2 Chron 16:12).

[35]C. S. Lewis, *The Screwtape Letters* (New York: Macmillan, 1961), pp. 126-27.

[36]The metaphor of dive bombing is suggested by Dallas Willard; the metaphor of cooking is suggested by J. P. Moreland. I have greatly benefited from the insights and personal advice of my colleague and friend J. P. Moreland. An audiotape of a lecture on prayer by Dr. Moreland is available from the Biola Library Media Center for a nominal fee, (562) 903-6000: "Prayer as a Spiritual Discipline," October 4, 1999.

[37]Aquinas notes, "As Augustine says, it is lawful to pray for what is lawful to desire" *(Summa Theologica* 2.2 Q.83, quoted in John R. Tyson, *Invitation to Christian Spirituality* [New York: Oxford University Press, 1999], p. 176). Tyson notes, "This is not, literally, a quotation from St. Augustine; it comes from Thomas himself (IV, *Sent.* d. 15, q.4a, 4b), but the sentiments are certainly in keeping with Augustine's point of view" (p. 176 n. 45).

[38]Rice, *Prayer,* pp. 142-43.

[39]Larry Dossey, "Prayer Is Good Medicine," *The Saturday Evening Post* 269 (November/December 1997): 53. For further details, see *Prayer Is Good Medicine: How to Reap the Healing Benefits of Prayer* (San Francisco: HarperSanFrancisco, 1996).

[40]Rice, *Prayer,* p. 150. Rice framed these statements in 1942 when speaking on "rights" did not carry our contemporary baggage.

[41]I have emphasized prayers for personal needs and desires since these kinds of requests are not typically treated in discussions of prayer. Of course, we must also intercede for others in need (e.g., Heb 13:3).

[42]Richard Foster, *Prayer: Finding the Heart's True Home* (San Francisco: HarperSanFrancisco, 1992), p. 183.

[43]A more detailed version of Debbie's suffering and death is available in Gary Habermas, *Forever Loved: A Personal Account of Grief and Resurrection* (Joplin, Mo.: College Press, 1997).

[44]Ibid., p. 58.

[45]Foster, *Prayer,* p. 182.

[46]Keith Ward, *Divine Action* (London: Collins, 1990), p. 167.

[47]William L. Craig, *No Easy Answers: Finding Hope in Doubt, Failure, and Unanswered Prayer* (Chicago: Moody Press, 1990), p. 56. First John 5:16-17 identifies a circumstance for which we will not receive an answer.

[48]Rice, *Prayer,* p. 65.

[49]Rice, *Prayer,* p. 193.

[50]Flint, *Divine Providence,* p. 217.

[51]P. T. Forsyth, *Soul of Prayer* (Grand Rapids, Mich.: Eerdmans, 1916), p. 14.

[52]Carson, "Matthew," pp. 391-92.

[53]Bernard of Clairvaux, *On Loving God,* trans. Jean Leclerq and Henri Rochais, Cistercian Fathers Series (Kalamazoo, Mich.: Cistercian Publications, 1973), 13B:23-33.

[54]Ibid., p. 27.

[55]Ibid., p. 28.

[56]Ibid., p. 29.

[57]Ibid.

[58]Foster, *Prayer,* p. 3.

[59]Robert Mounce notes, "Schweizer reports that, according to rabbinic law, burying property was conceived of as the safest possible course of action (p. 471) and therefore would absolve the servant from any liability" *(Matthew,* New International Biblical Commentary [Peabody, Mass.: Hendrickson, 1991], p. 234).

[60]Foster, *Celebration of Discipline,* p. 37. Foster continues, "In addition, I sought the wisdom and experience of past masters of prayer by securing and reading every good book I could find on the subject. I began studying the pray-ers of the Old Testament—Moses and Elijah and Hannah and David—with new interest" (pp. 37-38).

[61]Henry T. Blackaby and Claude V. King, *Experiencing God* (Nashville: Broadman &

Holman, 1994), p. 134.

[62]Willard, *Divine Conspiracy,* p. 175.

[63]Henri Nouwen, *Making All Things New: An Invitation to the Spiritual Life* (San Francisco: Harper & Row, 1981), p. 80 (emphasis added).

Author Index